I0879481

Paul Thomas Anderson

Contemporary Film Directors

Edited by Justus Nieland and Jennifer Fay

The Contemporary Film Directors series provides concise, well-written introductions to directors from around the world and from every level of the film industry. Its chief aims are to broaden our awareness of important artists, to give serious critical attention to their work, and to illustrate the variety and vitality of contemporary cinema. Contributors to the series include an array of internationally respected critics and academics. Each volume contains an incisive critical commentary, an informative interview with the director, and a detailed filmography.

A list of books in the series appears at the end of this book.

Paul Thomas Anderson

George Toles

**UNIVERSITY
OF
ILLINOIS
PRESS**
URBANA,
CHICAGO,
AND
SPRINGFIELD

1 2 3 4 5 C P 5 4 3 2 1
♾ This book is printed on acid-free paper.

Frontispiece: Paul Thomas Anderson directing *Punch-Drunk Love*

Library of Congress Cataloging-in-Publication Data
Names: Toles, George E. author.
Title: Paul Thomas Anderson / George Toles.
Description: Urbana : University of Illinois Press, 2016. | Series: Contemporary film directors | Includes bibliographical references and index.
Identifiers: LCCN 2016018921| ISBN 9780252040368 (hardcover : alk. paper) | ISBN 9780252081859 (pbk. : alk. paper)
Subjects: LCSH: Anderson, Paul Thomas. | Motion picture producers and directors—United States—Biography.
Classification: LCC PN1998.3.A5255 T86 2016 | DDC 791.4302/33092 [B]—dc23 LC record available at https://lccn.loc.gov/2016018921

To Melissa Steele

Contents

Acknowledgments

I am deeply grateful to Justus Nieland for his initial suggestion that I consider submitting a proposal for the Contemporary Film Directors series, and for his ongoing support at every stage of the subsequent writing process. His own volume on David Lynch was a steady source of inspiration to me throughout my work on *Paul Thomas Anderson*. My opportunity to present a portion of the manuscript to Justus's students and colleagues at Michigan State University came at just the right point in the revision process. Justus's and Jen Fay's notes on the manuscript were immensely helpful in giving me a sense of the book's true shape, enabling me to tighten my argument and (I hope) give it the right structure. My debts to Jim Naremore have been accumulating throughout my academic career. Like so many others, I have benefited incalculably from his scholarly example and encouragement. His reader's report on the manuscript provided yet one more instance of his luminous generosity and insight.

Ryan McBride gave me invaluable editorial assistance when I was trying to find ways to shorten and refocus the study. His recommendations were invariably right, but they were coupled with a deep understanding of and sympathy for what I was striving to accomplish. That made the cutting far less painful than it otherwise might have been. Dave McGregor assisted me not only in tracking down every published or taped interview that Paul Thomas Anderson has granted, but highlighted all the commentary within them that might have bearing on my study. Rob Gardiner tracked down interview sources in the final phase of manuscript preparation. I would also like to thank the students in my Paul Thomas Anderson seminar for their limitless enthusiasm about

Anderson's work and for allowing me to test some of the ideas that found their eventual place in this book. I have had many Anderson discussions with my brilliant colleagues in the Film Studies program at the University of Manitoba: Jonah Corne, Brenda Austin-Smith, and Faye McIntyre. Faye proved especially influential through the course of our many talks about *There Will Be Blood*. Charles Warren was the first outside of my family circle to read a complete draft of the manuscript and, as always, supplied the perfect balance of approval and provocation. Other friends in film who have either read a portion of this study or engaged in memorable conversations about the director with me since my Anderson obsession took hold include Carol Vernallis, Megan Parry, Jonathan Ball, Trevor Mowchun, Mark Betz, Joel Hughes, Rob Gardiner, Kerri Woloszyn, Jeff Crouse, Murray Pomerance, Bill Rothman, and Gil Perez, the last of whom I deeply miss. V. F. Perkins, Joe McElheney, Corey Creekmur, Susan White, Tom Gunning, Jonathan Rosenbaum, Adrian Martin, Geoffrey O'Brian, Jason Jacobs, and Lisa Trahair must be mentioned as lodestars for the sort of close reading I am committed to. Deborah Oliver has been the most brilliant, incisive copy editor I've ever had. It seemed that no mistaken detail in any shot description could escape her notice. Gretchen Derige supplied crucial help in the preparation of the filmography and index. Jennifer Comeau smoothly guided the manuscript through production.

I am fortunate to have three film-besotted children to spar with and be inspired by in every imaginable sort of conversation. Sam, Rachel, and Thomas, the time you spend with me is a consistent cause for wonder, laughter, enlightenment, and hellzapoppin' gratitude. My greatest debt is to my wife, Melissa Steele, to whom this book is dedicated. She makes everything possible. She is my ideal reader, my best friend, the holder of the keys to the imagination, and a daily demonstration that love is indeed a many-splendored thing.

Note to the Reader

Except where indicated, all quotations from the films are from the release versions. Quotations from the shooting scripts are clearly designated.

Paul Thomas Anderson

Words and Music: The *Magnolia* Crisis

Wise Up

> "To take an interest in an object is to take an interest in one's experience of the object, so that to examine and defend my interest in these films is to examine and defend my interest in my own experience, in the moments and passages of my life I have spent with them. This in turn means for me defending the process of criticism, so far as criticism is thought of, as I think of it, as a natural extension of conversation."
>
> —Stanley Cavell, *Pursuits of Happiness*

This book offers a considered, thematic and stylistic account of my viewing experiences of three films by Paul Thomas Anderson and their backgrounds—*Punch-Drunk Love* (2002), *There Will Be Blood* (2007), and *The Master* (2012). I also engage with related works of literature, philosophy, and the films to which Anderson's narratives owe some debt. My original plan for the study was to examine Anderson's entire career.

After all, he has so far directed only seven feature films, the most recent an adaptation of Thomas Pynchon's novel *Inherent Vice* (2014). The more time I spent in the company of his work (where he consistently functions as both screenwriter and director), however, the more I became persuaded that the three films I eventually settled on, for all their differences, were strikingly linked in ways that had not received much previous attention and that they shared unusual preoccupations. These numerous, complex linkages seemed to warrant treating them as a group, though I would hesitate to characterize them as a trilogy. *Inherent Vice*, a woozy, end of the sixties comedy of manners disguised as a detective film, laced with Pynchonesque paranoia and befuddlement, was released too late for inclusion in this book.

In an excellent essay on *The Master*, Geoffrey O'Brien begins by describing the territory that Anderson repeatedly explores in his narratives:

> [The America] where we live . . . [is] a country of deep loneliness—that same loneliness that permeates all of Anderson's films, and against which his characters are forever forcing themselves into protective families or parodies of families, a population of paternalistic strangers, adoptive sons, surrogate mothers, fake cousins. All his films . . . have found their way to the heart of a peculiarly American disconnectedness. The freedom to be left alone turns into a desperate drift: a desperation measured, often, in hyperactivity and baroque elaboration, as if keeping frantically busy could stave off a lurking sense of emptiness. From the start his films seemed to need to prove themselves with every composition, every line of dialogue, every cut, every music cue. The aggressiveness of style was a declaration of ambition; intending to astonish, the filmmaker made himself so visible that he was one of the characters, another creature of compulsive energy looking for a way to manifest itself. (292)

O'Brien deftly captures the feel of Anderson's recurring landscape of disconnection. He goes on to speak of the expressionist treatment of milieu in the films, as though in each narrative there is an attempt both to acknowledge, naturalistically, the claims of material reality and at the same time "to reconfigure the real, to bring it into line with the most extravagant desire, and it is that [latter] attempt that magnifies to the utmost the sense that the world is not merely implausible, but fundamentally unbelievable" (295). O'Brien evokes the essential dynamic of

Anderson's films and their mad dreamer's aspect. In diverse ways, each of them frames an appeal to the knowable world to manifest itself on more visionary terms—the terms of a deep desire that is impossible to articulate or satisfy.

Hard Eight (1996), Anderson's splendidly eccentric debut film, was premised on the magical appearance, out of nowhere, of a shrewd and honorable older benefactor who takes a lost young man in hand. The naive recipient of the surrogate father's largesse is moved in a trice from his "no-prospects" circumstances in the sticks to the imposing, garishly charged and disreputable wonderland of Vegas casinos. The benefactor, Sydney (Philip Baker Hall)—though his own resources are limited—opens every door possible for his young acolyte. His casino version of Oz is a realm in which new connections are easily, breezily formed.

Boogie Nights (1997) and *Magnolia* (1999) are San Fernando Valley movies, imbued with urgent, crackling life. Anderson sought to make the valley (where he grew up) into a place of mythic consequence, like Faulkner's Yoknapatawpha County. If he were to approach the locale with an attitude of sufficient, affirming grandeur, the region could yield action on a scale appropriate to other myths of American self-making. Anderson's rendering of the valley is hyperbolically vivid, a place teeming with "characters" trying to find openings in their constricted situations and breaking out with incandescent gusto. Though their aspirations are, more often than not, touchingly small-time, Anderson fully honors their fantasies of renewal. Anything paltry can become large in the rendering, especially if the external world is depicted, intermittently, as an Expressionist fever chart of characters' gift for ardor. There is ample opportunity to meet likeminded dreamers on the social periphery, which in Anderson's valley films seems thick with mystery, exotic danger, and human flow.

It is my sense, however, that *Magnolia* marks a significant transition, taking Anderson to the end of one way of dramatizing possibilities, and gesturing—in the midst of an only half-recognized crisis—toward another. The millennial space carved out in *Magnolia* attests to Anderson's faith in a world where talk and group activity are plentiful and transformative. He pursues a vision of provisional community and reconciliation, though it is underwritten throughout by a relentless emphasis on estrangement and neediness. By the time of *Punch-Drunk Love*, which bears some canted relationship to romantic comedy, Anderson's created world has become sharply and fearfully diminished, and its population thinned out. His central male character, Barry Egan, is a pathological introvert, ill at ease with almost everyone he encounters, who has immense difficulty making himself understood—to others, to himself, and to the viewer—by means of language. The spaces Barry Egan occupies and moves through seem a curious mixture of impersonal strip mall topography and emanations of his baffled, tormented psyche. It is increasingly a challenge to determine where the cloistered self leaves off and its physical surroundings begin. The boundaries between mind and matter are porous, in a dreamy way, and the soundscape Anderson designs to supplement the surrealism of the images is a clangorous amplification of Barry's ferocious swarm of fears. *There Will Be Blood* and *The Master* repeat and further complicate this "estranged solitary" design, as though Anderson has become transfixed by the specter of damaged male souls in arrested development, living at remote distances from their buried needs. These three films seem to go into exile from any settled forms of social behavior, shifting into reverse and undoing the work of civilizing influences. We encounter outwardly grown men in uncomprehending struggle against some impasse: the residue of stunted childhoods. The visual environments where these men are first encountered—a grim corner of an office, a hole in the ground, an army landing craft in wartime—externalize this impasse. The business of childhood is indeed never finished for Anderson. The departure from traditional, readable narrative structure seems to be a necessary corollary for Anderson's deepening fascination with human unknowability. The forms of his films, like the landscapes they depict, are fitted to the haunted, withdrawn central male figure's dilemma.

This book offers little direct commentary on Anderson's life history or his frequently tempestuous conflicts with producers and studios. (A vivid picture of Anderson's predilection for high-stakes struggle and his abhorrence of compromise are portrayed in Sharon Waxman's *Rebels of the Backlot*. Waxman also strives to place Anderson in the context of his 1990s "independent filmmaker" generation. As is the case with most directors, however, his stronger, more important affiliations are with artists of an earlier period.) The biographical facts that interest me most are those having to do with his shadowy upbringing in his crowded, sister-dominated family—three siblings and four half-siblings. Paul's father, Ernie Anderson, had reasonably successful careers as a disk jockey, television and radio announcer, and voice-over artist. The looming presence throughout Paul's childhood of his father's authoritative voice—shape shifting and disembodied, a genial, hidden ghost in the machine—has noteworthy ramifications for the phantom father figures (benign or sinister) in Anderson's movies. Even more momentous, in my view, is Anderson's oppressive, apparently contentious and unresolved relationship with his mother, Edwina. In the multitude of interviews he has granted since the release of *Boogie Nights*, Anderson consistently deflects questions about his relationship with his mother. The possible reasons for this silence are worth pursuing, even in the absence of biographical particulars.

Many reviewers have noted the preoccupation with father-son relationships in Anderson's films and the emphasis on surrogate families with an absent, muted, or, in the case of *Punch-Drunk Love*, perfectly child-mirroring maternal presence. I would argue that the foreground conflict with father figures and male doubles in Anderson's later films is an elaborate screen for the far more complicated, perilous, irrational drama with the hidden mother. The first scene in *Hard Eight* reveals a young orphan who has rashly lost the $6,000 he requires to give his deceased mother a proper burial. The final image of *The Master* focuses on Freddie Quell curled up on the beach next to a prodigious, naked, female sand sculpture (a memory image) with an especially prominent breast. Frank Mackey's most closely guarded secret in *Magnolia*—one that his journalist interrogator, Gwenovier obliges him to confront—is that his mother is no longer living. Frank (Tom Cruise) terminates the interview in a furious, agitated state after Gwen (April Grace) asks him: "Frank, can you talk about your mother? . . . Frank, can you?" One of *Magnolia*'s many puzzles is Frank's reason for burying the *fact* of his mother's death, for which he bears no responsibility, and which poses no obvious threat to him.

In *Boogie Nights* (1997), the most blistering, hyperbolic scene depicts Eddie/Dirk's mother (Joanna Gleason) ambushing Eddie (Mark Wahlberg) when he returns home after a late-night adolescent spree. She denounces him at frenzied length, seeks to destroy as many of his bedroom wall decorations as she can get hold of, and evicts him without granting him a hearing. Anderson, who, as I previously noted, pointedly avoids the topic of his mother, Edwina, and his relationship with her in interviews, spoke on only one occasion about this scene's personal import, in 1999:

> When his mother comes at him like that, she's really crazy and out of control. She's kind of without motivation to a certain extent. I think one of the greatest mistakes I've made in the past and that a writer can make is, "What's the character's motivation?" Well, a lot of times it's so fucking confused and so polluted that you really have no idea. That woman is pretty nuts, and I think it's sometimes hard for an audience to grab hold of a character whose intentions aren't clear. You don't really know what the fuck she's yelling about. You know she has an odd jealousy toward the neighborhood girl he's banging, so she's upset about that, but her actions are so manic, you can't get a hold of them. I was just really glad that the actress in the scene didn't require a lot of clarity on her behavior, because I couldn't have given it. I really wrote what made sense, and what made sense was sometimes so illogical. There are some people who saw it and said, "That scene doesn't make sense! Why is she going crazy?" And I would just say, "You know what? I've never been able to figure it out. But it sure makes sense, and I've sure been there." (Konow, 2000)

In an earlier interview, published closer to the time of *Boogie Nights*' completion, he ducked questions about his mother and then went on to explain why: "I've been reluctant to talk about that because maybe I'll deal with it in another movie. It's not so much about trying to guard privacy; it's about trying to guard, in a mysterious way, the stories I might tell. I don't want to give away the ending. I also don't want to be the guy who's dealing with this mother for 30 years" (Rensin). An *Esquire* interviewer in 1997 pressed him to elaborate on a possible connection between the Julianne Moore surrogate mother in *Boogie Nights* and Dirk's mother (with her possible autobiographical connection) with a carefully worded question: "The movie [*Boogie Nights*] is in many ways about family, but both the main character's real mom and figurative mom (Julianne Moore) have what you might call boundary issues. His real mom, Joanna Gleason's character, is beating him up, and he's fucking [his adoptive mom] Julianne Moore's [character]. So is this coincidence, good scriptwriting, or a Freudian slip?" Anderson replies, "You've got it. It's all of those," and further agrees with the interviewer when the latter points out that "the first time he fucks Julianne, it's like an adoption—he gets reborn, renamed even" (Udovich).

One of the main strands of argument in my book is that Anderson continues to "guard" the story of his mother that "he might tell," perhaps imagining that he is "deferring" it for another movie, but the story is always working its way, with obdurate, ghostly force, into his narratives about fathers (real and surrogate), and carries the real burden of the narrative mystery—the shaping force of its formidably "illogical" sense. The "motivation" of Anderson's male protagonists in the three films I study becomes increasingly skewed, deformed, and unfathomable, and in each case the mangling pressure derives from the protagonist's inability to secure a crucial "lost" balance and alignment with absent, not-quite-buried maternal shades. Literal mothers recede further and further into the background—part of an unspecified, unrecoverable, impossible-to-overcome past in which some significant damage and severance have transpired.

The animating myth and subterranean logic of Anderson's films since *Magnolia* is a remaking of the mother out of new materials, and the piecemeal recovery of mother's nurturing power, which is as much feared as it is sought after. I think the quest for an archetypal female form and voice—the restored mother, brought back from "death" and reintegrated, as in *A Winter's Tale*—accounts for Anderson's characteristic sabotage of traditional narrative form. *Punch-Drunk Love*, *There Will Be Blood*, and *The Master* all focus on incapacitated, near-outcast men whose environments both mirror their mentalities and imprison them. Anderson, with ever-greater audacity, removes the lynchpin of traditional narrative logic, and in *The Master* he dispenses with laws of causation almost completely. It is as though the *form* of reason driving the protagonists' actions is also the form of reason (radically defective) governing the film's world. World and protagonist reinforce each other's delusions, and dictate the seeming necessity of internal stasis and preordained routes to fallacious goals. Both "forms" of reason—internal and external masculine prisons—are doomed to fail without the miraculous intercession of unreadable events, mystical voices, sounds, and surreal images alive with obscure, insistent promptings from a realm "elsewhere."

The rest of this introduction examines what I take to be the contradictory pressures at work in the avowedly autobiographical, densely verbal *Magnolia*, which may have necessitated a change in Anderson's method and technique in the films that followed. I argue that the "Wise Up" musical number is the place where Anderson confronts a crisis of truth telling and attempts to resolve it by replacing speech with music. This segment, and the later hailstorm of frogs sequence, which I treat only briefly, expose several other facets of Anderson's filmmaking that are key to my study: Gaston Bachelard's intuition of the instant, Robert Duncan's concept of emergence, and formal strategies (doubling/pairing, disruption/containment, a spiritual preoccupation with innocence and grace) that take on even greater prominence in the three films I examine separately. Finally, the endangered and dangerous, indecipherable self, after *Magnolia*, receives relentless attention in Anderson's creative vision, along with the ambivalent solicitations of a "disconnectedness" that alternately comforts and destroys.

* * *

The "Wise Up" sequence is one of Anderson's great, flabbergastingly chancy set pieces. To understand its narrative function in *Magnolia* and its powerful emotional effect, one must first consider the logic of its placement in the narrative structure and how it serves as both an answer to, and a release from, the "pushed-past-the-breaking-point" verbal turbulence that precedes it. From the beginning of his career, Anderson has been drawn to operatic, bipolar contrasts between scenes of savage eruption and antidote scenes of containment. The latter frequently create a contemplative, interior space in which the outpouring of malignant energy is diffused and, to some degree, cleansed. Anderson's lead-up to his relay of restorative melody—in which the same song is unwittingly passed from one afflicted soul to another in their separate coops of isolation—has been a grueling scrutiny of the same individuals in public settings, each at the end of their tether. We are given what amounts to a "domino effect" of escalating breakdown scenes, a "cusp-of-the-millennium" cascade of rage and panic, swelling like a contagion and penetrating every sector of *Magnolia*'s nine storylines. All the major characters are cracking open concurrently, and the stream of hurt and invective flows from every direction uncontrollably, like a biblical flood. It is hard to know whether the need for reprisal or the need for atonement is the greater force of expression, and which of these needs speaks in a louder voice. Impending death from illness, family alienation, the humiliation of a child, the tremors of addiction, and a scalding misogynistic rant are among the "alarms" that are sounded and then blended into an audio endurance contest of unstrung woe.

This collective voice of frenzy is suddenly diverted into the more subdued flow of a single rambling speech. Bedridden Earl Partridge (Jason Robards), one of two older fathers in *Magnolia* dying of cancer, and whose mind is wandering in its final extremity, embarks on an epic eight-minute monologue. Anderson aptly refers to this desperate lament as a "Eugene O'Neill speech." The frantic hullaballoo of the other characters, who can hold nothing back, is unnervingly supplanted by a helpless, hopeless creature for whom the end is very near. He is the last runner in the "fever of life" gauntlet. Earl, like the other "carried-away" voices, is *possessed*, in his case by regret for having wasted the love of his first wife through successive acts of sexual betrayal and emotional abandonment. He insists, while confessing to Phil (though it seems he is mostly talking to himself), that regret, far from being useless to him at this juncture, is indispensable to him: "you fuckin' regret what you want. You can use that, okay?" His meandering speech, as filled with anguish as any of the wild voices that have gone before him, transposes the language of eruption into a softer key, one in which energy and breath are scarce and must be husbanded. Though he declares that he has squandered the love entrusted to him, bemoaning the fact that his story is not a good one and does not hold together, his steady emphasis on the centrality of love shifts the film's atmosphere from desolate fury to something more inward and gentle: a groping tenderness. The rainstorm that fills the darkness outside becomes attuned not to violence but to tearfulness, the "what'll I do?" of Earl's blank, childlike trembling.

To accompany the final stretch of Earl's speech, Anderson switches visually to some of the characters whose accusing outbursts we have witnessed. They are now silent and solitary in their separate outposts, trying to figure out their next moves. Earl's speech confers a kind of benediction on all the perplexed, vulnerable faces we behold. His frail voice is now the common shelter in which the stricken, faded-out speech of the other characters seems to gather. Near his bedside, his nurse Phil (Philip Seymour Hoffman), fighting back tears, fills a baby dropper with liquid morphine and releases the contents into Earl's mouth when the old man's power of utterance gives way. At this juncture, the musical number "Wise Up," performed by Aimee Mann and many of the film's exiles from happiness, gets underway.

In the *Magnolia* shooting script, Anderson describes the blurred transition into the musical number as a form of "hoodwinking": "I thought the best way to do that number was to have it creep up on you" (205). The first singer, Claudia (Melora Waters), appears to be half-listening to the song on her apartment stereo after doing a line of cocaine. She feels moved to join in with the song because it is one she knows, and its lyrics have an immediate application to her own predicament: "It's not what you thought when you first began it . . . you got what you want, now you can hardly stand it." Each of the eight subsequent characters who takes up the lyric from where the last singer left off resembles Claudia in the shared condition of isolation, in the "discovery," whether the character is awake or unconscious, of a connection to the song's injunction ("wise up"), and in the attainment of kinship with Mann's voice, which has somehow found them. She enters them as an abiding spirit, appearing to *know*, in the way of singers, both who and where they are. A trial release from their various entrapped states is gained, in some but not all cases, by the capacity simply to repeat the spell-breaking reminder: "it's not going to stop until you wise up."

Anderson's characters in *Magnolia* are split into doubling pairs—a strategy that persists and is further complicated in his subsequent films. "Wise Up" allows us to diagram how the pairs' situations mirror

Claudia (Melora Walters) is one of the nine characters singing over Aimee Mann's "Wise Up" in *Magnolia*

and oppose each other simultaneously, resulting in one sort of avowal or awareness being reversed, thrown into question, and brought to an impasse.

Two figures closely connected to Earl Partridge—his present younger wife, Linda (Julianne Moore), and his estranged adult son, Frank—are both discovered by a tracking camera in parked cars, in separate locales. Linda, overwhelmed by panic, guilt, and confusion about who she is and by the strain of long-term addiction, has passed out as a result of a suicidal overdose of her husband's pain medication. We observe her in shadow behind a car window streaked with rain. Linda, in effect, dreams her portion of the song, which has to do with "signing away the deed" of life and compiling lists (too late) of impossible needs. Having found a means to avoid the unbearable spectacle of her husband's death, Linda seems involved in some peculiar race to the finish line with him. Frank, we have just learned from Earl's final speech, was abandoned by his father while his mother was dying of cancer. He was essentially left on his own to take care of her and watch her die at age fourteen. During the song, Frank appears to be contending against his entrenched persona of a coldly self-sufficient, ruthless operator and misogynist. He sings his way past the repeating phrase "it's not going to stop" and arrives at the blockage-dissolving phrase "till you wise up." Frank, in effect, is singing unconsciously in opposition to Linda, Earl's "replacement" for his mother, as she reenacts his own mother's disappearing act, slipping toward death. Frank's show of strength as he presses against his steering wheel feels "borrowed" from Linda, whose own resolve and dim sense of purpose ebb away.

In another pairing are two elderly fathers dying of cancer, both with an alienated adult child. Jimmy Gator (Philip Baker Hall), who has steeled himself against remorse and self-interrogation, tries to push thoughts of his cancer and the daughter he sexually molested (Claudia) out of mind as he sings a fantasy phrase about being "sure there's a cure" and that he's "found it," thereby stopping time. Earl Partridge, who, as we have seen, tried to evaluate his many relationship failures unsparingly in his lengthy, half-delirious monologue, lies unconscious, like Linda, while Phil sits at the foot of his bed and sings that "it [Earl's suffering] is not going to stop." Earl, from his own dream space, seems to have found the "cure" that Jimmy vainly pretends to see, having taken it upon himself to "wise up." He confronts the derelictions in his life unflinchingly and finds it fitting that the "story sense" he attempts to make of his life "falls apart."

A third pairing involves two quiz kids, one young and the other middle-aged, grappling in their separate realms with the unanswerable question, "What Do Kids Know?" Donnie Smith (William Macy) sits in front of a giant commemorative portrait of the check for $100,000 that he had won decades ago, money that his parents stole from him. He sings about drinking to kill the pain as he mulls a plan to "retaliate" against the boss who just fired him. He wishes to retrieve some of what his parents robbed him of; he will become a thief himself to punish the parental thieves who got away with it and abandoned him. Young Stanley (Neil Flynn), singing as he sits over an open volume in a darkened library, conveys a counter-message with his stillness and centered position in the frame. Earlier he wet his pants and hyperventilated during a live broadcast of *What Do Kids Know?* in futile protest over being exploited on every side. He now appears to be marshaling inner resources after a day of great upheaval, waiting to see what happens next. There is strength in his passivity. Donnie's passivity, by contrast, seems to render him blind as well as weak. He is anxiously bent on futile action.

Stanley's arrival in the song comes right on the heels of Frank, who is striving to undo his own exile, and his adamant long-term refusal to look inward or backward. Frank, in effect, turns into Stanley, the somber child who seems arrested in the midst of his (presently) useless heap of knowledge and his powerless verbal fluency. Frank's dying father is matched by Stanley's father stretched out in bed, impenetrable in his sleep by a child needing to break through to him. The remaining characters who take part in the song are not literal children, like Stanley, but operate as further extensions of the confounded quiz kids' childlike qualities. The policeman, Jim Kurring (John C. Reilly), though he has been through a divorce and has a job that is fraught with ghastly encounters, seems strangely imbued with innocence. He has a totally uncynical attitude toward his life and a way of relating to even the most troubling aspects of his police work that feels utterly engaged and without callousness. Claudia, though a cocaine addict, a victim of her father's sexual abuse, and someone incapable of ordering her existence so that its turmoil might be reduced, partakes—in a fashion that seems difficult to account for—of Jim's unextinguished, grown-up innocence.[1]

Central to the predicament of all the paired and split male figures in "Wise Up" is Jim Kurring's accidental, humiliating, "childish" loss of his policeman's gun shortly before the song begins, and his frantic, unsuccessful, flashlight search for it in the rainy darkness. The loss of the gun (a marker of aggressive, assured masculinity) is implicitly a collective experience for Anderson's group of broken, fearful, and vulnerable men. They have each been returned, by different routes, to a condition of childlike helplessness, which is tied—if only by desperation—to increased openness. Frank Mackey is in many respects the most complicated figure in his charged relationship to "gun" loss. As he contemplates paying a visit to his dying father, many things are simultaneously threatened, among them his embattled hatred and fear of the female, the foundation on which he has erected his false, fiercely barricaded public persona. His terror at his mother's "weak" dependency during her final illness and his resentment over the massive caregiving demands placed on him as she prepared to abandon him by dying (when he was barely an adolescent) have grown hopelessly entangled with his father's neglect, absence, and show of *strength* in withholding love. Frank's split between the "not going to stop" and "wise up" poles of his internal debate are amplified when he at last sits beside his father's unconscious body, repeating several times the imprecation "you fucking asshole," while in the very next breath acknowledging his dread of abandonment—losing love and strength once more: "don't leave me, don't leave me."

The missing phallic gun establishes linkages as well with other missing, stolen, rerouted objects. Donnie has illicitly acquired his paternal employer's keys, one of which breaks off in the lock of a door he strives to reopen—intriguingly, not in the act of robbing his "father," but in the effort to cover up his earlier break in by returning the money he had robbed. The spread and theft and spilling and hiding of "medication" that forces addiction and pain killing (to the point of near-lethal overdose in Linda's case) occupy the same porous category. Pills and cocaine are used in much the same fashion the "gun" is—to hold a person together who is otherwise in danger of falling apart. Linda steals some of her husband Earl's painkillers for her ironically "self-integrating" suicide attempt. One of Earl's dogs eats some of Earl's pills that Phil, faced with too many concurrent demands on his attention, drops on the floor. He can't find all the pills scattered across the floor, mirroring Jim's fruitless gun search in his panicked attempt to retrieve them. The dog dies as a consequence of Phil's failure to gather them all up. Jimmy Gator's medicated grogginess and on-air collapse during the quiz show is made to seem interchangeable with contestant Stanley's desperate need to pee, and the shaming release of urine down his pants leg—which renders him unable to perform his designated role as boy "know-it-all."

"Wise Up" ends with Stanley urging capitulation with the phrase "So just give up." It is significant that his words are offered by a voice that hasn't changed yet. His voice rises to a boy soprano pitch to blend with Aimee Mann for the song's concluding high notes. Stanley's last correct answer on *What Do Kids Know?* before his cave-in involved his singing aloud in French a fragment of an aria from Bizet's *Carmen*: "Love is a rebellious bird that no one can tame." (The boy soprano switches genders, as it were, to perform Carmen's self-exonerating lament.) The "Wise Up" sequence is therefore bookended by two victimized children of different genders (Claudia and Stanley), with a number of other child "remnants" interspersed between them. The three grown-ups in the group (a stepmother and two aged, spent fathers) are all hovering near death. Aimee Mann's voice is assigned the monumental task of drawing a musical line strong enough to somehow integrate a fractured group psyche—or, put another way, to bring a single psyche, resembling Anderson's, out of its massive disarray, so that it may live again, into the light. The female Claudia, aligned with Aimee, must be the untamed bird that can fly—through the force of music—all the way to shivering, waiting Stanley, and release him from confinement.

* * *

The "Wise Up" sequence, though occurring well before the end of *Magnolia* and serving as a preamble for the even more fanciful rain of frogs to come, feels—at least in memory—like the emotional climax of the film. The song brings the most prominent characters in the film into powerful, fleeting alignment. Their disparate voices, identities, and quandaries converge persuasively through the simultaneous reception of the same music, which each of the listeners recalls with a set of private associations, and then imitates until the song becomes a solvent of paralysis or discord. Anderson insists on music's capacity to break up the "frozen sea" within us—in this instance, if one is visited by the right fragment of song in a moment of abandonment and takes possession of it in a voice that risks a matching "exposure." The number charts a movement past solitary struggle to a vision of unified brokenness, yearning and quiet release. The uncanny (one might say unearthly) plausibility of this movement is what gives the "Wise Up" interlude, for some viewers, its affecting power. The many voices congeal, independently, into a single expansive consciousness, and the one song, addressing a host of different demands, becomes an unlikely instrument of persuasive integration.

Anderson takes a mammoth risk by inserting a musical sequence so late in his narrative, without any preliminary warning or formal preparation for an eruption into song that is as serious as it is surreal. The split between the utopian impulses of the musical and the dire extremity of end-of-millennium melodrama makes our transition into the song a tonal collision, which initially dislocates us. Anderson further heightens the viewing challenge by having the atmosphere of the musical performance so transcendental and laden with narrative consequence. "Wise Up" is designed to be an extended moment of major significance for all the beleaguered participants. Self-confrontation and a keener awareness descend on the singers, as it were, in one fell swoop, like a Paraclete from radio heaven. Far from disguising the song's deus ex machina properties, Anderson insists on laying the mechanism bare and reveling in its obtrusiveness. The entire fragile edifice of the film might well collapse if the "Wise Up" sequence registers as nothing more than bathos and authorial hubris. Anderson briefly jettisons one well-established framework of representation (messy, snarled-up realism) and replaces it with a framework that is overtly choreographed, stylized, and highly compressed. He paradoxically makes his gentle, formally and emotionally contained musical montage *dangerous* by so brashly disregarding the rules of proper film storytelling and constructing his climax on a foundation of coincidence. He arranges it so that the characters arrive at their separate turning points in perfect synchronization. This consolidated awakening seems governed by serendipitous grace and authorial fiat rather than by dramatic necessity. And the number recklessly flirts with absurdity, apparent in such decisions as beginning the song with Claudia snorting her cocaine and, later, having two singers (Earl Partridge and his wife, Linda, the latter in the midst of a suicide attempt) performing in states of unconsciousness.

Despite, or because of, its numerous infractions, "Wise Up" attains sublimity. Anderson, in Leslie Jamison's apt phrase, "cranks up the volume of the pain stereo" for so many scenes of seemingly cathartic but in fact stymied verbal release in the half hour preceding "Wise Up" that the viewer *longs for* an alternative mode of expression. The *composed* (in the widest sense) song supplies that new mode, allowing the internal action of the film to regroup and begin afresh, just in the nick of time. The many wrangling voices that Anderson himself has whipped up to fever pitch fall still for an interval, and in their place appears a voice from the *outside*, that of Aimee Mann, who finds a way to bring the whole of the film's jumbled community under her sway, for the duration of her song. Something large seems to be at work as Mann's ability to break through mental resistance spreads. And yet the impact of the number depends crucially on the perfect ordinariness of the depicted activity. Nearly everyone can call to mind the familiar gratification of recognizing a song that "speaks" to the moment's concerns and needing to take hold of it in one's own voice in some private place, safe from prying eyes. One after another, the characters attend to Mann's phrases as they blend their voices with hers, and in so doing acquire a different kind of mirror for their own perceptions.

Eileen Rizo-Patron, seeking analogies for the "intuition of the instant" in Gaston Bachelard's metaphysics, refers to "the sudden daunting realization of personal responsibility for the recurring errors and habits that rule over our thwarted lives" (xii). This description nicely captures the burden of truth that the song delivers to its captive auditors. In *Intuition of the Instant*, Bachelard considers the mystery of how instants of intensity can yield repose. Or rather, the intense instant yields *to* repose, becomes the gateway to it: "The *immediate* experience of time is not the experience of duration—elusive, difficult, and abstruse as it is—but rather the sober experience of the instant, apprehended in its immobility. All that is simple and strong in us, even all that is enduring, is the gift of an instant" (19). Bachelard then moves from an examination of the gift to thinking about the way the attention lays hold of the instant's promises. "Since attention has both the need and the power to recapture itself, it is in essence to be found entirely in its resumptions. Attention is also a series of beginnings; it is constituted by those mental rebirths that occur in consciousness when it heeds time's instants. . . .

If you watch a cat stalking its prey you will be able to see the *instant* of attack suddenly inscribe itself upon reality" (21). Finally, and most suggestively, Bachelard argues that "attention is always born of coincidence. Such a chance event is the minimum of novelty necessary to focus the mind" (21).

As I noted earlier, "Wise Up" commences with Claudia mentally split between the stereo playing in her apartment and the line of cocaine she has prepared to inhale. The song *coincidentally* enters her awareness while a separate action is in progress. The words bear some relation to her act because she fully attends to them while she succumbs to a familiar destructive pattern. The words are not merely heard but remembered from prior listening occasions. She claims the words by singing along with them, becoming in the process their coauthor. Joining a song, one paradoxically becomes more aware of the words one *chooses* to imitate and absorb, than one is conscious of one's own words—authored, as it were, when we speak to others. In Bachelard's terms, the words "recapture" Claudia's attention, allowing her to begin afresh, and like the cat in its instant of attack, to have the words sharply "inscribe themselves" on her reality. The song itself has *future* phrases, a destination that it has not yet arrived at. But Claudia, in her instant of realization, has scarcely an inkling of the song's solution of awakening, which lies just ahead. She is caught by the threat of endless repetition. She does not feel herself (yet) in the power to escape what she "once wanted"; it is a power foreign to her, since the thing she wanted has taken over. She wonders, as she achieves the release that the cocaine brings, whether this sort of fulfillment is something she ought not to be able to stand any more. "Now you know," she sings. But does the knowledge of this *instant* accommodate anything but the certainty that the circling back to surrender will never stop?

Bachelard describes the "complex instant" as "brimming with simultaneities," which, as in a poem, "shatter the simple continuity of [duration]." Privileging as always the instant over duration, Bachelard regards the latter as "shackled time" (*Intuition*, 58). In "Wise Up," we behold a succession of individuals occupying different spaces, as it were, simultaneously. They overlap each other in their shared singing relationship to the same song and take each other's place, one after another, as transmitters of the music's power to undo, to make happen.

One phrase or set of phrases gives way to another, with several returns to the exact same words. Each singer borrows strength from the song for the instant he or she vocally inhabits it in solitude. The impression of solitude is steadily diminished as the ever-progressing melody is once more passed to another, wholly absorbed participant. The song forms by increments its own secret community, whose bonds seem to proliferate without being directly experienced or known. The *coincidental* sharing of the same melody presses the viewer to bridge within herself or himself the marked split between despair and affirmation in the group psyche.

It is chiefly Mann's pervasive presence as primary singer that is sensed by each "blending" performer and lifts him or her out of isolation. Privacies that run deep enough to elude the knowing self are touched in incommunicable ways by the singer's soft, uncoercive avowal of intimacy. The found figure assents through simply echoing the sounds that produced connection. But what precisely does each moment of "assenting to being found" yield? It is fittingly difficult to say. With the growing hollowness of assertive language in the cumulative din preceding "Wise Up," words began to feel like a blankness into which various declaimers, while breaking down, futilely flung their will. Language refreshes itself in music by "starting over again," in a sort of nursery hush, with a maternal voice (Aimee Mann's) making the world over, as one does when crooning a lullaby late at night. A recurring feature of Mann's way of interpreting her lyrics is to keep oscillating between fearful sorrow and a hesitant but spacious joy, a sense of blessing. The words keep repeating, but the meaning shifts as the emphasis alternates between "it's not going to stop" and "'till you wise up." There is a rising and falling movement throughout, depending on whether the singer's moment coincides with a solace phrase ("you're sure there's a cure and you've found it") or a hopeless descent ("it's never going to stop"). The predominant phrase-by-phrase sense is of continual reversibility of feeling; the mood doesn't stabilize. In Bachelard's terms, it is a "stimulated ambivalence—an active, dynamic ambivalence" (*Intuition*, 59) as each instant lifts, then climbs down. Antithesis seems to ride on the intake and outflow of breath. What the voice avows it must give up, so that avowal can once again occur. The instant seizes both the burden and possibility of needing to begin once more. Something is purely present, but then yields to echoes or intimations. "Misfortune flowers," as Bachelard puts it, in a beautifully ambivalent phrase.

What *emerges* in "Wise Up," depending on which character carries the tune, is ongoing transformation, a seizing of a different sense than what came before, but then a circling back to a sense before that, which in the interim has acquired new meaning and novelty. Attention is recaptured as the instant arrives, transfigured, *now*. "The paths toward purification," Jean Lescure writes, "presuppose the possibility of reiterated births. They call for the instant to shatter temporal fate, for discontinuity to authorize surprising advents" (quoted in Bachelard, *Intuition*, 70). "Wise Up" precipitates one rebirth after another, though an instant is the length of each awakening, and is the all or the very little that the rebirth encompasses. It seems—as we watch and listen to the sequence—that an "all" has found its way inside the very little.

What I term *emergence*, a term borrowed from the poet Robert Duncan, is a mode of revelation that gains ever more prominence in Paul Thomas Anderson's films. It occurs in the aftermath of an extreme disruption of film convention, a scrambling of narrative logic, or an abrupt departure from daylight sense. While appearing to honor the daylight sense of the "Wise Up" lyric's warning and spiritual hope, the song's actual effect is an intensification of *uncertainty*. The construction of continuities coincides with the building of a labyrinth of divided outcomes. We learn almost nothing about how the characters are benefited by their moment of transport. Is the weight of the ceaselessly repeated song phrase "not going to stop" cumulatively more decisive than the balancing phrase "wise up," with its implied possibility of regeneration?

As "Wise Up" fades, we cut to a view of a deserted city street in the rain. We may notice (within the same long-shot composition) a distant traffic light reversing its customary sequence, moving from red, to yellow caution, to green. Then the rain too abruptly ceases. A written weather prediction appears onscreen ("Rain Clearing, Breezy Overnight"). Literal doors begin to open immediately in the new sequence as Jim Kurring picks Claudia up at her apartment door, then opens his car door (with his key in mammoth close-up) as he commences what he regards as an "innocent" date. Donnie knocks on a neighbor's door, then proceeds to borrow a car from her to facilitate his planned robbery. (The kind, elderly female neighbor's door and the garage door behind

A misleading forecast as the frog storm approaches in *Magnolia*

which her car awaits are forcefully shown in the act of opening.) Frank arrives in timely fashion at the door of his dying parent's home and is eagerly welcomed by Earl's nurse and three amiably barking dogs. Just before Donnie leaves *his* home—with the intention of breaking into his former employer's warehouse—he contemplates himself briefly in an oval mirror, repeating a mantra: "You know, you know, you know." After "Wise Up," the world of the film opens up to a flurry of purposeful activity, suggesting widespread release from impasse and bondage. But this impression of "united" character awareness is as deceptive and misleading as the weather report. A convulsive storm of frogs will soon descend on the San Fernando Valley.

Stanley's despairing "So just give up" does not provide a clear preparation for the immediate (though temporary) cessation of rain. Donnie's "You know, you know, you know" does not indicate that he knows what has to be done, or why he is acting in the way he is. An open door can signify emotional progress and an admirable readiness to take chances. It can just as easily express regression (in Donnie's case), the shock of exposure, and the need to conceal oneself from close scrutiny. The first door-opening after "Wise Up" supplies us with positive and negative facets of door logic, with the simple device of a reverse angle. Jim arrives at Claudia's door, eagerly anticipating his second encounter with her and the date he has taken a chance on. When the camera cuts to Claudia on the other side of the doorway, we observe that she is high on cocaine and shamed by Jim's appearance of friendly receptiveness and trust. She is also anxious lest anything she thinks she knows about herself be accidentally divulged to him. Everything she sees argues for concealment. From her perspective, too much openness is pure threat. A song that intervenes as an act of grace to bring about a collective spiritual shakeup and rescue is equally concerned with reinforcing blockades. The song does not confer more awareness than, in the next breath, it spirits away. What remains when the song is done—what it leaves behind instead of knowledge—is a richly self-contradicting doubt.

The emergence of the irrational, grotesque, or indecipherable event in Anderson narratives is more often than not meant to disrupt or dissolve a chain of causality associated with the patriarchal order—a masculine mode of logic based on gaining or preserving control. The female counterforce in Anderson films is often quiet in its operations, an attempt to subdue (through unaggressive assimilation) and otherwise contain out-of-control energy. "Wise Up" is quiet containment of this sort, though Anderson's decision to resort to a full-fledged, uncategorizable musical set piece could also be regarded as dissonant, insufficiently grounded, and untenable, as many of *Magnolia*'s initial reviewers found it. Aimee Mann's songs provide a basis for male replenishment in a realm separated, by a brief but crucial distance, from the spoken word. The female vocal presence (like an enveloping sonic mother) emerges out of nowhere in "Wise Up," supplying both an authoritative primal source (and force) to its listeners, and at the same time giving backup to those who searchingly join their sounds to hers.

The frog storm unleashed near the conclusion of *Magnolia* functions as a more eruptive version of the female divinity or hidden force that intervenes in the "Wise Up" sequence. It can scarcely be claimed that the frog onslaught appears in the narrative without advance warning, since the film is honeycombed with references to 8:2, the source of the Exodus story of the frog plague (Exodus 8:2). There are, all told, at least fifty of them (Lane, 19). The main purpose of these signs and portents is not their capacity to foretell but to be strangely invisible—hidden in plain sight. Neither the film's characters nor the viewer are in a position to interpret the recurrent harbingers accurately. They are a kind of ordering principle, certainly a pattern, but a pattern whose value is bound up with "veiled" witnessing. Even more significant than the overdetermined but nonetheless inaccessible 8:2 is the biblical verse that immediately follows it, 8:3: "And the river shall bring forth frogs abundantly, which shall go up and come into thine house, and into thy bedchamber, and upon thy bed" (King James Version). The bedroom is the crucial territory that the frog downpour will "smite," and I would construe it as a return of the female repressed.

On a first viewing of *Magnolia*, one is likely struck by the disproportion between the sound and fury of this epic biblical event and its somewhat modest narrative consequences. Closer examination of the frog deluge reveals a substantial number of noteworthy outcomes, though they are still "small-change" incidents for such an otherworldly cataclysm. Here are the most telling effects: the interruption of Jimmy Gator's suicide attempt and its replacement by a more depersonalized, Rube Goldberg–style comic death, involving skylight shattering, TV demolition, and a resultant chance fire; the magical return of Jim Kurring's lost gun; the flipping of an ambulance conveying Linda to the hospital after her overdose, which does not result in her death but in her bizarre (comic) arrival at the hospital's emergency entrance by prolonged skidding; Frank's exchange of a single wakeful, possibly conscious look with his father, Earl, as Earl dies; Donnie being granted belatedly (and, again, comically) his wish for damaged teeth to match the bartender's he is in love with, who is obliged to wear braces; and Stanley being struck by the sheer wonder of this extravagant release from a rule-bound world ("This is something that happens," he says aloud to himself). Finally, and to my mind most importantly, Claudia's mother, Rose (Melinda Dillon), abandons Jimmy Gator after the full, horrific weight of his deceptions are exposed to her, in one of those Bachelard intuitions of an instant, and who, after a hazardous car ride in which she is bombarded by plummeting frogs, is reunited with Claudia as the storm peaks. While they cling to each other, Claudia repeatedly cries out "Mommy . . . Mommy, Mom." Rose, in response, declares that things are "okay" now, that she will protect her daughter from the storm, and that the two of them will henceforth be all right. The camera intercedes further by closing in during their embrace on a tiny message at the bottom of a painting that hangs in Claudia's room: "but it did happen"—as though commenting equally on the brazen fact of this emotional breakthrough and on its unlikelihood. The following morning, we watch Phil awaken Frank with a phone call from the hospital, where Frank's stepmother, Linda, is recovering from her overdose. We part company with Frank in a hospital corridor, searching for her room.

In this labyrinth of divided outcomes, convergence, and coincidence (like the narrated "historical" stories that open *Magnolia*) are presented as inevitabilities, by "dark dreambook" logic. Random chance and irrational derailments of one system of sense lead to mysterious potential cures. Necessity, which so often exhibits a harsh visage, forms provisional alliances with demonstrable human needs. The frog storm threatens two mothers with death, then spares them, in a manner that feels both haphazard and ordained, so that they can find their way, by different routes, to "frozen children" who need to be revived. Two fathers—caretakers of a failed masculine system—die in the mothers' place. The frogs are a flushing-out of Jimmy Gator's monstrous secret, evil that must be violently "returned to sight" before being drowned out. He is the prime mover, it seems, for this widespread infestation ("into thine house, and into thy bedchamber, and upon thy bed"), the unforgivable sinner who attracts notice from the heavens. After Jimmy is eliminated, Jim's lost revolver drops from the sky. Maleness "regroups" in a man-child bearing the same name as the one who could find no path to restitution.[2] As one of his final acts, Jim raises the question "What do we forgive?" as part of his fantasy scenario of a "cop" being interviewed for a reality TV show (this question is raised by Jim in a portion of a final monologue that doesn't appear in the finished film). Donnie, a hapless criminal whom Jim has saved and forgiven (choosing not to arrest him) gives voice, through mangled teeth, to the confusion that everyone in the narrative has grappled with: "I really do have love to give—I just don't know where to put it."

As Aimee Mann's singing voice resurfaces at the close of the narrative, she seems the bearer of strange tidings and dreams of possible escape routes whose meaningfulness is chiefly sanctioned by the *reality* of her presence. Claudia watches from her bed beside a window carrying morning light, as the figure of a man—his back turned to the camera—slowly approaches her. It turns out to be Jim, but the way his coming forward is photographed defamiliarizes him, emphasizing the difficulty of being known and trusted by another. Love between these two, on a better footing than either has experienced previously, is certainly conceivable. Will Claudia and Jim find where and how to put this love that they each presently require? Claudia appears almost able to envision it before the camera abruptly ends its scrutiny of her, and the screen goes black.

* * *

Speaking about his collaboration with Aimee Mann in one of his interviews following the release of *Magnolia*, Anderson said:

> Aimee was the person who turned me on to the investigation of who you are and what your background means to you . . . [She] and I have been friends so long that I've been able to watch the evolution of her songs. And not just that, it's that she's my friend and I can call her on the phone and get in touch with certain things that are going on in her songs that were created, at least in some ways, in relation to things that were going on in my life. And hearing things in your life re-created by another artist really gives you a greater awareness of the way things are going on around you. (*Magnolia* shooting script, 204)

Aimee Mann is not only the most significant female collaborator Anderson found for *Magnolia*, she is the decisive female presence in his entire body of work thus far. Her voice and music in *Magnolia* lay the groundwork for subsequent versions of female infiltrations of the narrative landscape. The singer-composer is both separate from the film's world and its most potent internal miner, the one whose unconstrained "manifestations" of spirit penetrates—with grace, sadness, and enviable freedom—the narrative's core. "I always hear the music before I write, or as I write," Anderson observed, in another *Magnolia* interview. "Even structurally the movie becomes a little like verse, chorus, verse, chorus, bridge" (Onstad, 2000). He speaks at greater length in the published *Magnolia* shooting script about music as a vital bridge to clarity. His then-girlfriend, songwriter Fiona Apple, "taught me something I'd never really known: Honest and clear *is* possible and good and it makes for better storytelling" (viii).

I would phrase the long-term lesson of *Magnolia* for Anderson somewhat differently. I think Anderson, in the course of making *Magnolia*, underwent a gradual, initially baffling sea change. He repeatedly stressed in interviews after the release of *Magnolia* that the film's 190-page screenplay was written entirely from the gut, that his method was to let everything pour out torrentially. Declaring how one has been damaged or damaged others, how one needs to fight back or dispose of one's cargo of guilt, initially strikes us in *Magnolia* as an efficacious, time-honored means of achieving self-awareness—by breaking through barriers. Although such confessional effusion is marked by repetition, awkwardness, and a floundering compulsion to discharge whatever leaps to mind, there is an underlying sense that the characters in *Magnolia* understand what afflicts them, and that their breakthrough will be attained by means of a purified utterance. Judging from the increasingly taciturn, oblique, and mysterious screenplays Anderson has written since (the adapted, prodigiously talkative *Inherent Vice* screenplay is the exception)—each of them built around a character unable to articulate his dilemma and who is manifestly at odds with spoken language—I think it is reasonable to argue that Anderson came to distrust remedies available to the free-swinging orators of hurt. "From-the-gut" candor wore out its expressive capacity. Anderson decided that the art of truth telling was necessarily more oblique. Direct confrontations of psychological "issues" could perhaps only mine the surface. The huffing and puffing of outward grapple are often delusively theatrical; the harder truths of the inner life may well prove inexpressible. After *Magnolia*, Anderson becomes fixated on how to break the overweening confidence of verbal dexterity, making talk instead either a halting muddle or a "veil of deception." He begins to seek out the voiceless desolation that lies beneath the beasts we have a name for. His characters need to be "reborn" not only in the Bachelardian sense (in the luminous uncertainty of each momentary intuition), but with silence asserting a claim prior to and perhaps greater than learned speech. Each of his main characters seems to be working to undo some deep, obscure hurt that an oppressive archetypal speaker has visited upon them. Speech avoidance, in part, signifies an attempt to rid language of its original polluting power and the sinister, coercive entanglements it engendered. He makes a firm shift of allegiance from characters who know what they have to say and who mean what they say, to figures who only mean *how* they say things.

In *Punch-Drunk Love*, the film that follows *Magnolia*, and which I examine next, Anderson arranges to have the narrative arrival of Barry Egan's prospective love interest and mystically tinged mother replacement, Lena, coincide precisely with the mysterious delivery of a harmonium outside his workplace. The harmonium is presented as an object version of Lena, which Barry must find the courage to retrieve, protect, and learn how to play. It is in disrepair when Barry first gets hold of it and stashes it in his otherwise forbiddingly sterile inner office The instrument is as much an

The harmonium that Barry (Adam Sandler) rescues from the curb in *Punch-Drunk Love* represents his wish to connect with Lena

embodiment of his own embattled "female" identification (he is under relentless siege by his seven domineering sisters) as it is of Lena's otherness. Like Aimee Mann's singing, the harmonium is a refuge from the treacherous demands and omissions of "overheated" verbal discourse.

The Sledgehammer of Eros in *Punch-Drunk Love*

> BARRY: (*while kissing Lena in bed, fully clothed*) I'm sorry I forgot to shave.
> LENA: Your face is so adorable. Your skin, and your cheek. I want to bite your cheek. I want to bite your cheek and chew on it. It's so fucking adorable.
> BARRY: (*pause*) I'm looking at your face, and I just want to . . . smash it. I just want to fuckin' smash it with a sledgehammer and squeeze it, you're so pretty.
> LENA: (*no pause*) I just want to chew your face and scoop out your eyes and want to eat them, chew on them and suck on them.
> BARRY: Okay. This is funny. (*Nodding.*) This is nice. (*They kiss.*) At the restaurant, I beat up the bathroom. I'm sorry. (*She hugs him.*)

I now focus on the poetic concept of emergence in Anderson's 2002 comedy, *Punch-Drunk Love*, with particular emphasis on its manifestation in the love scene (quoted above) in which Barry Egan (Adam Sandler), after finding the courage to pursue his love interest, Lena Leonard (Emily Watson), to Hawai'i, whispers to her in bed his desire to "fuckin' smash [her face in] with a sledgehammer." The second episode I explore at length, one that delivers visual and auditory shocks related to the verbal shocks presented in the bedroom scene, occurs near the beginning of the film: the curbside delivery, by taxi, of a damaged old musical instrument—a harmonium (portable organ)—literally moments after a disastrous, perhaps fatal, flipping of a vehicle on the same street. The harmonium, in effect, dislodges the mysterious, seemingly horrific car accident from narrative view and memory: we will never be concerned with it again. The distressing linkage in the bedroom scene of Barry trying to discover an appropriate language to express his love with an incongruous wish for violence is a psychic variation on the earlier, equally baffling juxtaposition of the harmonium and the terrifying assault and suppression of the accident involving the Jeep Cherokee. I am interested in developing an idea of "poetic emergence" as it functions in indecipherable, affronting film episodes such as these. It is useful to distinguish between narrative events that at least loosely conform to our sense of the rules and genre conventions that a film has "bound itself to" and the less common experience of emergence—which I define in my discussion of the "Wise Up" sequence in *Magnolia* as a wrenching of form, an overturning of daylight sense that permits something genuinely unknown to come forth from concealment. I conclude my analysis with reflections on how emergence relates to Anderson's unusual employment of allegory throughout *Punch-Drunk Love*'s narrative.

The U.S. poet Robert Duncan writes at length of emergence as revelation in his magisterial critical study, *The H.D. Book*. Duncan is not directly concerned with film, but his reflections on what poetry requires to come into its full power seem to have a clear bearing on the eruptive moments that Anderson devises for crucial occasions of shattering in each of his own feature films. Duncan hopes to identify the ways in which a fittingly radical poetics might include all of the things that contemporary culture "excluded or hid from itself," and how particular poems or acts of poetic vision gain access to them once more. Duncan testifies to poetry's sovereign capacity to move us beyond the sensible, beyond reason-respecting terms that some forms of realism mark as the domain of the real. His "recovered" categories have to do with "hidden or lost traditions of thinking about Eros, hidden or lost modes of conceiving of time and space, hidden or lost ways of representing the self or person, [and] hidden or lost understandings of the source and nature of form" (8). I follow Duncan's lead in conceiving of emergence in film poetically. Images and sounds may retain their affiliation with narrative logic, genre conventions, and the phenomenal world—Duncan calls the last of these the What Is—while, simultaneously, something of a different order emerges from a hidden place. What comes forth may feel "irrational," spiritual, or phantasmagoric, as it struggles to reconnect us with an entity or force we have mentally banished from the world we are prepared to recognize as our own. In a way that is beyond casual, we have lost sight of this forsaken thing struggling to break through to consciousness, and thus have also lost the sense of it. Emergence is a forceful coming back to light, a return of something to consciousness after a long period of exile. It may well feel like a first encounter rather than a repetition. One can recollect what is emerging without understanding that memory is involved. The power of the return can be enhanced if one can feel the linkage with something that came before, without being able to firmly place it.

In film, emergence occurs at points when the codes we rely on to make sense of film stories and participate in them temporarily give way. They are too limiting, a viewer may feel, to account for what is being presented. There are suddenly unfamiliar demands being made, and to meet them we must lose our moorings—become adrift. The sights and sounds that throw us off course are manifestly unintegrated, unstable, combustible. Thinking about what is being released from hiddenness acquires an explosive quality. Our very placement in the narrative is, for an interval, drastically under siege. Even if the effect presented is quiet—for example, Barry whispering his desire to Lena—we sense a violent disruption of our mental patterning. As we try to pacify one or more unsettlingly discordant elements with comprehension, the elements seem to exceed our powers of containment. Emergence, as I conceive of it in film narrative, has to do with the abandonment of laws that bind, namely our "natural" cultural assumptions and glosses. Emergence, for Paul Thomas Anderson, is about stretching old units of social measure and containment until they crack open. Something jets out, spills over like the oil in *There Will Be Blood*, while concurrently a reliable way of securing meaning drains away. We might think of the loosening of narrative law as a failure of a convention (say, of genre) to do its customary work. Perhaps a convention must suffer exposure *as* a convention in the act of breaking, as we've seen in the case of "Wise Up." A convention becomes poignantly visible as it fails, stripped of the disguise that made it appear natural and worthy of unself-conscious assent.

So, we lose our footing in a convention while something unanticipated or unrecognizable emerges from hiddenness. The coming out from hiding—which implies a prior time of being forced into hiding—is a crucial dimension of emergence. What else does emergence have to do with losing orientation, or, more metaphysically, with being lost? If we think about Barry Egan's condition of lostness at the beginning of *Punch-Drunk Love*, which nearly everything in his environment, appearance, and behavior seems to ratify, the film is suggesting that he and we must become even more fully lost, that we must cast away whatever need we have for the security of placement or adjustment if we are to find a route to a remedy. The estranged person must go deeper into estrangement in order to reduce his entrapment. Adam Phillips writes compellingly about children having to discover or invent "the experience of being lost" to supplement whatever actual lostness is present in their life circumstances: "They, we, will spend as much time as we can getting lost to protect ourselves from the experience of being lost" (*On Balance*, 173). He makes an important distinction between getting lost and *being* lost: "Getting lost might involve working out, as far as one can, what kind of excess not being lost involves one in. One gets lost when there is the excess of an object of desire in the vicinity; one is lost in the absence of this promising excess" (174).

* * *

The *Punch-Drunk Love* dialogue between Barry and Lena cited earlier forms part of a remarkable feat of emergence, in the enlarged sense of "coming forth" that I've been outlining. But before we can ascertain what it is that breaks loose from the worn-smooth signs and passwords of romantic comedy, we must attend to what those depleted, "exposed" conventions convey to us in their own right. We need to specify what the romantic and comic contexts leading up to the bedroom scene seem to have prepared us for. What do we think we have been led to understand and have faith in as this couple begins to make love for the first time? Our sense of their closeness, and what has been settled between them in the sexually fragile atmosphere of the Hawai'i hotel room, is suddenly no longer sharable or knowable. When precisely does this loss of security occur, and what are we to do with the pure potentiality—dangerous and dumbfounding—that replaces our comfortable connection with the lovers?

Barry Egan is played by Adam Sandler, whose comic persona, in film after film, is strongly associated with mock outbursts of essentially harmless anger. Anderson endows the character of Barry Egan with Sandler's familiar trait but makes a crucial revision. In Barry's case, the rage that frequently erupts from him, uncontrollably, is real. Because he can neither govern nor comprehend it and keeps it in a repressive compartment entirely separate from his "good" qualities, his rage has the capacity to do serious damage—psychic as well as physical—to Barry and whomever seeks to draw near to him emotionally. Barry has no means of evaluating his bouts of fury. He can scarcely acknowledge that they've happened and cannot bear to dwell on the strange actions engendered while the fit is happening. (In this respect, Barry's outbreaks directly parallel the handling of the Jeep accident at the beginning of the film. No sooner does the horrible collision erupt, seemingly without sense, before our eyes, along with a deafening sonic accompaniment, than it is swept off frame and narratively forgotten.) One might call Barry an innocent—a savage innocent—and that impression persists even when he is flying apart.

What Barry does recognize, fully, are his fears. Cues to panic abound in his world. His carefully managed daily routines in his equally sterile office and domestic environments are designed to stave off the forces of terror as much as possible. Nothing in his living spaces is allowed to be self-expressive in matters of taste or personal inclination, given the likelihood of Barry's nature being more subject to attack, if he isn't burrowed in. Behind every piece of evidence that he is pressing for more life (and Barry feels such evidence is incriminating) is an anxiety worm, eating up whatever dares to show itself. Barry's childlike sweetness and mumbling affability are a kind of cringing social uniform—like his confining blue suit—meant to camouflage his ever-present distress. He is mortified by his fear, going to great lengths to prevent it from leaking out shamefully in his dealings with others. (Barry has one devoted lieutenant at work, Lance [Luis Guzman], who appears to take everything Barry says at face value and to acquiesce without questioning his reasoning. Barry is comfortable with Lance because he mounts no challenge to any of his assertions and requires no explanations. He is Barry's Sancho Panza as a "little-brother" figure, and like Panza with Quixote, he accepts with minimal understanding the "madness" of the man he dutifully accompanies.) In all other relationship circumstances Barry is outwardly deferent, often servile. His deference and docility are a bit confounding, even repellent, since they are so bound up with a compulsion to appease. Barry's benign qualities cannot flourish if they are merely shame-induced coverings for dread. Nor does he have the slightest suspicion that his fear is continually feeding his rage, its dark, secret twin.

Anderson's plan for the viewer in *Punch-Drunk Love* is to keep him or her confined in an uncertainty comparable to Barry's own. We are encouraged, for example, to doubt the seriousness of Barry's anger, because of our secure awareness of Adam Sandler's customary comic distance from such outbursts. Genuinely demented rage would also clog the gears of romantic comedy's forward movement, placing major obstacles in the way of the comedy's ostensible goal: the joining together of a "sane-enough" couple. No matter how persuasive Sandler's disconcerting descents into derangement may be, in their aftermath we attempt to ameliorate or evaporate the *too-muchness* in what we have witnessed. We wish, just as Barry Egan does, to insulate his gentleness—the "*true*," childlike Barry—from contaminating contact with his blind, lashing-out moods.

Yet Anderson also obliges us to contend continually with the densely experimental style of *Punch-Drunk Love*, a style mammothly concerned to rattle our conviction that Sandler's Barry is a comfortable, accessible entity. Among the imposing features of that style are these: the camera's off-center manner of framing Barry; the jangling sounds that accompany his ordinary efforts to navigate his nondescript environments, a noise network that is expressionistically attuned to his atavistic inner life and that seems to prod Barry and viewer alike toward a nervous breakdown;

the steady impact of minutely calibrated perceptual shocks to Barry's system (legible on Sandler's face and body) as he processes even the most innocuous external stimuli; the swirl of blending, flowing color patterns that appear to be composing a separate but related story within the story. All of this delirious instability persistently ratifies Barry's lostness and the agitations that are his psychic inventory. Set against these challenges is the viewer's *need* that Sandler's persona still be available and operative. We cling to the promise of Sandler's buoyancy and the remnants of his innocence like a life raft so that the logic of the romantic comedy form will not entirely disintegrate.

Prior to the bedroom scene, Barry has taken the immense step of committing to a first-time plane trip, then flying to Hawai'i in pursuit of Lena, a woman about whom he knows next to nothing. He does know that she has declared her interest in him and that she has demonstrated an almost alarming degree of patience with his idiosyncrasies. (The viewer is as unsure as Barry is of what to do with Lena's unwavering attitude of bemused devotion. Maybe we regard her with a measure of suspicion. Lena could easily have an unrevealed sinister agenda, matching that of the woman Barry "connects with" on a pornographic chat line.) In their encounters thus far, Barry has inadvertently revealed much about himself to Lena that should prove disconcerting to her. In no instance, however, has she responded to him with the apprehensiveness that his self-exposure would appear to warrant. So Barry is now resolved to throw his inexhaustible caution to the wind, following her to a faraway, unknown and therefore undoubtedly hazardous (in his eyes) island. He has managed somehow to clear a number of additional hurdles once he lands in Hawai'i and succeeded in meeting up with Lena in the crowded lobby of the Royal Hawaiian, where the two forcefully collide in silhouette and embrace fervently. After an unbroken string of surprising gains, Barry accompanies Lena—following her lead—through a perplexing maze of impersonal hotel corridors (the film abounds in colorless pathways of this sort) and has dared to reach out to hold hands with her as they draw closer to her room.

The camera greets Barry's initiative in taking her accepting hand with a conspicuous iris-out effect. Anderson employs this device not simply to overemphasize, comically, the act of hand holding, but to defamiliarize the "simple" ritual of touching another—whereby Barry braves the dan-

Having tracked Lena down after arriving in Hawai'i, Barry (Adam Sandler) calls her from his "hotel room" in *Punch-Drunk Love*

Barry in the first of several mazes in *Punch-Drunk Love*

ger of increased intimacy. By reanimating a dawn of cinema technique for sequestering a luminous detail from everything around it, Anderson confers a beautiful naïveté to the camera act of paying heed. For Barry, this protective securing of a woman's hand is a momentous declaration of closeness. A man who is so self-conscious that he has no casualness whatever at his disposal completes a basic act, assertive and vulnerable at once, and in so doing transcends himself and becomes half of a couple. The taking of the hand, the iris-out tells us, is something to be not so much recognized as deciphered. What might this move signify, in its unforeseeable potential for two with such scant knowledge of each other to go on? One might be inclined to argue that, for Lena, holding hands is a less sizable or meaningful leap of romantic faith than it is for Barry. At the very least, she grasps the convention in a fashion that Barry cannot match. But for Lena to ignore a host of distressing signals and lead this jittery, unbalanced stranger to her room with neither hesitation nor reserve requires a canyon-wide jump on her part. To offer her hand to Barry seems to him a great pledge. He might well take it to mean that she is promising "everything," and Barry's imagined everything is clearly inordinate, engulfing. He is a creature with a possibly bottomless need.

An ellipsis places us inside Lena's room, indeed on the unsettling expanse of her bed, which the camera slowly reconnoiters in a close-range tracking movement (from foot of the bed to headboard) as though it were yet another type of corridor. Somehow difficult boundaries have been traversed since the previous shot, and Barry's body, still clad in its blue suit, is resting atop of hers. Foreplay has been initiated—we assume by her—and Barry seems involved in a disconcerting experiment, with no better than a frail hope of meeting his lover's expectations, however modest they may be. The camera comes to rest on a close-up of their heads. Light seeps in from a window behind them. It does not quite manage to warm them visually, and it competes with a liquidy test-pattern band of blue (matching the shade of Barry's suit) horizontally stretched across the lower third of the frame. Though the blue partition does not claim additional space for itself during the extended dialogue exchange in this shot, it conveys, almost subliminally, an impression of water rising. Barry seems to hover precariously above this realm of fluid light. Because the blue rhymes so perfectly with his clothing, a pulling motion is gently established, menacing Barry with the possibility of sinking, even drowning, in this still lake.

Punch-Drunk Love erratically conforms to romantic comedy structure, despite its many odd deviations from it. Anderson needs that structure to ground the viewer, to give her some sense of narrative direction and orientation. That structure alerts us to the fact that a crisis is looming. The progress of the unlikely romance has been too smooth and swift. Barry appears well out of his depth, and under pressure to express himself in ways that he is not sufficiently self-controlled or self-aware to navigate. Lena, who has been so bafflingly receptive to Barry's internal kinks and bizarre besottedness, must very soon hit against or trigger some grotesque flare-up of misconduct that will exceed her vast tolerance. At the very least, Barry is sure to disappoint himself (and to some extent Lena) with his fumbling anxiety as he approaches the monumental hurdle of lovemaking. His childishness peeps forth in his first words to her: he apologizes (in an elongated, doleful "I'm sorry") for having overlooked the *rule* of shaving before commencing his sexual task. As the camera cradles both of them, calmly, and brings us closer, we brace ourselves for Barry's stumble. The tightening of our proximity to the pair of large heads adds a measure of discomfort, but it also creates a space of palpable silence in which our attention must nestle with a kind of held-breath discretion. We fear for both Lena's and Barry's precarious well-being in this small sphere of tender, bodily trust they are ushering in. Barry's shuttered psyche seems, at this moment, placed in our keeping. We feel that he is on the verge of wronging or harming Lena somehow, without meaning to, and himself as well. We also anticipate that she will recoil from this finally unacceptable wrong, as she has every right to do. We do not want to add to Barry's impending woe by wronging *him* with a too-hasty repugnance at his failure, whatever form it may take. It is disconcerting to acknowledge that we don't know him well enough to predict what he will do to her, or how to account for its significance.

Lena's response to Barry's apology for neglecting to shave combines gentle reassurance with sexual daring. She tells him that his face is "adorable," marvels at the appetizing texture of his skin and cheek, and, suddenly but calmly turning feral, expresses three times the desire to "bite" him. That she finds his face "fucking" adorable instills in her the strong urge to sink her teeth into his cheek, or at least the urge to say so. Barry pauses, giving himself time to process Lena's declaration and intention. (The viewer feels comfortably ahead of Barry's effort to make sense of what she has told him. We have no trouble parsing love talk that conveys the hope of a "sweet devouring.") Concluding that he has caught her gist, he proceeds to quietly divulge a desire of his own. Like an eager-to-please pupil, he mirrors what he takes to be the substance of her disclosure and shows his courageous readiness to exceed her in unrestrained truth telling. He begins by announcing that he too is contemplating the face in front of him; his demeanor and intonation make it clear that Lena's features are an enticing sight. The face gives him ideas, which he shyly endeavors to put into words. He is confident that the melody of Lena's own "biting" wish is carried forward and impressively amplified. "I just want to . . . smash it. I just want to fuckin' smash it with a sledgehammer and squeeze it, you're so pretty."

Something utterly unprecedented in the language and thinking about relationship available to romantic comedy emerges from hiddenness here, in the Robert Duncan sense of meanings yet-unmade and untried that I described earlier. It is the most drastic, mettlesome Anderson signature moment in a film where such audacious ruptures are plentiful. One's first impulse, as one reels from the speech's inscrutable effrontery, is to laugh. Adam Sandler, a comedian, has once more said something that "crosses the line" in a freakishly nonsensical manner. The apparent vein of tender seriousness in Barry and Lena's trial-and-error romantic exchange was perhaps *merely* a setup for a monstrously excessive joke. The avowal not only disrupts the rhythm of the scene but (if we believe that Barry means it) also shatters the shaky veneer of the character's sanity. Barry is now utterly marooned from the viewer's capacity to read him at all. His recuperation by renewed contact with social norms—no matter how elastic these norms may prove to be—seems, at this moment, unlikely.

Further evidence that the speech is predominantly comic in intent is found in the structural symmetry of Lena's initiating speech and Barry's simple-minded response to it. If we place Barry in the category of the artless child-man who mimics a female adult's *pattern* of speech without following the tricky *figurative* speech of her avowals, then his egregious mistake makes manageable comic sense. What works against our effort to make comedy resolve the problem of Barry's speech intention, and thus relieve us of the necessity of taking him at his word, is Barry's recurring collision with his propensity for violence in many previous scenes. His eruptions have been consistently distressing to viewers because, contrary to our expectations and possible hopes, the violence has psychological grounding in Barry's fathomless rage. The expression of this rage, whatever its source or root causes, is unbearably defenseless and not to be taken lightly. We must return to the difficult proposition that when Barry whispers his desire to smash Lena's face with a sledgehammer, he means what he says, at some crucial, still-to-be-ascertained level. Surely it is possible to give voice to a violent impulse, to own up to a fury at one's core that is joined to the wellspring of love, and to mean it without *knowing* exactly what one is saying. How often the most excessive words, tumbling out of us without filter or calculation, fall short of conveying the full complexity of truth. They go too far but still can't reach to where they need to go. Barry is attempting to locate his love within the immeasurable, frightful vulnerability that is opening up and pouring out inside of him, threatening to dissolve the barely formed person that he is. He speaks here, unduplicitously but with dire effect, out of his innocent but still-terrible relation to a necessary violence.

Barry is like Psyche before her betrayal of Eros, when she is wandering, untutored and without a plan, in Eros's palace. Apuleius, in his version of the myth in *The Golden Ass*, describes the contents of love's palace as standing undefended before Psyche, who regards its plenitude without knowledge: "No single chain, bar, lock or armed guard protected it" (Duncan, 87). The feelings that engulf Barry as he "lets go" with his love are so immoderate that he is even more likely to shatter at their emergence than when he is swarmed by fear. He is confusing himself with Lena, in the meld that loving engenders. When he talks about the smashing or shattering that must happen if he is to be released from his fraudulent, stifling shell, it is as though it were being done to *her*, literally and by proxy. Breakage is emphatically not mere metaphor. Barry senses that all the boundaries are loosening and that he is crumbling away with *unthinking* haste. He needs to bring Lena right along with him, make her mingle in the smash-up of the inadvertent nonperson he used to be. His common speech is drenched, like sleep talk, by spurts from the unconscious.

Barry hopes that his sledgehammer urges harmonize with Lena's own talk of chewing and biting. She has somehow ushered him into a nursery of speech acts, where, like creatures just acquiring language, they can say anything, testing the reality of their power to make a dent in an obscure, resistant world. The shooting script version of Barry's speech is much longer, more cushioned with explanation and points of safety. It begins with his assurance to her that "I-I-I-I-I-I-I don't want to hurt anything ever, but . . ." (76). This soft, anxious-to-clarify testimony seems less truthful than the more succinct, primal utterance Barry is left with in the film. Can there be any doubt that Barry has wanted, and felt driven, at times, to "hurt things"? But, as I have argued, his destructive, retaliatory instincts are inadmissible, debarred from conscious knowing, and produce so much guilt when there *is* a detonation that they must instantly go into hiding. Barry's condition returns him, often and helplessly, to what Christopher Bollas calls the "unthought known," which Joan Richardson characterizes as the place of "earliest being, in-fans—literally, that 'cannot speak'—the condition of being without words, for an extended moment living and feeling in the light and shadow of our first object, the mother" (125).

* * *

In the bedroom "sledgehammer" scene, Barry is trying to acknowledge the curious idea of *shared* existence with Lena in a manner that does not recapitulate the bullying, infantilizing concern of his phalanx of seven sisters, whose oppressive extension of mothering makes love identical with humiliating subjection. To their incessant invasions of his psyche by constant, demand-filled telephone calls has been added the phone sex caller he reaches out to earlier in the film, whose proliferating threats and attempts to communicate blur together with his siblings' claims on him. Sex talk and family love talk are virtually indistinguishable. In fact, with the phone sex caller the initial promise and expectation are that Barry (once he has entrusted a female gatekeeper with all his "personal" information, in strictest confidence) will be introduced to a voice whose sole aim is to draw forth his desires uncoercively and gratify them without judgment or reprisal. But from the onset of his fantasy exchange with her, his partner's "sweet talk" has an edge to it. Barry is dealing with another interrogator, like his sisters, but one who lacks any of their concern for his welfare. The sex provider's speech proceeds with aggressive haste and a transparent pretense that knowing something about him is part of the pleasure. The air of intimacy is, unsurprisingly, impersonal, and the push to make him unburden himself amplifies his status as a man without qualities to call his own. His desperate hope for closeness, a semblance of human contact, is treated as though it too were an assembly line item, identical to that of any other customer.

On the morning after her glassy-voiced coaxing to reveal his secret cravings, the phone "lover" calls Barry back. She rapidly transforms into an ever-closer approximation of his sisters, making peremptory demands for further money, assistance, and compliance, and refusing to take Barry's resistance seriously. She follows his sisters' preferred tactic of relentless follow-up calls. The consequence of this fusion is that the "private" realm of sex has been infected, indeed taken over, by the most painfully constricting patterns of his upbringing and current family imprisonment. Barry's suppressed proclivity for violence as a means of escaping the python grip of family love is imported into the part of his psyche guarding itself against sexual inundation. (We earlier saw his resources for suppression fail him when he shattered glass partitions compulsively at a family gathering. The glass shattering is a corroborating response to the ramp-up by the sisters of their verbal assault on him. They repeatedly call their brother Gay Boy and retell—probably for the 1,000th time—the story of his destruction of a glass door as a child.) Giving in to sexual impulses may well result in his manhood being further shredded in a duplicate "family blender."

When Barry refuses to heed the phone sex caller's extortion threats, her boss in Utah, "Mattress Man" Dean Trumbell (Philip Seymour Hoffman), dispatches a posse of four brothers to travel to Los Angeles and attack Barry, which they do, first when he is alone and later when he is with Lena in the narrative's second car crash, after the couple return from Hawai'i. The transformation of sibling gender swarm from female to male provides Barry with a dreamlike arena where he can release his hostility toward his sisters at one remove, in a stunningly efficient, righteous frenzy. The sledgehammer of bedroom fantasy becomes a real tire iron with which, in a clockwork ballet of focused rage, Barry smashes two of his assailants' faces in and repeats his earlier attack on glass by shattering several windows in their pickup truck. The brothers' interference with the progress of his love for Lena—represented by the violent, deliberate car collision—suggests that all the "sisterly" demands of the phone sex caller and the pressures of an endlessly repeating family invasion pattern have not been overcome or left behind. Barry's trust in the newfound realm of sexual intimacy is extremely fragile. The past pursues him in misshapen, unrecognizable forms. The brothers, the collision, the need to explode, all feel like the unshakable forces of Barry's own nature: a repetition compulsion disguised as a means of escape. Lena's face sprouts blood as Barry's car spins round and round. He gazes at her wound dizzily, both seeing and not seeing what it signifies. His car has been struck, in effect, by the violence in himself that he aspires to keep separate and distant from Lena—something she must not know about him because he has not yet come to terms with it himself. Anderson's shooting script for *Punch-Drunk Love* designates a shot in which the camera "pushes in on Lena . . . as she notices Barry going pretty fucking crazy" (81). The film wisely removes this act of beholding. Lena is given no reaction shot. She disappears from view until Barry returns to her in his car, recapitulating Barry's trip to the bathroom in their earlier restaurant date, where he tears the facility to pieces and then calmly walks back to their table, where she waits for him.

Barry's triumphant settling of scores with the marauding brothers is, in my judgment, less a victory over Barry's fear than it initially appears to be. Lena sits dazed in his car as he, equally dazed, leaves his vehicle and, with dreamlike clarity, seizes the role of avenger. This savage eruption following the car crash returns us to the car accident Barry witnessed, like a melting jellyfish, at the beginning of the film. He has thrust the first incident from his mind as a seemingly necessary denial, a denial of his fear that his own bottled rage has caused the Jeep to flip over. This repudiation summons—by the opening's dream logic—the harmonium to arrive in its place: thus, to *take* the place of his destructive impulses. Just as hints of Lena's magical redemptive red attire—linked to the harmonium—peep out at Barry during his travels through a variety of color-deprived indoor labyrinths, so a series of large vans turn up with eerie frequency in the city streets, quietly menacing and perhaps carrying as their hidden freight Barry's own destructive powers. It is important that we see his real and projected foes as standing in the same blocking relation to him as his sisters. What is outside doubles as what is inside him, yet again. The phone voices, for example, are both "out there" and a cascade of noise *within* Barry, the gibbering fretwork of his sparse self-definition. And the fearsome antagonists he contends with are equally embodiments of his unreckoned-with drive to lash out, to tear himself to pieces. Lena's wound as a trigger for his "calm" explosion allows his violence to be a spontaneous expression of love. But we are mistaken to think he has achieved clarity in his rampage.

Because Barry has experienced love with Lena in a space cleansed of obstacles, he expects (when the brothers crash into him) that he can yield to violence in a similarly "cleansed" space, with impunity. He wants violence to release the same freeing intensity that he has found in his successful pursuit of love. He discovers in his surrender to it the same inviting lucidity and force, but in the street brawl his explosion of pent-up energy attains a clarity that is only delusive. In its aftermath, Lena grows dim for him. He almost forgets her connection to him when he leaves her at the hospital. The summons to further retributive rage takes precedence over love's harmonium, and it takes a trek from Los Angeles to Utah with a new weapon in hand (a phone receiver with a severed cord) for Barry to discover a better means of confronting his nemesis, Dean Trumbell, than through "simple" brutality. (It is not clear how Barry makes this journey. He suddenly shows up in daylight, on foot, in front of the Mattress Emporium, which rises up before him, like a destination in a vision. Anderson suggests the possibility of a magical 650-mile hike across the desert. A flurry of psychedelic colors bridges a scene of Barry talking with directory assistance on a black phone and then reappearing, with a white phone receiver in his hand, in a wide empty space, moving forward toward Trumbell's lair.) Trumbell, like so much of Barry's world, opposes him through an act of doubling.

For Friedrich Schlegel (1767–1829), the key philosopher of the Romantic movement, the universe "was an infinite and infinitely bewildering chaos." Art, according to Schlegel, attempts to express this chaos and give it approximate shape through an endless doubling process. "Art was . . . the dialectic fusion not of one pair of opposites, but of many pairs, all of which, shading off into each other in subtle nuances, were the periphery, as it were, of the same mysterious center that was the heart of the paradox," making *emergent* "the essential 'duplicity' [duplicity as doubling] of art, which reflected the 'duplicity' of man and the 'duplicity'—the infinite plenitude and infinite unity—of the world itself." This process cannot be brought to a "happy" resolution. "A Romantic ending," for Schlegel, is always by necessity "a temporary one," a moment in the cycle of approximations, "and [the Romantic text itself] a monument of a necessary failure" (Rosenbladt, 57–58).

Barry somehow projects himself across the desert to track down the overseer father figure, Dean Trumbell, whose minions have hurt Lena, and who looms large as a threat to Barry and Lena's future domestic (and sexual) tranquility. Locating him in an elastic film instant in his Mattress Emporium in Utah, Barry reduces this distant, controlling patriarch to manageable archetypal size. He does so by seeing through the facade of power Dean has erected. Barry unearths Dean's own fearfulness, uncertainty, and comic failure to uphold a stable image. He detects the "duplicity" of his double, who cannot withstand close scrutiny. Barry, having acquired self-knowledge and new intuitive powers in the course of his "long walk" with the disconnected phone, recognizes all of Dean's evasive maneuvers and defenses as inflated replicas of his own. He does not need to engage him in meaningless physical combat. All that is necessary is to see through him and to stare him down. This anticlimactic encounter is a beautiful comic corrective to the confining revenge logic of the street fight with the brothers. Barry confronts Dean (who possesses his own blue attire—jeans—and now wears a blue barber drape as well for his haircut, administered by a female employee who suggests Delilah trimming away Samson's strength with her scissors). He proclaims that he has a love in his life that gives him a strength Dean can't imagine. What he demands of Dean is a declaration of no further harm, a simple "air-clearing" fiat: "That's that." In the face of Barry's love-bestowed centeredness, Dean wilts and capitulates.

* * *

So much for shadows of the oppressive father. Barry's seeking-out and overcoming of the mother proves more daunting because it involves Lena directly. Let us return to the bedroom "sledgehammer" scene, where Barry must find the image of the unappeased, paralyzing mother in the lineaments of Lena's face and must acknowledge that part of his desire is the longing to hammer it. The wish to hammer the mother is a need to find a face that is distinct from all the entrapping substitutes. He would break through the Medusa demeanor of the toxic nurturer (who can only demand and impose) and find an accepting, uncoercive face in its stead. Once he makes contact with a love that does not reduce and crush, he can perhaps disentangle love from his reflex capitulation to suffocation disguised as care. Barry's inner and outward protest has never been claimed by him; it dwells like an outcast in unmarked terrain. To be equal to the challenge of sex (and its powerful tributary, love) he must borrow—like a mini-Prometheus—some of the fire that belongs to his rage. In so doing, he reverts to a child's state, which always means something more and other than what we think. He is renewing himself as a child of appetite and daring, as opposed to the child in the corner, head lowered. It is only by laying claim to his violence that his love can be made real. Not to make contact with it is not to emerge with Lena.

Barry, face in shadow, whispers to Lena in such a way that he relieves himself (for now, at least) of his painful load of self-consciousness. His voice is delicate and lovely and his demeanor entirely responsive as he offers her his hideous song of smashing. He would crush her face, and in so doing, prove his readiness to shield her from all harm. There is something of Lennie here, from Steinbeck's *Of Mice and Men*, who doesn't know his own strength, doesn't know better than to squeeze the "soft animals" he loves until they strangely die. Barry possesses vastly more intelligence than Lennie, but his fledgling feelings lag well behind his thinking. While he *has* his intelligence, his feelings "have" him, and it is a puzzle to consider what advantages there might be in letting this arrangement persist. What does it mean to let your emotions have you? It is fitting—indeed, expected—for small children that inordinate feelings "have" them in their grip most of the time, as part of natural development. The volatility must be experienced and accepted as belonging to one's body and psyche before they can be rationally evaluated and brought down to manageable size. A hemmed-in child-man like Barry Egan can easily be deemed insane when going through the same process belatedly, but perhaps in his case as well, the broadest possible confusion about being "had" by one's emotions is indispensable. The trick is to find human company safe enough to allow one to conduct in another's presence these long-delayed but necessary experiments. The unruliness must come forth, monstrous elements intact, before a true sorting-out can commence.

A greater shock than what Barry actually says to Lena occurs immediately afterward in her response to it. Anderson's direction of Emily Watson here has her continue with her previous line of erotic invitation without the slightest pause or the faintest hint of a reaction (76). This is not evidence of distraction on her part or a failure to absorb his meaning fully. We have the awed, initially dismayed impression that she embraces his avowals as though she had been anticipating confidences of just this kind. No shadow flickers in her expression. Apparently, she finds nothing in his threat to draw back from and nothing which need disrupt the continued play of shared "craving talk" they devise together. She leaps beyond us in intuitive understanding without our being able to grasp how she did so. Because she becomes an enigma at this point equal in its challenges to Barry's own mystery, we might well entertain doubts about *her* sanity, as well as his.

Lena's response confounds and dismantles genre expectations yet again. We have been thoroughly alerted, as I noted earlier, that sexual initiation will pose major obstacles for Barry. We expect that Lena will finally see that self-protection dictates distrust and will draw back abruptly, in shock, from what Barry heedlessly shows her about himself. The time is right—if not long past due—for a rupture in their relations. Too many large obstructions in a row have been almost effortlessly disposed of. Yet instead of turning away, Lena speaks even more voraciously of face chewing, upping the ante by adding Barry's eyeballs to the projected meal, "eyes" she proclaims she will scoop out before "eating, chewing, and sucking." There is no discord whatever in this rhetorical contest of passion. "Anything you can do, I can do better," she seems to be saying, like the sparring sharpshooter lovers of *Annie Get Your Gun*.

Lena and Barry mutually accept the proddings of excess in what Rimbaud has called the "immense unruliness . . . of the senses." In fact, it is Barry who is momentarily brought to a halt by Lena's unbridled talk, as though *her* extremity were the thing that warranted questioning. Barry says "This is a *joke*." He comes to grips with her eyeball coveting by cautiously deciding to regard her effusiveness as pretending, of a kindly sort. "Okay. This is funny." (He accompanies this statement with a nod, as though inner confirmation of a nervous hunch is immediately required.) Her excitement, it appears, holds no perils for him. Although he is uncertain about her state of mind with respect to him, he discovers, perhaps with a little jolt of surprise, that he is not afraid.

At this stage they commence more sustained, committed kissing, which Barry experiences—in a manner that seems noble and debilitating at once—as a demand for further truth telling. He must divulge a shameful secret on the spot, and receive pardon from Lena, if he is to be sufficiently pure of heart to receive additional embraces. "At the restaurant, I beat up the bathroom." This prior destructive seizure of Barry's during their first dinner date is an action he has kept secret from Lena and, to some extent, from himself. It emerges as something both that is painfully clear and that needs, after becoming visible, to *be cleared*. He emits a small, half-strangled "I'm sorry," the phrase he endlessly repeats in the film as an alternative to actually feeling regret. He wants her to know what he has done, but perhaps he isn't contrite about "beating up the bathroom." Maybe he shouldn't be. Once more Lena appears to be emotionally in advance of him, with a spirit mother's omniscience, demanding neither clarification about this incident nor reasons for any additional worrisome lapses. She meets his abashed mood shift with a spirited embrace, which again arrives too swiftly and spontaneously to be the result of a *decision* to reassure. She exhibits the mystifying, unshakable calm we have come to associate with her, and the effect is otherworldly. I am moved by the incredible fact of her calm not being somehow delusional, or an act. She is not in mental flight from suppositions that are beginning to weigh and prey on her. The scene ends with the assurance that all obstructions to exalted lovemaking have, against staggering odds, been lightly swept away. Whatever muddle remains, the vital linkage that Barry dared to put his faith in prevails.

But as Anderson treats us to an old-fashioned blackout effect, signaling sweet concord and the imminence of matters not for our prying eyes, we may still marvel at how unknowable the lovers remain. We do not know them and cannot quite figure out how they have picked up signals that lead them to imagine they know each other, even in the most rudimentary sense. Customarily, in romantic comedy, when one of the central courting pair is bedecked with character defects and swathed in eccentricity, an ample explanatory framework is provided for the more "normative" character's attraction or gradual succumbing to the problem figure's initially well-masked allure. In *Punch-Drunk Love*, Lena seems more drastically in need of causation accounting, given her headlong pursuit of Barry and inexhaustible patience with him, than perhaps any steadfast lover in the genre. Yet Anderson, where Lena is concerned, goes to great lengths to keep the usually well-stocked cupboards of character "causation" factors strikingly bare. What Anderson does show us, near the beginning of the film, is Lena seeking out Barry at his workplace, just after the harmonium is unaccountably dropped off by a Checker Cab van at the curb near his warehouse. Later, we are told that

On the pretext of arriving too early for an automotive appointment, Lena (Emily Watson) meets Barry in *Punch-Drunk Love*, handing him her key

Lena had once seen a photo of him in the company of his seven sisters. She remembered the image of Barry, a loner in this female crowd, and made an effort to procure an introduction. This is almost the full extent of what we learn about Lena's impulse to pursue him romantically. The only additional clue is her statement that, as an only child herself, she is curious about someone raised in a crowd of siblings. The harmonium and a photo we never so much as glimpse are the entire basis for the woman's resolve to connect with him. Somehow Lena feels that Barry's "risk" in retrieving the harmonium is a recognition of who she is, a meaningful bid for attachment.

Anderson is insisting, against the accumulated counsel of love story conventions, that explanations of the ready-made variety are useless. They do not grant us human knowledge that matters or takes us anywhere. The sense of adequate character knowing (the legible mechanism of psychology or typing) is generally too cheaply bought. It is artificial and becomes nonsense by affording too much sense, at the expense of mystery. Anderson would have us believe, with Robert Duncan, that we do better when placed in the dark and held there, as Psyche is with Eros, when she is enjoined not to cast light on him, or everything will go awry.

* * *

Anderson's preparation for the harmonium's emergence in the film's opening sequence is the staging of a ghastly, earsplitting accident on the city street—a large event in cinematic terms, and impossible to ignore. We cannot see what causes the Jeep Cherokee to flip over, which augments our interest in the action. But what proves more perturbing than the *fact* of the accident is its prompt disappearance. As I noted earlier, the immoderate crash seizes the viewer's awareness and, in the next instant, escapes from the narrative without leaving a trace. It has no overt plot repercussions and seemingly no hold on the narrative's future. It could be argued that this preliminary flash of car chaos prepares the way, by a kind of occult forecast, for a rhyming action much later in the film: the later rear-ending of Barry's car by the Stevens brothers' pickup truck. This deliberate attack by the bent-on-intimidation Stevens clan occurs right after Barry and Lena pass through a slowly opening garage door in Barry's car, reminiscent of Barry opening a similar garage door manually in the film's opening sequence. The first garage door lifting resulted in our initial glimpse, together with Barry, of daylight and the outdoors, and was followed swiftly by the scalding sight of the car crash. But the urge to connect these two crack-ups does not clinch the meaning of the one we encounter at the beginning. Its meaning continues to feel suspended, withheld; the later repetition of its out-of-nowhere explosiveness in another key does not dispel the first accident's nimbus of terror and impenetrability. If anything, the senselessness of the opening mishap seems to overspread, by a kind of contagion, the clearly intended later collision.

The linking of a high-impact visceral incident with its immediate removal from view (a wiping-away from what we might call the movie's mind) makes us attentive to the *scale* of things when "emergence" is at issue, and of how onscreen time-flow necessarily alters as emergence—in this case, of both the car wreck and the harmonium—takes place. Robert Duncan identified various conditions as characteristic of poetic emergence: a break with intelligible order, an influx of seemingly haphazard elements that make strong demands on the reader, and a resultant disorientation as the reader fails to place the new things in any sort of adequate arrangement. The "coming forth" exceeds our powers; we can't subdue whatever the images release to us. Recall Duncan's arresting phrase: "hidden or lost modes of conceiving of time and space"

(8). Time requires a separate rhythm, a different pulse and rate of flow to handle the onset of mystery. For a radically new perception to escape the dictates of custom and ingrained response, pressure must be brought to bear on both our spatial placement and its enclosing time frame. Time needs to find a scale of its own to match the intensified scale of the erupting action. It should thoroughly partake of the chaos-inducing sabotage of familiar narrative pattern and progression. Time can be made to freeze or meander or compress in conjunction with the sudden defamiliarization of space. Our effort to process the disturbing new experience may create a split between its existence as a physical happening and as a mental event. The emerging incident won't consolidate its claims as one or the other. And time as well splits between "natural" unfolding clock time and the stuttering dream time of consciousness.

Let us consider the different sorts of time rhythm and time pressure at play in the releasing of the harmonium into the film's world. Lostness and emergence combine here to especially powerful effect. Gunther Schuller, speaking about rhythm experiments in the late compositions of Brahms, describes Brahms's exceptional attentiveness to the "science of the beat": "What Brahms was after was to create a tension, a tug of war, between the actual heard rhythm and phrase, and the underlying metric pulse" (quoted in Ross, 302). Anderson's time sense operates here in a similar fashion. As the sequence begins, Barry brings a telephone conversation inquiry about a possible "mistake" in a Healthy Choices promotional campaign to a premature close because of his intuition that something in his environment needs to be checked. He moves into a pitch-dark interior space after leaving the fluorescent glare of his desk in the corner of a large, windowless warehouse room. We not only lose touch with him briefly, apart from the ghostly sound of his footsteps, but we are also disconnected from our placement in time. We are adrift, for a tiny interval, from time constraint and the sense of how exactly we are moving forward. A mild anxiety accompanies this severance of contact with the reliable present tense. We are on the verge of feeling lost, and that uncertainty is amplified with the abrasive, menacing sound of the garage door being jerked open. Light forcefully, almost punitively returns as we cross the threshold with Barry to the drab outdoors.

We seem to be released, along with him, into a different time zone. The metric pulse of the outside world seems instantly differ-

Punch-Drunk Love opens with Barry on the phone in a corner of his manufacturing shop

ent from the squeezed-in time at Barry's warehouse desk, where we have previously heard an off-kilter telephone exchange take place, punctuated with the erratic pinging and plunking of pipes. The exterior light diffuses into the distance rather than stabbing Barry—as it did at his desk—with a sharp, sterile pressure. At his work desk in this Kafkaesque enclosure, Barry's senses seemed as squeezed shut as the dead time that hemmed him in. Once outside, Barry shoulders the obligation of actually looking around him. He scans the out-of-focus environment for telltale signs of malevolent agency. He does not command the prospect he surveys, however. The camera circles him briskly, as if taking him hostage. The first full unleashing of conspicuous camera movement sets up another temporal rhythm—like a dizzy square dance "dosey doe," supplanting the rigidly stationary entrapment of the warehouse room, with its cold blue vastness and intimations of a superfluous human presence. The outside is intent on actively cutting loose, separating itself from Barry's control and his diffident, undisclosed intentions. Barry's walk strives to keep time-motion compatibly slow and cautious, but time seems determined to rush unfettered, quickening its pace and leaving his anxious monotony behind. The camera inquisitor impatiently vaults ahead of Barry's last revealed standing position onscreen, undertaking the task of approaching the long city street on its own.

We are now unsure of Barry's exact whereabouts. Has he left the vicinity of the warehouse garage door and walked down the alleyway toward the street? Perhaps he lags some distance behind the camera, which is heading a bit too rashly in that direction, possibly serving as a kind of advance scout. It is equally likely that Barry has elected not to venture too close to the street, that he is still hovering around the garage door, an out-of-the-way onlooker, as the camera investigates the surroundings without him. In this scenario, which will shortly be confirmed as the correct one, the camera proceeds on its own initiative, offering a separate route to wary inspection as it approaches the somehow instantly worrisome stretch of roadway. The camera's risk-taking carries with it a sense of violating a prohibition. It is looking for trouble, insistently pressing forward to a place where perhaps one should not go. This very act of trespass may be the force that calls the fearsome crash into being. Such is the hidden but plausible logic of emergence in this episode.

There is further time tension even within this embrace of forward motion. Something about the appearance and flapping noise of the two canvas-wrapped chain-link fences that we pass between en route to the thoroughfare, and something in the fragile presence of tall street lamps shedding wan light in the distance, causes us to hang back a beat even while the camera presses ahead, bent on revelation. The drag on the camera's new audacious pulse seems to include Barry—wherever he is physically—in the "on-edge" disposition of our looking. As the camera's view of the daunting road widens, our preliminary notice of the streetlamps gives way to the more active pairs of headlights of a few approaching vehicles (at different distances). The lights bear down on our now-settled position as curbside observers. Similar to a relay handoff, the camera's movement and time sense shift to the possible story invasion by the advancing cars. The camera halts, and remains motionless, as the vehicles in the far distance gradually seize focus while drawing nearer. They have time to declare quietly and with seeming ordinariness a likely workplace destination. Morning traffic progression carries its own sense of time: a slightly foggy, unconscious drift toward a waiting structure—that of the job, which Barry himself blandly embodies.

The sudden flipping over and violent, booming slide of the first of the two vehicles to arrive (as it is almost upon us) tears to tatters the trance-like state of the routine drive. Time "snaps to attention" and *condenses* with ferocious alacrity. We feel that whatever time is held within the framed image converges with this chaos-consumed Jeep. As we imagine the unseen driver trapped inside it, hovering between life and death, perhaps already lost to time, our feeling of time motion is jarringly arrested. The Jeep Cherokee screams "Help" and "Helplessness" in its death whirl. Emergence takes place during this freeze-up, coalescing with its almost namesake, emergency. The camera does not move to track the Jeep's final landing place. The accident noise is subsumed by the stronger squeal of brakes as a cab thrusts hugely into foreground space, and comes to a halt. We have a visceral emulation of "shock" in the cutting back and forth between Barry's dismayed witnessing of the double event. The cab arrives with the same abruptness and compression as the accident, filling the frame with vehement Day-Glo orange, a narrow checkered band identifying the vehicle as a taxi in the midst of the color. The presence of the street behind the cab is consumed by the more emphatic "now here *this* is" of the urgent fresh arrival, the taxi tarrying briefly as it delivers something. The harmonium, too obscurely lit to identify as yet, is dropped off at the curb, and then the cab too is swept from view as it races off.

What is the scale of time in this episode? In literal duration it amounts to almost nothing, but in its actual reception by the spectators (the viewer and Barry), these volatile moments are full to overflowing. Time stands still, in other words, while somehow simultaneously overflowing its banks. It floods space, with the sense of everything converging in a fierce moment of consequence, and then drains away before we have *room* in time to account for what it has brought into presence and summarily removed. The cab slides into place before us like a repression screen, blocking out the sight of flying debris from the still-in-progress accident. A sliding side door opens toward us and a figure within (observed mainly as a pair of hands) hastily withdraws a large object from the cab interior and, without the slightest hesitation or confusion, places it squarely by the edge of the roadside, as if making a scheduled delivery. The cab's manner of arriving with a squeal of brakes and speeding off in another shriek of sound conveys the same mingled sense of emergency and efficient attainment of purpose. The cab's arrival swallows up in the blink of an eye the time of helplessness and impending doom, while taking over the space the accident has just carved out for itself. Instead of being absorbed by the forces of disorder and the prospect of human loss, we are pressed into the separate, insulated time of a vehicle keeping to a tight, metered schedule, and making (with no other admissible concern) a split-second delivery. The energy of destruction becomes nearly indistinguishable from the energy of purposeful shipment and relinquishing. (The object, in effect, is violently relinquished, or dumped, to the curb, with no assessment of the dangers close at hand.) The time of someone's deliberation and reason for sending this object so hurriedly, as though in response to an urgent plea ("I need it now") and the timing of the cab's dispatch are unavoidably superimposed over the time of senseless uproar, the hideous sprawl of a random "out-of-left-field" event. The viewer has no choice but to link these two time frames together. We are made to regard the proximity of the two vehicles' emergence and almost simultaneous vanishing as a stunningly peculiar feat of cause and effect.

Such a "twinning" perspective can easily entangle us in dark speculation about the malignant properties of the object left behind. If we remain alert, we are given enough time to make out that it is a musical instrument, with what looks like piano keys. An ominous vibration, lingering in the air from the crash and panic-freighted delivery, envelops our first inspection of the harmonium. Whatever the instrument literally is, it seems indelibly stained by the horrible road disaster that its arrival displaces. The violence is, to an extent, siphoned into the harmonium, as something it has the power to account for, in the narrative's future. For now, the deposited object *wants* to be noticed, whether for good or ill, by Barry, as the point-of-view shot of him reacting to it from the middle distance confirms. He shakes his head, in a manner that indicates he didn't *mean* to see either the accident or the object, apparently refusing the harmonium's preliminary appeal to acknowledge a connection with it, and thus some sort of complicity, as well.

Almost immediately, the normalizing reintroduction of Barry as "real-time" witness to the dreamlike street incidents is shaken up as the camera resumes its independent consciousness and mobility. The camera appears to deny Barry's posture of refusal by manifesting an eagerness to move closer to the harmonium and lay claim to it, but perhaps it also picks up on, and embellishes, a secret wish of Barry's, hinted at by the tentative half-step forward he initiates just before we cut away from him. The camera approaches the harmonium covetously in a slow tracking motion and then examines it at close range, for what one might call a "stretched" moment of intimate beholding, swaddling the now benign-looking little piano in a soft, magical silence that contrasts powerfully with all the preceding audio din. This rapt inspection alters the time mode decisively yet again, introducing a diffident rather than nightmarish dream time. The harmonium is by no means conclusively identified as something that *belongs* to Barry. It does not coalesce for us as a gift expressly meant for him that merely awaits his decision to grab hold of it. The harmonium indeed beckons in some fashion, but from within an undispelled obscurity, laced with qualms.

The next cut surprises us with a view of Barry back at the warehouse desk where we first encountered him, in the midst of a business call. This transition suggests both an indefinite time lapse and a decision on Barry's part not to join the camera (and us) in its preliminary survey of the still forbidding, danger-charged musical contraption. Movie conventions require an interval to restore order and *mend* themselves so that something in the narrative will hold steady enough for us to proceed. We will gladly rejoin the adventure that has begun with such unraveling disclosures (call them feats of emergence), but we seek some assurance that there will not be instant, further exacerbation of our apprehensiveness. We can only be *so* lost, and remain participants in the narrative. Thus we welcome the chance to retreat to the comparative security of an intelligible, manageable operation. We embrace the task of observing Barry performing a recognizable act (talking on the phone)in his moderately strange work milieu (this irksome prison, whose painted blue walls perfectly match his suit. Watching him conduct business over the phone alleviates our sense of overwhelming strangeness on the loose *elsewhere*. The fact that we have returned to the warehouse desk to discover Barry engaged in phone activity similar to that we remember from our initial view of him serves to normalize, to a surprising degree, the warehouse interior and its prescribed behavior patterns. Their inimical, alien feel in the film's opening scene has largely worn off.

The time flow in Barry's now-domesticated corner of the warehouse is unobtrusively asserted as the "new normal" as well. In contrast to all the dislocating shifts and slippages in the different temporal rhythms offered in the brief segment we have been considering, we seem to have settled back into an ordinary, reliable time frame. Perhaps we have been given the clock with which the rest of the movie's diverse and bizarre modes of duration needs to be synchronized. Barry himself mentions in his phone conversation the problem posed by "time difference" in scheduling further communication with the supplier he is talking to. Time is one of the many things Barry can't get clear or reach an agreement on in his reasonable "call of complaint." However gently he reviews the failings of the equipment order he has been sent, the male voice on the other end of the line—a great literal distance separates the two speakers—refuses to process or accept the grounds of Barry's dissatisfaction. And yet, though the business chat is another minefield for Barry, both he and we are regaining our bearings. The work space proves an attractive refuge from the pileup of unreadable, actively aggressive signs emerging in the murky outside. The external world has already defined itself as too thunderous and vertiginous a puzzle to contend with. It is not the excitement but the incomprehensibility of what has transpired that we recoil from. At least for now.

At this point in the narrative, like Barry in the phone conversation that opens the film, we seek assistance in understanding what the rules are. If we are given time to study the "phrasing" of just-completed events carefully, we may be able to make the story rules bend a little to our advantage. The second phone conversation is stabilizing because it brings us back to action and space we have already seen. We are more settled in. Barry and a disembodied other male voice discussing a topic by phone, even though the subject is changed, tie events together. We are presented with a second effort to "straighten out a misunderstanding." Barry's first conversation was about finding an opening in the rules of a contest that might permit him to gain "free air miles." The Healthy Choice Foods promotion rules strike Barry as lax, able to be manipulated. We too are seeking to understand what openings as spectators are available to us. How can we play by the rules of this peculiar world and win some *free* "air miles" of our own? The vicarious air miles, if you like, of spectatorship. How odd it is that Barry, a man so wary of movement in any dimension, associates freedom with a surfeit of cunningly "looted" air miles. Barry finds a hole in the rules and will squeeze through it with the booty of a freedom that terrifies him. Barry's conviction that he may have detected something in the Healthy Choice Food contest rules that has escaped others' notice works on him like a heady criminal elixir. He feels giddily outside the law while remaining technically inside it. The possibility "emerges" for Barry, like a widening crack in the heart of reality, that the airless system he lives in has a flaw in it, muffled in the fine print of the rules, and that this flaw might be exploited by him for private gain.

Having noticed one such discrepancy, Barry can hardly look in any direction without further possibilities for sanctioned thievery leaping out at him. Lena tantalizes him with the choice of being either upstanding or underhanded when she entrusts him with her car keys and therefore her car within a few instants of approaching him, not even requesting an exchange of names. Lena's car has turned into the warehouse alley from the danger-strewn street and reminds us of the recent Jeep accident and its baffling aftermath by almost colliding with the harmonium as she enters the lot. Barry's meeting with Lena precedes his appropriation of the harmonium and, one might reasonably infer, somehow implants the idea, the fated necessity, of the theft. Lena herself mentions the piano to Barry, as though an outside observer were needed to corroborate its actual existence. We instantly perceive her to be a more dependable observer than Barry. When Lena says to him, "Can I ask you—can I trust to leave my key with you, and give it to you?" she gives direct expression to the dependability issue, in another key. He does not steal her car, but the thought of doing *something* wrongful has entered his head, and issues in the seizure of the harmonium. His volatile response to Lena is displaced onto the helpless—though still vaguely sinister—instrument.

In Barry's first trip outdoors, during a short-lived work break, everything he came into contact with *assailed* his senses and conspired to drive him back inside, where he might—with sufficient repressive effort—block it all out, persuade himself that what he encountered had never happened. From the moment he raised the intimidating garage door and left the warehouse, he seemed a fugitive, a person leaving the premises without clear authorization. He is utterly ill-equipped to ward off the shocks that bombard him unceasingly. Barry's second visit outside demonstrates a complete field reversal, beginning with the light, which has not only warmed up but flares with impromptu rainbows. When Lena seeks him out, as though it were expressly Barry she needed to have a word with, she runs toward him in a manner that could not be less alarming, even to one as drastically on guard as Barry. Her rapid approach prevents him from fleeing (his automatic survival impulse), and once she draws near enough to call out to him she sets off a chain reaction of good will in the now-benevolent alleyway. Everything appears to be streaming in his direction (in sympathy with Lena), wooing him to gather it in. All the appurtenances of this drab environment have suddenly taken a shine to him. Like this luminous stranger, they wish him well. The light and harmonium, the building, the alleyway, and the distant road seem placed in his keeping, along with Lena's car keys. One is confounded by the arbitrariness of this utter, near-schizophrenic transformation of elements, which takes place without any marked shift in Barry's own attitude or underlying mood. He has in no sense earned a reprieve by dint of effort. His new, more propitious standing outdoors comes to him in the form of grace; there is no better term for it. The topsy-turvy welcome the morning bestows on him makes us as wary as Barry himself is. We would be foolish to take the senseless, rapid removal of all menacing environment behavior at face value. Barry reinforces our own suspicions by ducking back into the warehouse after Lena's departure, flattening himself against the interior wall, almost hyperventilating.

After Lena is safely out of sight and Barry elects to snatch the waiting harmonium for himself, his way of doing it has the appearance of larceny. He has somehow found the courage to place himself near it, like an innocent bystander trying to be "casual" on an otherwise vastly empty sidewalk. He loiters for a long spell, considering how he might lift the instrument nonchalantly, and as he finally wills himself to reach out, he unleashes the hounds of hell in the form of a huge moving van frighteningly close to the curb, careening by at ear-shredding volume, seemingly inches away from the curb. The Allied Van Lines behemoth materializes out of nowhere, just as the earlier accident did. Its fearsome passage briefly blocks our view of Barry at the crucial moment of his grabbing the harmonium. When the moving van disappears, we glimpse Barry from the reverse angle, gripping the heavy instrument as he makes a flailing escape. He is framed as a tiny figure racing away from what resembles a dust-cloud cataclysm; the echo of the monster vehicle's roar still shudders in its wake. The scurrying fugitive is drenched in anxiety, and scattered tinkling chords—apparently emanating from the music box—sound a "Jack and the Beanstalk" alert that the culprit is making his getaway in plain view. In another swift reversal, Barry loses all trace of guilt moments after reaching the hideout of his office tucked deep in the warehouse and setting down his prize. Until now we have had no inkling that Barry possessed an office; he seemed to be a creature belonging to the corner of the warehouse room. He has the gratified demeanor of a seasoned abductor who has given his law-abiding adversaries the slip. Nevertheless, a large office whose walls are see-through glass seems to be a dubious hiding place for his treasure.

* * *

Somewhere in the course of Barry's progress through this test, we are likely to start questioning the *reality* of Barry's habitat. It may well happen right after Lena walks away from him into a roseate haze while Barry spies on her, or in the subsequent shots of Barry compounding his spying activity, pressed against a shadowy garage wall and slowly peering around the edge of his hiding spot into the distance at his quarry. (We are taken aback when we realize that it is no longer Lena but the harmonium that excites his voyeuristic attention. One kind of romantic looking opens out, as if by Wonderland dispensation, onto another.) I do not mean to suggest by my use of the unreal reality formulation the common movie albatross worry that Barry is merely dreaming or fantasizing—as a result of a deluded mental state—the world he encounters. I would argue instead that his environment is tied to his subjectivity more fully and intimately than is ordinarily the case for film protagonists. The geography posits some claim to autonomous, solid dimensions (i.e., a compelling otherness) but it is also, in a consequential sense, a space inside him.

The geography and its imposing inhabitants can usefully be approached as spaces and figures in an allegory, though not so insistent an allegory as to feel cumbersome. The shimmering edifice of Barry's tumultuous milieu resembles a vast, medieval tapestry: the landscape is there to chart the stages of a soul's exile and the soul's awakening to its need for a journey. The milieu, in its capricious, volatile character, takes seismic readings of the inner man. It provokes conflict between the most salient forces that dwell within him. It reminds him, by odd analogues and literalizations, of dormant or forgotten aspects of his self—-orphaned scraps and tatters of a lost and broken spirit. Part of the problem, of course, is how Barry can achieve a fitting relation to a scheme larger than his capacity for self-absorption. There must be a firmness, therefore, in the figments of Barry's imagining. The landscape wants to be made fully real—like a puppet dreaming of being a real, live boy—to escape its imprisonment in grotesque, debilitating confusions. The hallucinatory world must pass through the testing ground of a more capacious imagination. In this process, the landscape will mirror Barry's progress to health (or Healthy Choices) and, in so doing, gradually regain its own separateness and integrity. As much for its own sake as for his, his environment, in Anne Carson's resonant phrase, takes an active "interest in the nuances [of him]"; the nuances of the environment are Barry's nuances, and they are attempting to compose a path through a labyrinth (52). Once he solves the maze through which he is repeatedly shown to wander, he will have his place within a world that goes beyond him, that does something more than confirm, at every turn, his lostness.

In some ways, *Punch-Drunk* is an allegory such as psychoanalyst Melanie Klein might have devised: a stymied psyche proceeding to *know* itself through frenzied splittings. Eve Kosofsky Sedgwick has compellingly characterized the Kleinian narrative of conflict-raging development as "relations among multiple, semi-anthropomorphic objects . . . treat[ed] in terms of deities and daemons . . . able in themselves to damage and be damaged, to renew and be renewed. The traffic of projection and introjection is the vehicle for the primitive defenses of the paranoid-schizoid position—but also for the forms of reality orientation and creativity, through the treatment of the good internal object, that can mitigate or transfigure those defenses" (30–31). Klein's devouring cycles of "greed, envy, rage, and anxiety," Sedgwick argues, testifies to the "almost grotesquely unintelligent design of every human psyche" (125). For Sedgwick, everything in Melanie Klein's account of the psyche bespeaks "a ratio or relation between an internal object and an ambient surround" (32). Sedgwick supplements her account of Klein with a sentence that she derives from Marcel Proust, and offers as the crux of his mysticism: "The universe is *as* alive as anything it holds." A self can collapse and bring down with it "the whole ecology of value and vitality." But it can also be revived with the right "internal object" and feel (after a period of nullity) that it *belongs* to a living universe and is filled with its stuff.

Until Lena, Barry's "lightfoot guardian," is admitted inside him as an animate force, one that he acknowledges as having a claim on him, all the spaces he endeavors to occupy and form impressions of conspire against him. Barry seems to be closely conjoined with the even more damaged World War II vet, Freddie Quell, in *The Master*. In the special-features section of *The Master* DVD, Anderson includes the famous John Huston documentary, *Let There Be Light* (1946), which chronicles the treatment of various returning soldiers with combat-inflicted psychological and neural damage. Many of the symptoms that these veterans exhibit eerily match up with Barry Egan's afflictions. The harmonium is, of course, not "dead wood" like Barry, but an almost sentient entity, which is the means of bringing first Barry and then the things of his world back to life. As its name implies, it is a promise of harmony, a balancing of the life within and the world without. The harmonium is another version of Lena, taking up room inside his office. It is an instrument of the psyche, enabling him to produce truer sounds, and to release a long-suffocated voice, a voice that has been worn down to a near-whisper by a dense cabal of punishing circumstance.

Immediately after the love scene in the Hawaiian hotel room, we are shown Lena by herself talking on the phone (Barry's primary device for "failed communication" attempts) to Elizabeth, one of Barry's seven bullying sisters, who works at the same company as Lena. Barry, initially, is nowhere in sight. She may well be alone, which is a startling state of affairs, since until now Lena has not felt like a separate entity, a person in her own right, untethered to Barry's projections. Her head leans against her hand as she reclines on a hotel room sofa, conversing calmly and competently with Elizabeth about a work question. We try to read past her unruffled manner and hard to decipher expression in order to determine the emotional outcome of her lovemaking. When Elizabeth asks her directly about whether Barry has called her for a date, Lena tells her "No," and on the heels of this lie (perhaps designed to shield Barry rather than herself from sisterly interference and control), we suddenly sense that she is making eye contact with Barry. We discover just in advance of seeing him that he *is* present and a silent witness to the call. We cut to a shot of an unexpectedly immense-looking bed, with a pleasant tumult of bedspread and sheet rolling toward Barry like breakers on a beach. Clad now in a white terrycloth bathrobe, he matches all this cheery, undulating brightness. He seems pitiably small, unsure of himself and remote in the frame, though, as he holds a fixed, seated position, propped against the tall headboard. The whiteness links his cleansed-of-blue garment to hers. As the camera slowly closes in on him, there is a felt increase of intimate connection with Lena but not of assurance on his part. He appears to be a quasi-helpless, anxious boy performing relaxation under the watchful eye of his protector; he returns Lena's look with the air of a supplicant. The camera movement is gentle rather than aggressive, but there is still an impression of invasion carried by Elizabeth's fully audible voice on the phone. We hear her saying "you wouldn't go out with him because he's such a freak sometimes" as the camera brings us nearer to Barry. The words give our view of him a certain "pinning-in-place" effect. He seems able to register what is said about him, as though he and the viewer hear his sister's voice on the soundtrack with identical clarity. The voice reaches past Lena's mediating presence and bores into him. But then, another surprise. As Lena concedes to Elizabeth that he is "a little strange," Elizabeth instantly reverses course and leaps to her brother's defense. Barry seems less swallowed up by the bed island on which he sits as Lena magically mediates on his behalf. She lures the sister away from one of her standard gambits of unwitting emotional assault, and has her take on instead the unlikely role of impassioned booster.

The allegorical field tilts in this scene to grant Lena not only more prominence but more heft as a self-directing consciousness. Barry's awareness of her has developed to the point where he can handle, to a modest degree, the threat of her separation and distance, as he handled, in the love scene, the threat of intimacy without coming undone. Admittedly, Lena resembles a mother taking on an unpalatable task for a son not quite prepared to do battle on his own initiative. But she also gives evidence of penetrating and making common cause with his Don Quixote perspective on things. She is not a bewildered Dulcinea but a fellow errant knight, happily launched on a mad romantic quest. She is felicitously daft, if slightly more pragmatic, than her new partner. As Barry watches Lena speak about him in the third person to Elizabeth from the not-too-frightening distance of her bed, he must overcome the temptation of paranoia, which is a remarkably contagious state for someone like Barry, so freshly stripped and vulnerable. He manifests a reluctance—which the film's entire immersion in his point of view seems to confirm—to allow Lena to be split off from himself enough to declare her differences, and apartness, from his own needs. He is like Melanie Klein's infant in many respects, with its wild greed to ingest the Mother. Sedgwick, in her summary of Klein, speaks of the powerless child attempting to make himself safer by ingesting "good" objects, where they are liable to remain distinct and magically alive, doing battle with "bad" contents and vulnerable to being devoured or fatally contaminated by them" (132). Barry must learn somehow to love Lena by comprehending her capacity to be separate, without panic. She can disappear from his presence and control, and he can do the same, without annihilation or betrayal.

Barry must forge from his emerging psychic needs a secure place within "the middle ranges of agency," to replace the infant's greed and natural, survivor's insistence on all-or-nothing arrangements with something else. "You can be relatively empowered or disempowered without annihilating someone else or being annihilated" (Sedgwick, 130). Sedgwick concedes, with beautiful astuteness, that keeping one's foothold in the middle ranges is "a fragile accomplishment that needs to be discovered over and over." And it is fair to say that allegory itself poses obstacles to a figure's shift from an existence governed by static categories and compulsions to life in the "middle ranges." The law of perspective that Anderson favors as characters begin to contemplate the possibilities of separateness within merger is never far removed from death awareness. Death enters the picture in the deafening crash of the vehicle on the highway at the beginning of the film. The harmonium first appears as a blocking screen for the outcome of that crash. It replaces the crash with an equally loud, entrancing silence. The little piano's gentle, halting music only makes sense in relation to that primal conjunction of destruction and covering silence. Its proximity to unearthly terror persists: the music of love flows from it. The harmonium begins as a *wounded* instrument, and damage is integral to its form of beauty. The harmonium is repaired by Barry, but it appears to resist *total* repair. Anderson imagines "ideas, emotions, selves and other phenomena . . . [arising] in *new* relations" in the shadow of transience and irreparable loss, "a strangely spacious framework of impermanence and the acceptance of it" (Sedgwick, 70–71).

Anderson prominently and recurrently features a song on his soundtrack of *Punch-Drunk Love* that provides further clues to his approach to love's mystery. We hear Shelley Duvall's voice as Olive Oyl in

Robert Altman's *Popeye* (1980) singing, with charmingly off-key wistfulness, the Harry Nilsson song, "He Needs Me." The song is launched in *Popeye* when Olive spies on the sailor man, himself abandoned and homeless at an early age, as he tries to figure out how to take care of another foundling, Swee'pea. Olive sings, "And all at once I knew / I knew at once / I knew he needed me." She is taking on the burden of the sailor with and *as* a baby who needs her, unmistakably, despite his vaunted strength in isolation. Manifest need is by no means the most honored and alluring basis for romantic attachment. In fact, a too-powerful initial sense of a romantic prospect's undisguised need is likely to prove a forceful repellent. The needy or clinging figure, who apparently has difficulty standing on his or her own two feet, is construed as an impediment to one's own desire for freedom and emotional mobility. And it is distasteful to be overvalued too quickly; it cannot help but feel like a contemptible, disastrous misjudgment. The one who doesn't convey need openly will have greater success exciting need in another. We curiously seek to place ourselves in the keeping of those who don't show a natural inclination or fitness to meet our needs. Or perhaps the need is to conquer another's thrilling impulse to turn away, to leave us behind. We know the ache of viewing a beloved back as it moves—preoccupied, self-sufficient—away from our concerns, to concerns that rank above ours. Love is so much about calling back, making a figure turn around in time, forestalling the disappearance.

Anderson simply removes the customary thorniness surrounding too obvious or vehement a human need for attachment, just as Olive Oyl does when she repeats the phrase "He needs me" over and over again in her song. When it is not by choice, there is something horrible about being alone too much that contemporary art and criticism alike feel constrained about addressing, or even owning up to. We are supposed to know what to do by now with the condition of being on our own and supposed to be able to give a maturely positive account of ourselves in our productive separateness. We have to believe that effective rhetorical cures have been found for any lingering cultural shame or stigma surrounding aloneness. And once the rhetoric has done all it can, we are enjoined to be silent about the rest. Who wants to hear about old-fashioned regrets, uncertainty about the benefits of having no life companion, or the ache of solitude and unfulfilled need?

Judith Butler takes up this problem of the existence and preservation of a responsive, amenable "you" outside and beyond yourself by considering the "radically counter-Nietzschean approach to ethics" of Adriana Cavarero (31). Cavarero, in *Relating Narratives*, argues, according to Butler, that "I am not, as it were, an interior subject, closed upon myself, solipsistic. . . . I exist in an important sense for you, and by virtue of you. If I have lost the condition of address, if I have no 'you' to address, then I have lost 'myself.' In her view, one can tell an autobiography only to an other, and one can reference an 'I' only in relation to a 'you': without the 'you,' my own story becomes impossible" (32). About Lena in *Punch-Drunk Love* we can say conclusively that she responds wholeheartedly to Barry's need of her. She is not at odds with his need, ever, despite its being (in our eyes, at least) frighteningly large, inarticulate, and often infantile. She mingles without embarrassment the roles of mother-surrogate and lover. She removes the toxicity that we associate with doing maternal repair work in a midlife romantic relationship. Being a mother figure does not uproot the possibility for other kinds of devotion and passionate pleasure. She is taken with Barry for reasons that are never divulged and, once having been drawn to him (and his need of her), she sets about doing what needs to be done to release him from himself.

We readily respond to stories of abandoned or mistreated children, like Oliver Twist, finding suddenly, when things are at their bleakest, a male or female benefactor who can minister to their wounds, supply shelter and consistent affection in time to save the child's spirit, and to permit continued emotional growth. We are less sure of what to do with mothers in the guise of lovers who appear much later in a victim's life, crossing various role boundaries with a damaged being stuck somewhere between the wreckage of early childhood and the unintelligible demands of maturity. It is troubling to see a nurse, say, taking a premature romantic interest in a patient who is very much in the throes of a mental malady. We are quick to impute an undiagnosed sickness of her own to the nurse and to imagine that her sexual attraction and affinity are due to compulsions, projection, and a lack of self-awareness. Lena does not ignite, for more than stray moments, these familiar film noir suspicions. She appears utterly at home with herself, free of desperation, able to navigate capably the demands of a high-level job, and equipped with social graces, chief among them forbearance. We learn that she has been married before, but she seems to have come out of that relationship without recriminations or a craving for a resumption of miseries akin to those left behind. Anderson settles some of our concerns about her "sufficiency of motive" by making her the daemonic agent (a benevolent rather than a malign demon) of allegory. She clearly functions as a "making good" on the mystical promise of the harmonium delivered to Barry's warehouse. Her assortment of reddish raiment is designed to complement, in a gratifying, off-kilter way, Barry's stiff and stifling blue suit. Her dress amplifies the shine of the harmonium and, on her first, key-bearing appearance in the parking lot outside Barry's warehouse, her orange-on-the-way-to-red dress seems to provoke a lens flare that makes her presence an extension of the force of daylight. Like a figure in courtly romance, she needs to be pursued herself, after initiating her humble, faithful knight on a quest for both her and a lost truth about his own psyche. After Lena's first appearance, Barry's visual field will begin to accumulate more and more instances of red (clothed figures and objects), all of them connected to her and somehow leading him toward her, whether he catches the color flare clues of heart language or not.

Lena resembles as well the helper figures in folktales who appear to the hero, at various junctures in a journey, to comfort, encourage, and test his moral nature and the soundness of his emotional convictions. Angus Fletcher, in his extraordinary seminal study, *Allegory*, argues that the daemon is a guardian or intermediary who mirrors the hero's single-mindedness, and indeed shares his "possession" by the quest. The daemon can be seen as a sub-character of the protagonist, split off from the hero's psyche, and whose very constriction of meaning enables the hero's character to be revealed, facet by facet. There is, however, a vital "you" component within the daemon. She is Other as much as she is a semblance of one's secret, buried energy (the potential frozen within during some early crisis, and the subsequent workings of a curse). Her Otherness is linked to the protagonist's unrestrained will or wish to be rejoined to reality, conceived grandly and positively. She *is* the world in its elusiveness, its distance, and its confounding face of hospitality. In the bedroom scene in *Punch-Drunk Love*, we see Barry and Lena's mutual possession by this strange, single-minded quest to declare their need, without temperance, mitigation, or discretion.

"You can't do that." "Okay." Lena demands that Barry not abandon her in the hospital again in *Punch-Drunk Love*

Punch-Drunk Love stages moments of emergence that suggest that deliberateness, choosing, and rational control are not feasible conditions for becoming more, a larger entity. As in allegory, we see figures acting out of compulsion in the very midst of breakthrough, triumphantly demonstrating their lack of inner control (Fletcher, 64). Their surrender to the dominant compulsion in their nature (be it steadfastness or violence) is often the means for passing the trial that presently confronts them. Human agency continues to operate single-mindedly, perhaps narrowly, with the controls characteristic of possession. Perhaps Barry's growth is merely a movement from one mode of compulsion to another, more propitious sort. Anderson may be following Fletcher's idea that one of allegory's assumptions is "that men [and women] suffer from a primary illusion when they imagine they are in control of their actions" (64). Choices are made for us by our daemon, who arrives on our psychic property without warning, like the harmonium, and then takes possession. Barry tells Lena at film's end that he has purchased enough pudding to "redeem the [air travel] mileage" in "six to eight weeks" that will make it possible to "go with you wherever you have to travel." He was driven to make those absurdly excessive purchases but has still "reasoned *not* the need." "Redeeming mileage" is a lovely contemporary idiom for quest progress, and though the "mileage" is not yet redeemed, Barry has faith that it *will* be, in just a matter of weeks. What Barry knows about Lena is that she *has* to travel for her work and that he *has* to go with her. He knows that his right to do so somehow hinges on his compulsion to keep burdening her with the whole, shameful truth about any of his actions that might in any way concern her. He would not be worthy of her, he believes, if this truth-telling mania were to desert him. Lena will not be shattered by news of his latest extremity; her love, as punch-drunk as his own, seems receptive to every telling.

The Trail of the Ellipsis in *There Will Be Blood*

> "The word *ellipsis*, he'd been told, could literally be translated as 'to hide behind silence.'"
>
> —Rachel Cusk, *Outline*

Before the title "There Will Be Blood" appears onscreen—white letters in weathered, biblical font on a black background—we hear a slow-rising, ominous, atonal sound made by stringed instruments. The first music cue of Jonny Greenwood's austere, punitively flinty score deliberately echoes the barrage of agitated violin strings that leaps out at us in Lars Johan Werle's prologue soundscape for Ingmar Bergman's *Persona* (1966). What might *Persona*'s prologue tell us about the narrative workings of *There Will Be Blood* (2007)? Bergman repeatedly stressed in interviews how the opening of *Persona* (and indeed the whole film) was an expression of spiritual blockage (e.g., Bergman, 195–96). The torrent of images unleashed—after the direct acknowledgment of a projector arc lamp, the whirring cogs of the celluloid feeding apparatus and the numbered frames of celluloid leader passing through the projector gate—mimics consciousness in the act of disgorging. The images that tumble forth, in no obvious order, are, according to Bergman, a residue of old ideas, a residue of past preoccupations that he hopes to expel from his system so as to clear room for something living, not dead, as these images seem to be. He hopes to arrive at an empty, receptive state where it will be possible for him to start anew and regain the power to see and imagine on fresh terms: "My life just then consisted of dead people, brick walls, and a few dismal trees out in the park. In hospital one has a strong sense of corpses floating up through the bedstead. Besides which I had a view of the morgue, people marching in and out with little coffins, in and out. So I made believe I was a little boy who'd died, yet who wasn't allowed to be really dead, because he kept on being woken up by telephone calls" (Bergman, 199).

The sound accompanying this feverish "poem in images" is "stripped of all essentials. Just studio noises and music" (202). Eventually the prologue begins to gestate the dream intuition for the image field that becomes *Persona*. A boy on a hospital bed sees a large face emerging on a phantasmagoric wall—a movie screen, perhaps—behind him. A massive, initially blurred female countenance confronts him, which is slowly revealed to be an alternation of two faces that bear close resemblance to one another. The boy extends his hand toward the image and touches the visible, illusory faces, reminiscent of an infant reaching up from his mother's arms to explore the facial territory of the one who feeds him. The boy's mobile touch appears to bring these apparitions to life, or at least to the sort of memory life and projected life that film is able to confer. The eyes of the composite woman open, though it is unlikely that they see the boy in front of them who is seeking contact. *Persona*'s credits begin abruptly at this juncture of transcendent reaching and finding and not finding, amid a tumult of musical discord: percussive rattles, snaky glissandos, and booms predominate. *Persona* marks its departure from the "old and used-up" by tracing a path back to an all-encompassing maternal presence, a mother image that is equivalent to the face of the entire world. One of the film's narrative destinations will be the silence surrounding a mother's thwarted relationship with her child, a silence that must somehow be pierced by a female voice forced *out* of silence.

Silence, one of *Persona*'s primary subjects and mysteries, is also the core of Daniel Plainview (Daniel Day-Lewis) in Paul Thomas Anderson's *There Will Be Blood*. Plainview's silence, as in the case of *Persona*, must be understood as a kind of mask—the one alluded to in the film's title. An actor, Elisabet (Liv Ullmann), retreats into silence as her new identity, creating from it a place she hopes will be secure from the falsity, inadequacy, and garble of language. Silence is her means of self-repair and also provides her with protection against the claims of others. Her decision to refrain entirely from speech provides Elisabet with a grand role she can perform. Alma (Bibi Andersson), the nurse assigned to care for her, is obliged to accommodate Elisabet's commanding refusal to express herself verbally, though both know Elisabet could speak if she chose to. Silence grants Elisabet emotional distance and a striking measure of control over Alma. By slow degrees, however, Elisabet becomes ensnared in the silence that once gave her power. As it persists and becomes tainted by manipulative urges, the silence becomes a sickness. The burdens of silence I've described here are shared by the taciturn, remote protagonist of *There Will Be Blood*.

Lars Johan Werle's music for *Persona* has, as its most daunting task, making audible the contours of a teeming, twisted psychological silence. How does the psychological web of Werle's music become integral to a Western? Anderson and Greenwood's strategy is to build (at the very outset of the narrative) a sense of internal discord already stretched to the breaking point, before we are given a terrain or a specific character to contend with. The music that swells and writhes beneath a dark screen serves as a ladder climb to a jammed consciousness, somewhat akin to Barry Egan's in *Punch-Drunk Love*. And as with the musical space in the *Persona* prologue, the emanation from the projecting mind feels intolerably overburdened. The score seems about to splinter, to "lose its head." Unlike *Persona*, the neurosis that the sound releases in the opening of *There Will Be Blood* does not belong to a woman. The faces of the women unveiled at the end of the *Persona* prologue supply a fitting destination for the wrought-up string and percussion that led us there: such music is a recognizable home of female interiority. For Anderson, however, it is the single-minded frontiersman of few words, the somber man of action, that the score seeks out and defines emotionally in advance of our first meeting.

The music also infects, by association, our initial view of the rolling hills of the New Mexico desert. The strings put us in touch with the stifling heat of an alien landscape. The desert is instantly *heard* pitting itself against human intruders it has no use for. The dissonance conveys an intense bearing down, as though the mind of someone trapped in this bare region were being unraveled by its contact with the elements, driven mad by slow, heat-inflamed degrees. A John Ford Western typically situates us in similarly unaccommodating desert circumstances, but the majestic buttes of Monument Valley seem to rise up in sympathy with Ford's persevering settlers and lonely outsiders. It is as though these mighty landmarks in the desert waste were themselves expressions of human will, mute demonstrations (like the pyramids of Egypt) of what the will to prevail can accomplish. The romantic scores Ford favors usually draw plentifully from traditional Western songs, songs that domesticate yearning, lonesomeness and the pleasurably strenuous discipline found at military outposts. Greenwood's strident music, by contrast, resists accommodation of any sort. Things have already gone too far for that, it tells us. Whatever personage the score stands in for has nothing to do with tonality, and will not be coerced back in that direction. When the strings press up against the written words, "There Will Be Blood," they seem to embody the wrath of this Old Testament–style prophetic curse. The spaciousness and "breast of the new world" beauty that could be released in the opening shot of the pristine, undulating landscape are *cramped* by the music. We are enjoined to recoil inward instead of expanding to meet the terrain on its own grand footing.

The violins fade out after conveying us to the as-yet-unnamed solitary figure of Daniel Plainview in a dimly lit mine shaft. The silence indicates that the object of the music's search—what the dissonance expresses and identifies with—has been found: a mysterious loner whose face is obscured by shadow. A lengthy segment without spoken language commences, in which we contemplate a man at work in a deep hole. Though the absence of language and music is conspicuous and forceful, the film is not silent. The score is instantly replaced by the sound of a pickax attempting to cut through recalcitrant rock. We have shifted from an implied psychological interior, in Anderson's customary manner, to an exterior space and activity that seem to replicate it. A man who has elected to go far into the earth, by himself, is exerting all his strength to break through an obstruction. This inhuman barrier clutches, like a living adversary, a thing of value which it must be made to yield up. No amount of brute force is too much for the task at hand. "Show me your environment and I will tell you who you are," writes Boris Pasternak. In *Punch-Drunk Love*, Barry Egan's glass-enclosed warehouse office is his identity: fragile, too exposed, and stifling. Daniel's mineshaft, like Barry's sterile, "on-hold" space, is a work environment, a ground of being, and predicament all at once. Daniel blends in with the sounds, natural and manmade, that surround him. We are relieved to have the music of an overtaxed mind cut out. We prefer the sound of willed human effort to the agony of consciousness. The hole Daniel occupies by choice is one he has created himself in a harsh contest with recalcitrant materials. But the lower earth possesses a serenely impersonal dimension, as well. It does not cry out in protest, nor does it oblige Daniel to be humane in his relationship with it. If the earth gives any counsel as one labors within and against it, it has to do with withstanding punishment. It takes whatever one throws against it and accommodates the one who offers abuse. Whether it breaks or holds firm, the earth one strikes with one's tools has no regard for human presence. It expects no mercy and provides none itself.

Before we see his face, we watch Daniel sharpening one of his blades underground. He takes a break from savage hacking to give his implement a finer edge. The opening for thought of some sort that this rest provides is used by Daniel only to dwell on extending his control, improving his chances for a good "haul." We first contemplate his face as he peers upward toward distant daylight. After an ellipsis, we are given an opportunity to survey Daniel whole, as he sits crouching by a campfire above ground. He seems frozen in an uncomfortable, fixed position, holding a mug of coffee (or alcohol) as night descends and the desert wind rises. Daniel seems to be governing his thoughts by turning away from them, refusing the invitation to enter his own dark interior. He will not submit himself to loose introspection and its dangers. The wind ruffles his hair and causes the cloth flap of his tent to shift about. He is more securely fastened down than his tent is. He stares forward as thunder and lightning erupt in the lowering sky behind him, giving no sign of taking it in. Daniel is one of those isolated men of the frontier, who contrives a grand destiny, out of the sight and reach of others, at the hazardous edge of settlement. There are no automatic conditions placed on his dreaming faculty, but he seems to allow himself to consider only actions and where they might lead as "prospects." Thought for its own sake is useless. A man resourcefully going about his demanding business without companions is joined in spirit to every laconic stranger on horseback riding, free of entanglements, in the direction of adventure; the Western stranger seems always to have emerged fresh from some mysterious encampment in the middle of nowhere. The bracing silence enclosing Daniel as he surrenders himself unreservedly to work discipline augments, by steady degrees, the commanding force of his presence. Even if we sense a demonic narrowness of focus accompanying his fierce commitment, we catch glimpses of a mighty will forging ahead in these cramped circumstances.

* * *

When Daniel, in the next underground episode, prepares his dynamite for planting in the shaft, the quantity of challenges he calmly takes up readily expands spectator admiration to awe. It is still the beginning of the film. Daniel and his tasks are all we have to dwell on. This is the scale of the world that matters and must be managed. He seems fit to see to the demands of arranging a blast that he can survive. He appears to be repeating a process whose tricky phases are well known to him. Once he has wedged the dynamite in a rocky cleft and lit its lengthy fuse, he confidently arranges his tool bucket and climbs the homemade ladder that leads out of the shaft. We watch him place himself at a distance from the pit above ground and strive in the baking heat to haul up by recalcitrant pulley the tools left below before the explosion occurs. The load of tools hits a snag and the blast happens before Daniel has completed raising them. This mishap swiftly deprives Daniel of his aura of superhuman calm and competence. Daniel becomes smaller, more confused, and fallible as his calculations go awry and his plan is seemingly thwarted. We observe him from behind, obscured by dust. When he is clearly in view again he is stooped over, assessing the situation uncertainly. The damage appears (to him and us) only moderate and perhaps fixable. After a tense pause, Daniel rapidly regains his bearings and begins to descend the familiar, reliable ladder. He has not descended very far, however, when his composure shatters yet again. One of the wooden ladder rungs breaks. Daniel loses his footing and hurtles an immense distance to the base of the shaft, snapping one of his legs as he lands. The distance he tumbles is extended by our bottom-of-the-shaft perspective on the plunge. Daniel exclaims "No" (the film's first word) as he writhes on his back in unmistakable torment. While the camera scrutinizes his face in profile at close range, he gives further audible evidence of his agony—a series of hoarse, inhaling gasps.

The escape from the hole segment is composed of enigmatic ellipses, small and large. The first conspicuous gap occurs between the sight of

Daniel's (Daniel Day Lewis's) painful fall deeper into the hole in *There Will Be Blood*

Daniel sprawled, helpless and moaning, and the view that immediately follows of him sufficiently recovered and self-possessed to be hoisting his body with its torn limb up the length of the shaft by rope. It is clear that he is still suffering acutely (his wincing and low cries attest to that), but the main point conveyed in this shot juxtaposition is how rapidly and efficaciously Daniel is able to separate himself from a condition of powerless, frail passivity. He will not languish as a man in need, even with a freshly broken leg, for more than a subjective instant.

A second reversal, this one accompanied by a more pronounced ellipsis, transpires when Daniel locates a chunk of silver ore in the mine wall ripped open by the explosion. He forgets his leg injury almost entirely as he ravenously inspects the suddenly precious object, crooning, "There she is, there she is," as though he has unearthed, in the thick of torment, a living female object worthy of love. The music reenters at this turning point, still crawling with a sense of portent and overwrought mental process. Yet the images don't offer much support for the eruption of disquiet. The music seems displaced from the rendering of mental anguish. We can only connect it to his physical maiming if we require obvious "illustration." At the same time the music pulls against the elation Daniel evinces in his discovery, thwarting any *release* we might find in his transformed mood. The agitated string accompaniment also jars against our admiring involvement in Daniel's prowess as he concentrates his will and heroically completes his climb back to the daylight world above. Instead, Greenwood's orchestration evokes a curse being placed on Daniel as he pulls something out of the darkness; the sound "infects" the discovery of silver. The ascent from the shaft is sonically wrapped in warning, as though Daniel hubristically carries out more from the mine than he should. There are already forces in motion, our listening tells us, that will eventually demand propitiation.

The next ellipsis is the most outrageous and speculation-fueling blank in a narrative unusually rife with puzzling discontinuities. Anderson shows Daniel free from the hole but now confronting apparently endless mountainous desert terrain, broiling and unpopulated, which must be traversed if he is to survive. He appears to have no access to any animal or other means of conveyance that might make the journey at least conceivable for someone in his broken state. The camera briefly attends to him inching his way backward from a prone position before leaving him behind and surveying the landscape that offers such opposition. The music continues to conduct a kind of warfare on our nerves, prolonging its own supplementary resistance to Daniel's progress. And yet, no sooner do we make this assessment of impossible demands than we cut away from the desperate beginning of a long trek. We instantly relocate to an assayer's office at journey's end. As the camera reframes within the office interior, Daniel is revealed on the floor of the office, in almost exactly the same physical attitude he exhibited at the mine. Now he is in repose, though restlessly awaiting the confirmation of the ore's value and the issuing of his claim certificate. Even after this miraculous feat of endurance and travel, the music does not relent by modulating to a calmer or triumphant tonality. We stay with the same wasp's nest of dissonance we encountered in the previous scene.

What are we to make of the entirely omitted depiction of Daniel's epic struggle to cross the mountain waste and return to civilization? In its place we have a bare, matter-of-fact ellipsis, vaulting over the formidable hurdles of space and time without transition, but still more significantly over the actions he performs. These, more than anything else in his subsequent history, would serve to delineate his superhuman vitality. Anderson deprives us of the portion of Daniel's story that would immediately grant us emotional access to him. Were we to share Daniel's struggle, however briefly, we would grant him qualities of the primordial adventurer that might qualify our judgment of him as having a stunted temperament. His survival skills would balance our account of his cunning, grasping rigidity. But the ellipsis effaces the emotional link or severely reduces it. What does Anderson's use of the ellipsis tell us, here and elsewhere, about his approach to storytelling?

The narrative of *There Will Be Blood* mirrors Daniel's tight-lipped refusal to make known or shed any light on the physical or psychic ordeals he has been through. The "burial" of all the particulars of his trek render this harrowing, near-supernatural experience akin to all the other secrets of his upbringing and background that Daniel is not disposed to go into. The fact that he made it to the assayer's office in one piece and is now able to file his claim is, for him, the pertinent element in his exploits. There is nothing for him to gain by offering tales of crawling backward, parched and wretched—a creature barely distinguishable from a desert reptile. He would prefer to be regarded as someone who has pulled himself together and makes no fuss about it, who awaits the ore results with a semblance of composure, and who will sign his name to the legal document with an ornate flourish. This act we do witness, in extreme close-up, and it is the one that counts for Daniel. We see the name being painstakingly set on the document. The man doing the signing is absent from the frame, as invisible and factored out as he was in his desolate passage through the sunbaked hills.

Anderson's eradication of epic narration and crucial dramatic instances of character declaration displays the rigor of self-imposed abstinence. The pent-upness of the excised drama makes all of its scarcely conceivable action flow, in a transposed key, into the gesture of signing a contract. Before Daniel Plainview's name is ushered into the narrative, the office scene that leads up to it presents us but a single, perplexing view of him. He is recumbent near the assayer's counter, his hands interlaced restfully behind his head. A rifle and a sack are by his side. His good leg is raised up, in an almost-defiant posture of prideful ease. The camera is obliged to pan down from the bustling office to disclose him on the floor—an odd point of interest we might otherwise have missed, noted almost in passing. The camera similarly pans down the claim document before a fountain pen emerges to inscribe a first and last name. The signing is a disguised point-of-view shot, which provides a third ellipsis after the revelation of Daniel's resting form. We are, without knowing it, scanning the assay report at the same moment that Daniel is, before he sets down his name and takes ownership.

The determination of the signing is reinforced by the return of the swarming dissonance music, and we are instantly borne along its harsh current to a time four years hence (1902) and a new landscape (California). A rickety wooden construction rising up in the new setting is the sole indicator that Daniel's operations have shifted from silver mining to oil well digging. Much has altered in the outward circumstances, which we must absorb through scrutiny of the details of a long-take composition. Daniel is no longer completely isolated. The men in view apparently work for and with him. The crucial points of continuity are the music (still festering with anxiety), the prominent hole (Daniel's preferred habitation), and Daniel himself, who, by implication, is still the largely uncommunicative, driven figure we encountered earlier. We have traversed another ellipsis, but this one feels less disconcerting than the gap of the missing journey. We do not feel, with this leap, that we have been denied contact with something essential, despite the additional unidentified personnel and the questions arising from Daniel's changed plans about what to dig for.

However, the prolongation of verbal silence through another group of scenes is beginning to aggravate the viewer. Part of what the music now carries is the pressure accumulating from the avoidance of speech. It feels as though a contagion is spreading from Daniel to his work associates. The score's unyielding distraughtness throughout the temporal and spatial gaps marks a decisive difference from other Westerns. Musical treatment of exploration and other valorous achievement is by and large expansive, containing at the very least a suggestion of temporary release and upward movement. No amelioration is present in the scoring of Daniel's transition. In this episode, the music's grimly rasping undertow seems attuned to the persistence of masculine apartness in the midst of collective endeavor. The sound works to suppress sociability. Whatever attainments Daniel can lay claim to as a result of his continual striving in the four-year interval are minimized by the music's unbending aversion to a positive tonality.

The hole we gain access to in 1902 lacks the adamant character of the New Mexico silver shaft. Settled materials have been replaced, suddenly, with murky, liquid ones. There seems to be a tactical modulation on Anderson's part from male to female metaphors. We have shifted from implacable, crystalline surfaces to moist, mutable quagmires. Sinking in deeper is the fear and the desire now, whereas before the determination was to hold clear position on solid ground, even beneath the earth. The film makes an early analogy between breaking chunks of ore loose from an obdurate wall and the breaking of Daniel's limb. As his leg shatters after his fall to the base of the shaft, the wall he was attempting to blow open relinquishes a piece of silver, as though his own breaking were a fair and necessary exchange for the silver's release. (We see further logic of this kind at work later on in the film when a gusher is brought in at the cost of his adopted son H.W.'s hearing.) The silver ceases to be simply a valued object: it is tied to an unevadable display of vulnerability. The pain Daniel experiences seals a compact with a sweet, suddenly feminized acquisition. "There she is, there she is," Daniel croons to the chunk of silver ore. It is a preparatory outflow of sentiment from Daniel, which, in a subsequent variation, will be extended and enriched. Daniel's successful oil drilling (resulting in the death of a "feminine" partner) yields the burden of H.W. (Dillon Freasier), which is in fact a great gift.

Turbulent mythic materials are introduced in this first oil drilling segment. In a film that seldom concerns itself with overt female presence, the mysteries of female power are displaced into the liquid earth, into which miners descend, waist-deep, to forage for oozing treasure. Every human need presented in *There Will Be Blood* is conceived topographically and is tested out on hyper-tactile patches of space. The thick effusion that is manipulated, captured, and made to erupt and sometimes burn from the tunnels and hollows of the earth is always trying to acquire a psychic language in Anderson's framing of it. One feels that the search for oil, this fantastic residue from the far depths, is an unrecognized search for one's buried origins, hurt, and attachments. The release of the oil always stands in for communication, and not only the obviously displaced sexual kind. It is as though the pit must be made to speak in place of lost and estranged others who cannot, and also be made to speak for the unreachable core of the man drilling, who is intensely driven but does not know by what. The urge to strike it rich is the explicable cover for the unspeakable urges that lie in shadow below it.

* * *

After making *Magnolia*, Anderson spoke of putting "my heart—every embarrassing thing I needed to say—into [it]." In his next three feature films (*Punch-Drunk Love*, *There Will Be Blood*, and *The Master*), there is no recourse available for impetuous, unfettered outpouring of this sort. Instead, one discovers a clamping down on both what is known about the self (of the protagonist, certainly, and in fact of everyone else, as well) and what this besieged self has the capacity to articulate. Consider the following composition from the beginning of the 1902 segment of *There Will Be Blood*. A man is shown silently smoking a cigarette and holding onto a rope as he watches a process that he probably regards as wholly intelligible. Another man in the background sits near an animal he is tending, his eyes also cast down. Two other men are digging in the oozing sludge in a hole beneath the man holding the rope. The quivering rope, which the camera tracks down the well, puts us in mind of an umbilical cord. It is attached at the lower end to a sizable bucket that the diggers fill with samples of ooze and shale muck, as they lurch around in this female underworld, struggling for air. They are nearly overcome by the gas fumes given off by the material they cut into and shovel. We discover that one of the two well diggers is Daniel. We hear the clank of his tool against the resistant elements, as we did earlier, but we are struck by the fact that he is no longer solitary in his mind-numbing labor. We behold not only a fellow laborer but someone able to reach out to him and support him in a near-embrace as he grows woozy and bends over, on the point of collapse. Daniel gasps for air, after receiving, and acknowledging with a nod, the male comrade's help and physical contact. Daniel's audible intake of air is a variation on his gasping in pain after his earlier fall in the silver shaft. In the new hole, he stares upward while attempting to fill his lungs with clean air. The next shot—another jolting ellipsis—could be taken as an oblique answer to the question posed by Daniel's craning upward gaze: "What is he seeing, or trying to make out, in the light above him?" We are startled by the sight of a man framed by the wooden supports above the well with a baby in his arms, which he is gently bouncing to keep from crying. The shot begins with the man's back turned to the camera. We are given a second or two to wonder who this person is before he swings around to face us, the baby pressed to his chest. Somehow the Stygian well operations, beginning with the tracking of the umbilical cord and proceeding with the brief exchange of touches and other signs of male fellowship in the midst of a boggy female topography, have conjured an infant, who turns out to be real.

Though Anderson deliberately courts confusion in this segment, the man holding the baby, who is established as the infant's father, turns out to be Daniel's partner in the well dig. (The screenplay identifies the character as H. B. Ailman [Barry Del Sherman]; in the film he remains nameless and voiceless, existing only in his silent gestures and physical actions.) The central relationship of the film—between Daniel Plainview and H.W. (Dillon Freasier/Russell Harvard)—is introduced in this fashion: A man peers up from the depths of the earthen prison cell he has contrived for himself. He appears to be granted a vision of undamaged innocence above him while feeling asphyxiated and fighting for oxygen. But there is a break, a deceiving gap, between the two shots: the subterranean point of view and the aboveground emission of light. Daniel is, in fact, literally disconnected from the implied point-of-view shot, making the soft-lit image of father and son into a kind of hallucination, a floating dream of need and rescue. (This shot is reminiscent of the images of the giant female faces in the *Persona* prologue; the boy in his hospital confinement reaches toward them as a supplicant.) As the shot revealing Ailman and the baby continues, the camera begins to pan left with the pair, and by a subtle, ingrained logic we are briefly led to suppose that Ailman is about to hand off the fussing baby to his mother. Ailman pauses; his face assumes a softer, smiling expression as he gazes down in our direction and also (implicitly) toward someone near at hand in the frame. As one of his arms reaches out, the viewer is mildly disconcerted to come upon Daniel seated in the space visually staked out for the "mother." Ailman's reaching out and touching Daniel's hand echoes his first offer of physical support, of an intimate nature, in the well. On this occasion, Daniel does not look up to return Ailman's prolonged gaze, nor does he spare a glance for the baby. In a sense he is doubly turned away, since this shot contradicts our just-formed impression of Daniel looking up toward the child from the well.

We are made privy to Daniel's thought process here to a degree that has few parallels in the film's later stages. As a substitute for the baby—which the camera has just disavowed as *his* possession—we observe him draw a picture of a modest wooden derrick, modified from a newspaper illustration placed alongside it. The act of drawing mimics the prior close-up action of Daniel signing his name. Though that signature was completed just a few moments ago in actual screen time, in ellipsis time, the event occurred in an already-distant time and place. The drawing features a tilted timber support beam, and Daniel inscribes a double arrow with his pencil, suggesting movement of the tilted timber armature in two directions. The derrick drawing claims Daniel's full attention. It pulls him away from the distracting gestures of human fellowship into another private space. An idea takes shape within him, and the simple pencil sketch seems to galvanize it into fully formed being. The sketch yields to a constructed and entirely operational derrick, complete with a horsepower-driven pump. The crudity of the derrick does not reduce its impressiveness, and its lofty presence dwarfs the two men approaching it, one of whom is Daniel. He gazes upward again, as he did when he was choking inside the well, but now he is staring with apparent awe at his own handiwork. Situated at ground level with Daniel, we can't see the top of the structure, which has the effect of extending its reach to the heavens. The quick gestation of this ramshackle derrick creature, imbued from our first sighting of it with an obscure power, makes it a parallel childbirth directly aligned with the temporarily vanished infant. Daniel has sired a quintessentially masculine, mirroring object for himself, sprung whole from his fancy in a flash. Another rope descends as Daniel raises his head skyward, rhyming with the earlier umbilical cord in the well. Each of us tries to leave a mark on the earth in our sojourn here, to find or build or serve something that in some fashion embodies us, expressing our strongest passion and hunger. Daniel appears to have found his confirming image and identity "mark" with the towering derrick, and he immediately sets about ministering to it, cranking the wheel that raises a rope attached to a massive phallic drill. He is also intent, of course, on making the derrick his servant. He conceives of kinship, ultimately, as fashioning a thing in such a way that it will eventually do his bidding.

In the drawing-to-finished-derrick ellipsis, Anderson highlights the double direction potential of the structure Daniel sketches. The unbalanced beam in his drawing thrusts upward, with arrows in pencil at both ends of the beam pointing in opposite directions. One arrow implicitly points to the baby that Ailman holds as he stands close to Daniel, watching him plan for the future. This arrow is aligned with something that Daniel has not yet claimed or acknowledged by a genuine act of seeing. Nevertheless, Daniel will soon assume Ailman's role as H.W.'s parent (in his crude, hampered fashion) when his friend is killed by the collapse of a beam that Daniel designed and constructed as part of his machine. The second arrow leads to the derrick, part of a literal representation of its way of working. Daniel's idea is that the copy he sketches of a picture in a magazine story lets him "take over" possession of it. He owns the device he draws, and his marks, in effect, put his name to it. The derrick, when built, will stand for Daniel's fierce urge to prevail and will impersonally extend his visible authority. The preliminary sketch testifies to a tension basic to Daniel himself, a split focus and double direction that will inform all of the viewer's emotional dealings with him. The steady push of Daniel against all the external elements that resist his making headway has a kind of sublimity to it—the sense of bending a recalcitrant reality with surpassing swiftness to a grand, lonely purpose. The dream is intensely material, but it reaches downward to a mysterious, richly chaotic depth and also upward toward the firmament, God's domain.

* * *

There is something of Émile Zola's compulsion to endow his chosen fictional topics with an all-encompassing grandeur in Daniel Plainview's mania: to "force the whole universe" into his subject through his mode of attack. Zola's craving for "the enormous and for totality," though incessant, is "never satisfied," and in that plaintive shortfall we see Daniel's as well. His efforts gesture vainly toward an always spoiled, deficient, yet uncontainable immensity, which "thwarts" him as soon as it appears to submit. Even in Plainview's ultimate defeat, Anderson does not wrest him away from the sublime mode. That mode is present in the scale of Daniel's destructive action and the ever-heightened rhetoric in which he accounts for himself. There is sublimity as well in his extreme capacity to cast asunder his attachments. He is finally a figure who seems condemned to forego attachment altogether, but at some level he chooses this condition. Affiliated with his cutting of ties is our investment in the nomadic Western hero, the permanent stranger who appears out of nowhere, lingers awhile, like Shane or Ethan Edwards, in a vexed relationship with a community, and then (his freedom and his curse) rides off again—to disappear in the hills or desert, back from whence he came.

Equally pervasive in the rendering of Plainview's revenge and collapse is a countervailing ironic mode that insists on the man's smallness, emotional stuntedness, anesthetized psyche, brokenness. Daniel can form connections only with those people and things that seem made in his own image. Whatever does not reflect him adequately, whatever does not yield to command and contractual agreement, he instantly regards as against him. Daniel can only hold close what can be counted as a *holding*, and what is his can be counted on because it is within his grasp. We do not settle Daniel's case by seeing either the sublime or ironic version of him as one to be dismantled or rejected decisively in favor of the other. The oscillation continues throughout the narrative—at the micro-level, with which we have thus far been primarily concerned, and in the sweep of the general pattern. In Angus Fletcher's formulation, the merging of seeming polar opposites "proceeds by means of displacement and 'negation,' by which is meant that in the unconscious . . . anything can come to mean its opposite" (298). Hence, ambivalence is not only a constant in our response to Daniel but seems embedded in nearly all of his delineated actions. So it is, of course, present in his relation to "riches," which are thrillingly associated with divination, high-risk drilling, outpouring without end, holdings, and equally affiliated to filth, the stink and murk of the oil itself. Oil is a frightening garb, Anderson frequently shows us, for faces to wear.

Friedrich Schiller, in "The Sublime," wrote acutely about ambivalence in relation to sublimity. Lacking any previously formulated concepts of psychic ambivalence to work with, he intuitively cobbled together a grammar of ambivalence, showing how it operated inwardly, as well as a cultural determinant.

> It is at once a painful state, which in its paroxysm is manifested by a kind of shudder, and a joyous state, that may rise to rapture, and which, without being properly a pleasure, is greatly preferred to every kind of pleasure by delicate souls. This union of two contrary sensations in one and the same feeling proves, in a peremptory manner, our moral independence. For, as it is absolutely impossible that the same object should be with us in two opposite relations, it follows that it is we *ourselves* who sustain two different relations with the object. It follows that these two natures should be united in us, which, on the idea of this object, are brought into play in two perfectly opposite ways. (133, original emphasis)

Daniel's progression in the narrative does not lead, as one might initially suppose, to a concluding radical diminishment of his strength and sovereignty. His shudder-inducing monstrosity vies with his unholy joy in contention until the last moments of the film, without a clear tonal outcome. Daniel's failure to recognize the cure for what ails him, what has always ailed him, does not reduce him in conventional ways to the status of a pathetic object lesson. Irony may encircle his closing outburst against his preacher adversary, Eli (Paul Dano), with its riotously vituperative rhetoric and capping foray into violence, but it does not enervate his aloneness or demystify his madly defiant urges. Robert Warshow speaks about how the image the Westerner "seeks to maintain can be presented as clearly in defeat as in victory: he fights not for advantage and not for the right, but to state what he is, and he must live in a world which permits that statement" (111). For Warshow, "what the Westerner defends, at bottom, is the purity of his own image—in fact, his honor," and "his broad aims never correspond exactly to his real motives" (110). Warshow further maintains that the genre's very form seems to demand some version of the climactic showdown. "The Westerner would not fulfill himself if the moment did not finally come when he can shoot his enemy down" (110). I am quoting Warshow's complex delineation of the Westerner piecemeal, well aware that Daniel Plainview is a far cry from other aspects of the hero type that Warshow presents. Of course Daniel fights "for advantage" at every turn (he comprehends little else so clearly). And Daniel has few marks of "the gentleman," "the knight-errant," "this figure of repose." He resembles far more clearly the gangster hero Warshow forcefully contrasts with the Westerner—especially in his inability "to accept any limits or come to terms with his own nature, fearful, loveless" (106–7). Warshow fuses the two figures briefly when considering their shared loneliness and melancholy, but he goes on to claim that the Westerner's melancholy is due to a clear (and dignified) recognition that life is "unavoidably serious," and not, as in the gangster's case, because of "the disproportions of his temperament" (106).

The powerful ambivalence of Daniel himself and of our relationship with him is consolidated in the film's double ending. We are prompted to view Daniel's farewell meeting with H.W., the scene immediately preceding the bloody, operatic finale in Daniel's basement bowling alley, from a steadfastly judgmental distance. What we observe throughout his repellent exchange with his hard-to-acknowledge "son" is a man who has betrayed everything of importance in their connection, and, beyond that, misunderstood all that has transpired between them, including the workings of his own heart. He has clearly squandered his chances for a deeper, enduring tie with H.W., and he aims to block any possibility of future encounter or reparation. All of his actions here—though pitched to a potentially grandiose hysteria—work to diminish him, to display the flailing impotence behind his denunciations. He is a figure overmastered and done in by an essential stuntedness, and by a vast, buried hurt. He is too fearful to face up to the latter, so he settles for lying bluster instead. Daniel's mansion appears to be a pleasureless, squalid graveyard, where nearly every light has been extinguished. No comfort is visible, nor any animating motive for further enterprise. Daniel seems set upon demonstrating that everything of value can be left behind. He drags the world's unease back and forth through rooms that weigh him down with their pointless clutter. His lavish showplace has no ability to show what it adds up to, either to him or to possible intruders.

There Will Be Blood might, in fact, end here plausibly, amid desolation and paralysis. But instead Anderson reverses course and springs a mighty coda on us that, amazingly, reenergizes the playing field and grants Daniel the opportunity to harvest his doom a second time, this time like a robust tragic warrior, who is closing his accounts on his own madly majestic terms. His behavior in the killing scene, as he suddenly rouses himself and enters a glittering vortex of manic expression, might at first strike the viewer as continuous—in its delusion-based assumptions—with his chill banishment of H.W. It is not as though any sort of moral clarity or probity has been added to the mix. Yet what is undeniably efficacious, dramatically, is the spectacle of Daniel proclaiming, with a stature akin to Ahab's in *Moby-Dick*, what he is and achieving what he conceives as an appropriate self-authorized defeat by proving himself one more time. If he is not defending the purity of his image, in Warshow's sense, he is accepting the consequences of his own intransigence, his endlessly thwarted bid for sufficient sovereignty.

Daniel attains a qualified triumph over the large, well-equipped forces of irony in the bowling alley confrontation scene, where he destroys the doppelganger whom he regards as his major foe. He snatches the identity of prophet away from hapless Eli—a concluding act of Plainview plunder—and fulfills in an extreme fashion the prophetic imperative of the film's title before declaring himself finished. (Daniel's declaration of completion brazenly echoes Christ's last phrase on the cross, "It is consummated," offered as the Son "gives up His spirit.") Daniel comes into possession of his "out in the open" identity by enacting, with heartless joy, a wild stripping away of veils. He does not lie prostrate before the verdict. He capers toward it, embracing the absurdity of all his prior striving for self-enclosure. His slaying of Eli is in no sense justified, of course, and it represents the zenith of unbalance in the film. Nevertheless, once it has transpired, this unnecessary, superfluous deed (bludgeoning the man without backing, assets, advantages of any sort, *after* his complete, abject surrender) feels inevitable. Daniel batters away at the unacknowledged enemy he has struggled against from the outset: his sham sovereign self, with its ghastly weakness and brokenness. When Daniel declares to his butler, almost jauntily, that he's "finished," making a joke of the bloody mess in front of him and of himself leaning over it, the soundtrack exuberantly erupts with the vigorous, victory dance opening of the third movement of Brahms's violin concerto. The tightly coiled music that has been in stifling bondage throughout the film has at last broken loose into a jubilant freedom that cannot be contained.

It is not difficult to discern irony at work here, but the size of Daniel's outrage (out of all proportion to the offense he avenges) and the giddiness of his savage retribution somehow match the scale and feel of the music. There is a kind of devil dance frenzy to the music's outpouring of triumphant joy. Daniel's build-up to the execution of Eli is a gathering together of all his own themes: exile from home; rivalry; brothers seeking to establish primacy; an unreadable, lost mother; abandonment; "drainage" by covert means until the father-owner is left dry; the humiliating necessity of speaking self-condemning truths to others. Eli is obliged to reenact Daniel's earlier mortifying ordeal in Eli's church, when he was given a script to speak as part of a hard bargain. As Daniel was made to shout in the presence of a congregation that he had "abandoned my son," the full realization of his bond with that child and how, out of helpless fear, he had spurned and betrayed it, came home to him. For a brief, unendurable interval, he became nothing but his shame. He revisits that scalding moment of truth by forcing Eli to take on the burden of all that Daniel refuses to "take into account," the vast sickening spread of his weakness, bubbling up like the oil from his first well. Like Humbert Humbert's face-off with nebulous Quilty near the end of Nabokov's *Lolita*, the tone of righteous redress the accuser aims for keeps being diverted into a funhouse key. Daniel latching onto the milkshake analogy is apropos. Daniel acts out a vampire-like draining, demonstrating how all one's resources can be tapped and piped away without one's ever suspecting. Unbeknownst to Daniel, as he imparts his lesson to Eli with demonic gusto, there is a kind of reverse draining at work. Daniel is straining to pump all his unexorcised darkness into the abject Eli, transferring ownership of the horrid contents to him. It is a feat of sublime trickery that first manages to deceive his "begging for clemency" enemy, and then sweeps the confidence man root and branch into his own deception.

Paradoxically, it is Daniel's absolute loss of control at the very instant that he displays total mastery of the situation that permits him to become an absurdly towering presence. Daniel wildly overshoots his own mark and brings ruin to himself and his entire enterprise, but in the spirit of one who grasps suddenly that ruin (and not success of any worldly sort) had perhaps been the motive force from the outset. He surrenders entirely to the *despoiler* part of himself, drawn to sheer internal chaos, which has always been there. As he hurls at Eli all the names of his own failed, unknown psyche, and exterminates the "false prophet" he has exposed, he seems to achieve calm at last. It is the calm that succeeds a full emptying out. As Daniel so aptly and memorably insists, the issue, and the mystery, is indeed "drainage."

* * *

The peculiar logic of atonement and misrecognition in the ending of *There Will Be Blood* can be traced back through the film, giving us a way to account for Anderson's persistent use of the stressed ellipsis in his editing. Ellipsis is a familiar form of narrative economy in cinema. It has an obvious fittingness for Daniel Plainview's case, since the compression that editing ellipsis strives for matches up with the compression that seems to operate in his own nature: a rigorous sifting out of "extraneous" elements. The quality of presence that Daniel Day Lewis imparts to him consistently emphasizes a proud pushing down of unwelcome psychic material as well as the gaps in his responses to what others attempt to convey to him. Ellipsis is also a mode of hiding in narrative presentation that can actually serve (as in the example of Daniel's epic backward crawling journey across the mountains to the Assayer's Office) to accentuate more acutely what has been left out. Significantly, in Anderson's shooting script there are many instances of overt affection and declarations of love between Daniel and H.W. In the film, all verbal evidence of Daniel's depth of attachment has been removed (call it emotional ellipsis) and the visual evidence of closeness (the testimony of gesture) has been reduced. What survives has been rendered more oblique. Again, the excision or blockage of positive manifestations of Daniel's need for attachment and his efforts to build an intimate father-son relationship does not make the connection that we behold feel more tenuous or cold. Highlighting the constraints to easy emotional flow works to intensify our sense of how much is actually at stake. Anderson would have us be prospectors for the hidden ore of feeling, searching the seams and gaps for the inadvertent giveaway moment, the "flashes" of what might turn out to be precious matter.

Daniel's assertion to H.W. in the final banishment scene that he had originally taken on the boy strictly for use, for "show," for a controlled scheme of exploitation is, of course, a false revelation. Yet it may not be a lie, either. Daniel has, in fact, *managed* himself around H.W. from the outset, but not out of cunning. It is more a case of ongoing trepidation. H.W. has made a sizable breach in the wall of Daniel's fortress, and Daniel feels that penetration as a jeopardy. To let this opening in himself be too clearly seen or to give vocal expression to how much it means would place him at a disadvantage in all his other dealings. Or at least this is how Daniel calculates the risk. Others would quickly seize on his demonstrable weakness and prey on it. To protect the true grounds of caring from detection, he plays the role of the father *in public* that he in fact yearns to be. He imagines that he is creating safeguards for himself by making an authentic intimacy into a "manipulative" theatrical display. He further keeps H.W. in the dark about what their father-son bond actually consists of (including perhaps the identity of H.W.'s biological father, Ailman), so that the boy will not see more than is good for him and thus gain the upper hand. When H.W. loses his hearing in the blast that brings in Daniel's richest strike, Daniel construes it as a judgment on his own vulnerability. He has invested too much feeling in the boy, and as a result has brought down a fitting curse on their relationship. The oil has not failed him, but in the weakness of his immoderate, undisciplined loving, he has failed himself.

Deafness in a sense does not constitute a break with Daniel's old arrangement with his son, but a continuation. What palpable evidence of closeness there is appears less in the confidences that the father has shared about his business than in the quality of their shared silence: their way of being together as they walk or rest. Both of them seem to be refining their aptitude for watching and waiting. H.W. is rewarded by Daniel with the privileges of unspokenness—what *need not* be said aloud—and continues the pattern of silent accord established between H.W.'s biological father, Ailman, and Daniel, early in the film. The logic of ellipsis in the two men's quasi-marriage is that speech is always cleared away in favor of what is more natural between them: wordless communion in the performance of demanding, consequential tasks. H.W. is not merely the adopted child; he is meant to fill the place left vacant by an indispensable friend who has been snatched away, a friend whose significance to Daniel will not—perhaps cannot—be spoken about. The continuity of companionable silence is one of the features of H.W.'s acceptable manner of closing the gap, of sealing the void.

Without Daniel quite being aware of it, H.W. has been granted the role of guardian of his secret emotional life. The onset of H.W.'s deafness confronts Daniel anew with the terrifying muddle and muckiness of that feeling reservoir the child has been assigned to tend. H.W. proves too frail and unresourceful for the job. The child's disclosed *need*—after the dreadful impact of the explosion—is too great for the child to bear alone. As Daniel watches him cry helplessly that he can't hear anything, something massive is clearly forcing its way up within him. The love Daniel has allowed into himself is *causing* this frightening turmoil, but Daniel feels its pressure as so immense and uncontrollable that he must repudiate it (and its human cause) if he is to survive as a person he can recognize. The terms of Daniel's implicit contract with H.W. have been violated by this forced exposure of Daniel's need for the boy. Too much love has been revealed, has worked its way "out into the open," and if that love is acknowledged, too much *more* will be required of Daniel. It will exceed, vastly, the declared, modest and governable allotment. Thus Daniel turns away from H.W. as soon as he confirms the child's brokenness and painful infirmity. His affliction over the child's suffering is displaced onto the oil well. His immediate concern for fixing the well, that "problem with a remedy," allows him to channel all his psychic energy elsewhere. He finds an exulting excitement over his newly surging wealth instead of a terror over the upheavals of love. The external fire *can* be brought under control, as his helpless grief cannot. However, the choosing of the well's demands over H.W.'s demands is not the rational "investment transfer" of a heartless man. Daniel instead strives, paradoxically, to keep his love for his son safe by forcing it back into hiding. Only when it is below ground again will it not overwhelm and incapacitate.

Dream condensation is another aspect of Anderson's method of deploying ellipsis. All that is removed from view and kept in doubt while H.W. wails "I can't hear my voice, I can't hear my voice" and Daniel attempts, by way of response, to drown out his *own* loving voice, is transplanted to an earlier, extended long shot of Daniel carrying H.W. to the camp shortly after the explosion. The narrative information contained in that run might have been conveyed briskly, economically. But Anderson elects to stretch out the act to the point where it feels dreamlike and endless. The truth of the attachment is to be sought in this apt image of a man holding what he cherishes and fleeing (with a percussive, clacking heartbeat accompaniment) from all the amassed perils of his entire life history to a place of safekeeping, which cannot be found. When, shortly afterward, Daniel leaves H.W. on a table, although the boy begs him not to, he runs back to the flaming derrick. Once there, his first action is to cut away two support ropes (ties) with an ax. He is promptly hypnotized by the blaze, standing as witness to it for hours, as though seeking any pretext to avoid turning around to confront the more consuming flames of his son's love, loss, and need.

Anderson concludes the scene with two distinct shots of H.W. and Eli, each watching the fire from their separate enclosures. The view of Eli is dim and meant to confuse us, at least initially. We think we see H.W.'s features in his face before correcting our mistake. *There Will Be Blood* parallels Bergman's *Persona* again in its relentless concern with identity crossovers, with one face shifting without warning to another's terrain. Anderson creates temporary mergers that are, by turn, touching

Daniel is drawn to the consuming flame of the gusher that caused H.W. to lose his hearing in *There Will Be Blood*

and distressing. Daniel's rigid determination to keep all the categories in his world clear and separate is opposed by a visual scheme in which everything wants to blur together, repeat, and proliferate unshakable affinities.

* * *

In *Persona*, the search for the hidden mother is central to the two women's joint narrative. In *There Will Be Blood*, the search for the mother takes place in an almost womanless wilderness. This quest, while of critical importance (as always in Anderson) is much less direct, and is mostly conducted by symbolic means—for example, the cumbersome mining apparatus reaching deep into the earth for a "saving" strike. Recall how in Anderson's first feature film, *Hard Eight* (1996), the initial meeting has to do with a son, John, attempting to find $6,000 to pay for his mother's burial. The father figure, Sydney, who arrives—like a good angel—to assist him is, unbeknownst to John, the man who killed his father. Here, in miniature, is the story that Anderson will always be telling, with a mother needing burial but still perilously exposed at the center of it.

At roughly the midpoint of *There Will Be Blood*, we see Eli displaying his power and faith for the first time in his church by performing a lengthy exorcism on an old woman, Mrs. Hunter (Irene G. Hunter) afflicted with painful rheumatism. Daniel observes this ritual from an invisible point in the background during his first visit to this church. Although we are loosely connected to Daniel's point of view as an outside observer, he disappears from the frame entirely before the exorcism commences, as though somehow absorbed into it. We are given no reaction shots to gauge his response to what he is witnessing until the ritual expulsion is completed. Daniel becomes linked to the demon that Eli summons from the old woman and then violently casts out of his house of prayer. Daniel is, beyond question, a vital part of the battle Eli is conducting with malignant forces and with this weak, ethereal mother, but he remains the missing term, the ellipsis, in the visible drama. Anderson once again displays his strong preoccupation with shots (extended, as this one is, or brief) that are built around crucial missing terms: withheld but strongly implied figures. I say more later about how the old woman, Mrs. Hunter, becomes the missing mother who embodies both hidden power and frailty in this exorcism, but for now I note only that the missing term images closely resemble the requirements that André Breton formulated for the proper surrealist image. "(1) It embodies contradictions. (2) One of the terms of the image is hidden. (3) The image starts out sensationally, then abruptly closes the angle of its compass—i.e., it embodies a deception, a sudden shocking frustration of whatever we had expected. (4) The image possesses the character of a hallucination. (5) The image lends to the abstract the mask of the concrete" (Anna Balakian quoted in Fletcher, 123ff).

Eli (Paul Dano) casts out a demon in *There Will Be Blood*

In this final section about *There Will Be Blood*, I consider some of the missing terms, shocks, deceptions, and swerves to hallucination that contribute to the shape and significance of three death scenes and their immediate aftermaths. As in the church exorcism scene with Mrs. Hunter, a missing mother will elliptically emerge in each of the scenes. Death is perhaps the most potent summons for ellipsis, and the ultimate expression of a gap whose blankness is a constant, admitting of no further elaboration. And yet people must do things in response to a death: they attempt repair, recovery, substitution, or evasion so that the sense of the blankness does not prevail. The meaning of human effort or mere persistence is never entirely rubbed out by the force of nil. The "sensational" eruption of death or the mere collapse of life as death quietly snuffs out the candle is followed by closure of a lesser sort, which Breton refers to as the "closing of the angle of the compass" within the image field that remains to life. One of the "deceptions" that the surrealist image embodies is that death closes, but in doing so it opens an escape route. Death creates a gaping hole through which life can escape. Life can walk away from death, through the gap, and indeed is *meant* to walk away, into the hallucination of earthly doings. Absence and loss are, at least in part, freeing, a lightening of the load.[3]

In the speechless early section of *There Will Be Blood*, as I previously noted, we do not see much explicit evidence of Daniel's attachment to his coworker, Ailman, before the latter's death. He turns up beside him in the hole when the oil well digging is first introduced. Stress is laid on their comfortable shared "mutism," and on Ailman's readiness to touch and support Daniel when the fumes nearly cause him to pass out. This touching, which Daniel does not reject but perhaps gratefully receives, is the first instance of physical contact between characters in the film. Right after this encounter, a view of Ailman cradling the infant H.W. reinforces the warmth of closeness. Their intimacy widens out and becomes the warmth of a family circle, with Ailman as mother figure, when the camera reframes to include Daniel seated at his worktable, concentrating. Ailman's behavior suggests a wife giving her husband space to accomplish a task as she looks after their child. We next view Ailman at close range when he is alone in the well, grappling with the drill bit that Daniel has lost control of. The bit plunges deep in the muck, resulting in a propitious release of oil.

Ailman's onscreen life consists of only a handful of gestures leading up to his fatal accident—gestures that, in the absence of speech, reveal everything we are permitted to know of him and of what his presence means to Daniel. Thus each charged glimpse of Ailman warrants close inspection. None of his defining gestures feels random or inadvertent. Behold then, Ailman in a rain slicker wildly exerting himself to free the drill bit—like young Arthur's sword lodged in the stone—from the impacted sludge in which it is caught. A marked contrast is established between Ailman's uncontrolled flailing (his vulnerability to a disorderly, agitating process) and Daniel's calm, serene fixity as he gazes down at him from a position outside the well, backed by a streaming, radiant light. Daniel exhibits the fascination of the detached observer contemplating a figure who is vehemently possessed by what he is doing. The sizable distance separating the oozing pit from the light-drenched surveillance post delineates a gap between the "blocked" intelligence holding its knotted instincts in check and a stand-in for these instincts, furiously striving to loosen a "rigid phallus" from a frozen position. Daniel's entranced, acquisitive look may be divided between the craving for spoils (what will the loosened drill reveal to him?) and a captivation by the spectacle of his comrade wrestling with such untrammeled, messy vigor. The action Ailman performs is literally a violent freeing of what is caught and locked in place. We next observe Ailman peering upward toward the light, precisely rhyming Daniel's own earlier gaze upward when *he* was in the pit, growing dizzy. Ailman releases the dripping tool, which is then hoisted by pulley to a waiting Daniel. Daniel excitedly strokes the tube when he can reach it, then extends his oil-streaked palm heavenward, in a manner that suggests both hubristic triumph and the request for a blessing from a higher presence. The accompanying music is again slippery, tautly menacing, full of portent. The successful retrieval of the drill is sonically joined to a still-unfolding musical narrative of impending disaster. The score spurns the appeal of Daniel's lordly, upraised hand.

In another few moments, the aggressive, rope-hoisted tool of pent-up virility gives way to a "female" image of a small reservoir, encircled by viscous mounds of earth. Men pour buckets of dark substance into the glistening oil pool and are briefly linked to conventional female rituals of water carrying as well as to a male spending of fluid into a mysterious, fearsome receptacle. Ailman appears once more, and for the last time, in the company of one-year-old H.W., beside the dirty pool, compounding and echoing the spiritual gesture of Daniel's illuminated oily hand by anointing H.W.'s forehead, playfully, with a streak of oil. When Ailman approaches the reservoir, carrying his child, he and the oval receptacle (with which his maternal actions grant him closer linkage) are presented in a striking overhead shot. The framing not only serves to bind father and son to the liquid pool, visible in its entire extent, but it also prepares us for the death scene that immediately follows. Ailman will be felled by loose toppling timber from the well apparatus whose construction his friend and mate Daniel has supervised. The overhead shot equally intimates a godly protection of father and boy, building on Daniel's prophetic, upraised hand (a reverse point of view answer to that gesture, if you like) and a possible threat from above. Daniel's hand, recall, no sooner acknowledges the possible presence of a higher power than, almost by reflex, it challenges its supremacy. The music filling this bridging passage overrides any suggestion of a blessing conferred. It pushes us instead toward the unwrapping of a curse, as we hear what sounds like a pebble rattling around a sinister roulette wheel. An unlucky gambler is poised to lose everything.

There is a shock transition—marked by an ellipsis—that transports us from Ailman's kissing of his son's face to a return plunge to the depths of the well. Two buckets are being lowered and the camera traverses the darkness of their descent with them. Daniel and Ailman are once again revealed side by side, standing in the sludge at the bottom in matching rain slickers. I want to stress how Ailman's gentle paternal kiss seems to unleash the black downward movement of the ropes and buckets, as though love is one of the generating agents of the coming fatality. The image feels hallucinatory, to take up Breton's term again, and swerves from the open, clear attachment between Ailman and H.W. to a more hidden, obscure connection between the two workmen. As they fill their respective buckets to the brim and the ropes lift the trembling containers, the men's faces are spattered by the overflow. They assume roughly symmetrical poses as they both raise their heads and release loaded pails. Their paired watching powerfully underscores the fact of their togetherness: of one mind, as it were. As our upward view clarifies, we discern workers at the surface tugging on the ropes as the tense scoring at last fades out, surrendering to natural sounds. The sudden resumption of ordinary noise does not reassure us, however. Rather, the natural sound alerts us to a *hidden term* in the placid landscape image, and with eerie softness "closes the angle of the compass." Murky sensations are visually opposed by the peaceful prospect of rolling hills, calmly occupied men, the graceful fabric of a nearby tent, and the suggestion of daylight security. But at that instant, a timber support beam collapses, and from an unanchored point-of-view shot in the pit we draw back from heavy objects hurtling toward us.

Anderson briefly confuses us about which man has been struck down and about whether the accident has proven lethal. We are given an unusually long time to contemplate a man turned away from us, cowering from the tragedy in the well. His face hidden for a crucial interval, he becomes the missing term and possible source of deception in the image. His hoarse gasping recalls Daniel's struggle for air in previous episodes. Finally we are granted a sustained view of Daniel's eyes daring to peek out and confront the human wreckage next to him. There is no answering shot to exhibit what he sees. Daniel's eyes transmit shock, and though much of his face remains concealed from us, we receive a sharp intimation of dread, as well. Daniel is illuminated here as a man afraid to look at certain things directly.

Another ellipsis snatches us away from this dread of looking. In place of the victim we are offered the settled face of Daniel in full daylight, still bearing streaks of oil and garbed in his southwester. He now appears to be staring in a self-possessed, perhaps penitential manner at what we are misled to suppose is the corpse of Ailman. Instead of the corpse we are shown—in a variation of the Kuleshov experiment—the startling image of the toddler, H.W., looking back at Daniel. Unmindful of the tragic circumstances, he seems to be debating whether the presence of this comparative stranger warrants tears. It is the first time that Daniel and the child have acknowledged each other directly. And because the child is a surprise substitution for the image we anticipated (the dead partner), H.W. appears to take over at a stroke whatever accumulated, unarticulated feelings belonged to the relationship that the accident foreclosed. From the standpoint of character psychology, this ellipsis is as significant as any in the film. Within the gap between Daniel's dread at confronting his friend's fate and his tacit acceptance of responsibility for his orphaned son, there are two sizable and suppressed emotional burdens. A transfer of energy is dramatized here, which has the force of a strong metaphor: "metaphor as event," in Mary Ruefle's phrase. Ruefle, a poet, speaks of metaphor as "the time it takes for an exchange of energy to occur. . . . *A poem must rival a physical experience* and metaphor is, simply, an exchange of energy between two things" (131, original emphasis). Daniel transfers (through an obscure mixture of grief, will, need, and calculation) his attachment for Ailman, who has been snatched away from him, to the child, H.W., the "burden" Ailman has left behind. H.W. is what remains of his father, the chief evidence that he existed. Daniel defers and suppresses his grief by immediately taking up the responsibility for the child's upbringing, seizing the burden almost without space for reflection.

When I rewatched *There Will Be Blood* not long after my mother's death, I was astonished to discover that the narrative appeared to be saturated with grief, a condition that had previously struck me as present only peripherally, and rather abstractly, well removed from the issues of character that seemed central. Naturally, I wondered whether my own grief had seeped into the barrenness of Daniel's isolation and insisted on making room for itself in a psyche that offered it little sustenance. But Anderson's elliptical method of presenting the various threats Daniel is fleeing supplied evidence that his highly conspicuous wrath may indeed be contending, in secret, against the weight of intractable grief. Anne Carson, in her preface to *Grief Lessons*, makes an extraordinary claim about grief and rage's ineluctable kinship in tragedy:

> Why does tragedy exist? Because you are full of rage. Why are you full of rage? Because you are full of grief. Ask a headhunter why he cuts off human heads. He'll say that rage impels him and rage is born of grief. The act of severing and tossing away the victim's head enables him to throw away the anger of all his bereavements. Perhaps you think this does not apply to you. Yet you recall the day your wife, driving to your mother's funeral, turned left instead of right at the intersection and you had to scream at her so loud other drivers turned to look. When you tore off her head and threw it out the window they nodded, changed gears, drove away. . . . There is a theory that watching unbearable stories about other people lost in grief and rage is good for you—may cleanse you of your darkness. Do you want to go down the pits of yourself all alone? Not much. What if an actor could do it for you? Isn't that why they are called actors? They act for you. You sacrifice

> them to action. And this sacrifice is a mode of deepest intimacy of you with your own life. Within it you watch [yourself] act out the present or possible organization of your nature. You can be aware of your own awareness of this nature as you never are at the moment of experience. (7)

The answer Carson provides to the question "Why does tragedy exist?" is ahistorical. *We* (or *you*) are the answer. Our rage, we are reminded, explodes from us, but the explosion is nearly always about something else, "displaced grief." A confusion lies at the core of tragedy. The shouting and heedless destruction brought about by the tragic hero often transpires in a "blind," like that occupied by Daniel Plainview. We also encounter him in Carson's judicious phrase, "the pits of yourself." In the shielding company of an actor we descend into the pit of ourselves to be "cleansed," by proxy, of our darkness. And this cleansing is steeped in sorrow. Is this Daniel's actual mission, as he burrows into the earth? Let us say that *he* seeks to be cleansed of *his* darkness. He seeks clemency as he drives himself ever deeper into the pit of himself. Carson says we opt for distance, whenever possible, in such descents. We send actors down in our place and watch them sacrifice themselves so we can get charged intimations of how our own nature is organized. Experience doesn't give us enough clarity when things are happening. We need a substitute, a stand-in, one who is *made* for sacrifice, who can act it out for our benefit, so we can gain perspective, which entails a deepening intimacy with our elusive self and life. Grief is the crucial hidden term. Rage batters and thrashes about to distract the hero (and perhaps the spectator) from its presence.

Out of grief that can barely be countenanced, Daniel looks toward the tiny child, abandoned by his dead parent, and in the act of gazing at him feels an empty space inside himself beginning to be filled. The emotional place occupied previously by Ailman is shifted, as though in a deed transfer, to H.W. No doubt Daniel considers H.W. as a potential acquisition, an idea he can understand that blocks his view of a need he doesn't understand. The transaction may even strike Daniel as a bargain. Both Daniel's rage and grief seem pacified, initially, though both remain near, trembling in the balance as he takes on the task of caring for the "left behind" infant and, more complexly, caring about him. The shot that follows the first prolonged exchanged look between them is a two-shot of Daniel and H.W. sitting beside each other. Daniel, the newly self-appointed father, tackles the riddle of supplying nourishment. He coaxes a reluctant infant to accept a bottle of milk by dousing the nipple with whisky, the succulent poison Daniel thrives on. In Anderson's shooting script, this scene involves a mother conscripted from a flophouse to breastfeed the boy. In the filmed version, it is a half-drunken Daniel rather than a surrogate who picks the child up after he refuses to drink and then dandles and pats him.

Immediately following this action, and serving as a concluding image for the extended, language-free prologue to the main narrative, is another two-shot of Daniel and H.W., this time aboard a train en route to an unspecified destination. Their intimacy has advanced remarkably in the space of a single cut, and this final perspective on blooming tenderness is granted unusual duration. We have ample time to observe Daniel taking pleasure in gazing his fill without embarrassment as the toddler studies his face quizzically, then reaches up and touches him. Daniel is further delighted as H.W. fondles his mustache, rewarding this gesture with a spontaneous smile. The tension in this lengthy visualization of serenity comes from Daniel's voice, which intrudes into the train compartment without warning and demands abruptly that we split our attention between father-son and the sound and sense of smoothly manipulative speechifying. The voice is not part of the image's present tense. It lies ahead of the action by many years and commandeers the train, in effect, by forcing it to pass hastily through time and space, as if to catch up with it. Daniel seems, on the one hand, to have no impediment to his involvement with his son in a present that snugly encloses them, but at the same time this present recedes—as we listen to Daniel's "alien" voice—into the future. The voice bears us away from openness, mutuality, and Daniel effortlessly loosening up. Yet the image of these conditions persists for a long time in competition with the speaking voice. The image will not let go and simply dissolve.

Daniel and the narrative have instigated a break with the emotion that expands within the long take in the train compartment and are determined to settle elsewhere, at some remove from this still-ripening tenderness. And yet Daniel is equally intent on lingering with his acquired "son," as though there remained all the time in the world to play

Daniel takes pleasure in his new role of fathter in *There Will Be Blood.*

with him. The speech, we soon determine, is a piece of salesman theater designed to persuade its various audiences to make a deal with Daniel on his terms. The voice, as we grow accustomed to its honeyed, John Huston–like authority and flow, reasserts *control* in the narrative. It is a voice equivalent, for all its measured self-possession, of the coiled music we encountered previously on the soundtrack. When we finally get our first glimpse of Daniel's face as speaker in the newly established *future* present tense, and (a little bit later) with seven-year-old H.W. seated behind him, we recognize that both of them are engaged in a performance. Both appear masked, now, as they face the crowd, inverting the terms of the open-faced exchange they shared in the just-vanished train.

* * *

The second death I examine is that of Joe Gundha (uncredited). An employee of Daniel's about whom he knows almost nothing, Gundha perishes in the well "cellar" in a manner strikingly reminiscent of Ailman's death, his head crushed by a falling section of the drill. Daniel is roused from sleep in his cabin by his business associate, Fletcher (Ciarán Hinds), bringing him news of the accident. H.W. is unobtrusively in the background of this extended shot as the news is delivered, clearly alert to everything. His positioning behind his father may remind us of the place he regularly occupies in Daniel's public performances. H.W.'s mute witnessing establishes another link between Gundha's death and that of H.W.'s biological father.

Daniel's response to the report of Gundha's death is complicated by the insertion of a flashback—a device only resorted to this once in the narrative. How peculiar, then, that the flashback is devoted to the final moments of a stranger's life, as he stands completely unmindful of the threat poised to destroy him. The accident is shown, in large part, from Gundha's point of view, though it is resolutely a blind point of view. He comes into focus as a man emphatically marked for doom (we know the fatal accident has already happened) but who is absorbed by some other concern. This point of view is called into existence only so that we can witness its obliteration before anything of consequence is taken in. The flashback is narratively unmoored: Fletcher has not himself seen the accident; no one but the victim, Gundha, a now-severed perspective, is attached to it. Gundha is crushed into the mud with only the camera narrator as witness. When Ailman died, Daniel was right beside him, surveying the aftermath through an act of terrified peeking. Here Daniel is blanked out, except perhaps as the recipient of horrible news, which he then might imagine for himself. The flashback fills in a gap instead of creating or reinforcing one. It is, therefore, the opposite of the ellipsis, which promotes hiddenness. The fleeting Gundha flashback puts a face to a man who, in story terms, doesn't count for anything. He is not someone whose passing will engender complications for Daniel that can *force* him into a new course of action.[4]

Although nothing in Daniel's processing of the facts indicates more than exasperation at a botched operation and the possible loss of an expensive drill bit, this small episode furnishes another narrative channel where Daniel's grief works its way into visibility. In the scenes that follow the flashback, there is much emphasis on Daniel's apparent control and detachment. Nonetheless, the flashback releases a counter-current of memory and projective identification. The underground terrain it illuminates vibrates with old, unfinished, "half-raised" sorrow and is bewitched by it. Right before Gundha's appearance, Daniel's listening face disappears from view, to be covered over by Gundha's face in the hole, as he labors unwittingly toward the sight of his own death, or, to be more precise, the collapse of sight before it can take in what is happening. As soon as the plummeting metal drives Gundha into the muck, we return to a close-up, high-angle view of Daniel's face, as though he had been the co-recipient of the death-dealing blow. The viewer, minimally concerned with Gundha in story terms, may process the accident viscerally but is likely able to quickly relinquish it as a point of interest. It seems that we are free to let it go unless it generates more "useful" narrative implications.

Daniel appears to ratify the rightness of our determination not to linger over it. He rouses himself impatiently, and makes a disagreeable middle-of-the-night journey to the well where the accident took place. But, in fact, without our being let in on Daniel's precise inner whereabouts, there are clear indications that the disaster has a significant impact on him. The narrative, surprisingly, does linger over the death by dwelling on the details of its aftermath. Daniel seems to carry the burden of this loss as though he had, indeed, been an intimate witness of the tragedy from inside the hole. Our sympathy lags well behind his: he is unable to let go of the experience, however "secondhand" it may be. The view of Ailman's corpse that we anticipated in the earlier death scene, but which was elliptically denied us, seems to be delivered belatedly now, when Gundha's all but faceless form, unrecognizable, drenched in mud and blood, is hauled up and into the light on the deck platform.

The raising of this horror from the darkness and Daniel's confrontation of it may complete an emotional recognition that was blocked, evaded, or displaced at the time when Daniel lost his partner, Ailman. Daniel is framed from behind as he contemplates the victim. The body is below the cutoff point in the frame. Yet we have beheld the hideous form, coated entirely in wet filth, long enough ourselves to realize that there are no signs or traces by which this man might be identified. Daniel surveys the stranger's remains for an unusually prolonged "moment" before turning and giving a number of orders: that the corpse be washed and dressed in clean clothes, that a tent be set up to honor his death, and that the well be closed down until midday. Daniel also angrily remonstrates with the workers about the importance of "telling someone" when a man is in the cellar. He then quickly reins in his anger. While Daniel gazes down at Gundha, Anderson's composition includes a second male figure resting on the coiled ropes behind him, who seems impassive and genuinely unconcerned. This worker's disengaged stance and look further focuses Daniel's contrasting attentiveness and disquiet. Greenwood's score lightly intervenes, amid the sound of crickets, with a wavering thread of lament—a sound that rustles indefinitely, like a night breeze, rather than emerging decisively.

The next brief scene carries us inside the tent the men have erected. There is a remarkable prolongation of Daniel's on-screen involvement (direct rather than delegated) with the dead man's affairs. We watch him sorting through Gundha's photos and keepsakes in a tin box, and removing a cloth cross that he hands to another man packing up his effects. He pauses as he looks at the cross and concludes that Gundha's religious affiliation was a serious rather than a casual matter for him. The music has gained in agitated force, which bleeds into the next scene of Daniel walking alone through a barren stretch of desert. The preoccupation with Gundha's faith has stayed with Daniel and prompted this trip to Eli's chapel, which he has never set foot in. His manner of walking is deliberate but weighed down. The vacillation in the string accompaniment reinforces the impression that Daniel is striving unsuccessfully to break free from a difficult train of thought, or at least to regain mastery of his troubled mind. This current dilemma suggests that Daniel is being driven backward to grief, to the unfinished mourning for the loss of Ailman, and perhaps of others before him.

The narrative placement of Joe Gundha's death and Daniel's quiet contention against its disproportionate effect on him has everything to do with H.W.'s imminent accident and with Daniel's fiercely divided response to it. He will be lodged once more between grief and hysterical anger. And he will force the anger to *convert* and express itself as elation over the oil strike victory and his vanquishing of the fire that erupted in the well. But we are not done with Daniel's trip to Eli's church. He pauses at the door before entering (a church service is in progress), although the cause of his halting is not a reluctance to barge in, but instead a strong unwillingness to concede this act—his abrupt appearance in Eli's domain—to his adversary. Once he goes inside and takes a standing position at the rear of the church, he disappears for a considerable interval as a visible reactive witness to the exorcism being performed on the elderly, arthritic Mrs. Hunter. Eli's casting out of the demon (a ritual that includes, among other maneuvers, sucking the devil out through her swollen fingers) pushes, as I noted earlier, a female figure into the foreground of the drama for one of the only times in the film. She arrives as a possible veiled answer to the question, "What is Daniel grieving over?"

In her extraordinary study, *The Art of Cruelty: A Reckoning*, Maggie Nelson reminds us that it is "a hallmark of patriarchal religion, culture and psychology to have a repressed symbolic matricide at its root—a matricide cast as necessary for the human subject to leave the mess of nature and bodily dependency behind, and to become a full participant in subjectivity, language, and culture (all of which, in phallocentric discourse, are identified with the male)" (168). Nelson goes on to discuss the function of the abject in the work of Julia Kristeva—which always comes back to the violent psychic expulsion of the female: "While the abjection of the maternal may be necessary, according to Kristeva, to form a subject, its expulsion can never be seamlessly accomplished. The abjected maternal returns, via horror, repulsion, the uncanny, haunting, melancholia, depression, guilt, the inchoate but harrowing sense that one has lost, left, or killed something critical" (169). I propose that the grieving that Daniel undergoes involves not only Gundha's link to the maternal former partner, Ailman, but to a lost mother figure who precedes both these now-dead men, and whose existence is never mentioned in the film.

Mrs. Hunter gives no evidence of surviving strength. She epitomizes, in fact, pitiable vulnerability. And yet once Eli begins to fondle and sexually suck on her fingers to spring loose the demon, the force he seems to encounter and be, in part, possessed by, has a deep propensity for violence, sexual craving, and acts of malevolence. Before Mrs. Hunter can shed the symptoms of her ailment, Eli must engage her hidden tormentor in a public struggle. He must unreservedly surrender to his own righteous rage, if the spirit foe is to be physically expelled from the chapel. Mrs. Hunter is emotionally remote from her demon and disconnected from the mayhem of Eli's contest, but what he has spiritually excavated (another sort of mining) has initially dwelt within her. Her form is the only visible reference point for what Eli contends with. Eli's vehement "acting out" of holy wrath is, undoubtedly, performed with Daniel's presence in mind. Eli shows no awareness that Daniel is in the church watching, but he is surely mindful of his intrusion on the service. We are swiftly persuaded that some portion of Eli's channeling of demonic energy and his power over it is aimed at this temporarily concealed (from us as well as Eli) witness. In another sense, the exorcism is also performed on Daniel's behalf. The obscure pain that he has been carrying around inside him and that has led him to this church gathering is somehow incorporated into the ritual he spies on, just as his burden (over having abandoned his son) will be more overtly manifested in the later church scene, when he is made to confess his sin against H.W. while being baptized. In the later scene, Daniel's seeming reluctance to shout his guilt is braided together with a pressing desire for acknowledgment and release. In the Mrs. Hunter episode, the scourge of guilt is tied to the surrogate form of an old, helpless mother. What issues from "her," in Eli's paroxysm, is a ferocious will to inflict harm, suddenly unloosed and whirling with Eli in the air. The death of Gundha merges with a prior undisclosed crime against a female figure (perhaps a tormentor in her own right). Anderson wants whatever it is that is rising up and cast out here to remain unfathomable. The deepest thing cannot, should not be given a name, certainly not a curative and thus a diminishing explanation.

The questions of Oedipus, as Maggie Nelson paraphrases them ("What have I done? Am I a criminal?," 170), are Daniel's questions as well, though buried further down than Oedipus's, and never *fully* confronted. Daniel is both always avoiding his original crime and always

Daniel tells Eli's congregation that he abandoned his son in *There Will Be Blood*

looking for it. The most manageable place to hunt is under the ground, where the thing that is located can be transmuted, after self-punishing effort, into wealth. He doesn't, in fact, find the prior crime that belongs to him, that may even define him. In this failure he resembles Anderson's other madly circuitous questers. The viewer, as well, is prevented from securing firm knowledge of Daniel's original transgression, the pressure of which grants him, from our first sighting of him, his pent-upness. Daniel puts other burdens in his mind—lesser burdens that feel unwedded to thought, that can be disowned, disputed—substitutes for the primary offense, which he has no way to deal with. These burdens are shadows of the knowledge that Daniel cannot absorb. His innermost self, as Nelson puts it, is a "culprit" that avoids again and again, though only narrowly, being driven into the open (170). The other burdens Daniel reckons with (some of them crimes), having to do with murder, abandonment, loss, or neglect, may necessitate spurts of grieving in him, but anger repeatedly comes to his rescue and camouflages privation and need as the "forces of resistance," seeking to wear down his will. Daniel gets to finish his narrative, without the self-incriminating Oedipus realization and the self-administered punishment that follows it. He expends all his might, with ironic success, in preventing the knowledge that should be his from coming home to him. Daniel's marked absence as a responding witness to Mrs. Hunter's exorcism is tied to his concluding blindness. He is himself the ellipsis in the scene where a demon is identified by Eli and powerfully expelled.

Having been freed for the moment from her suffering, Mrs. Hunter is led into a slow dance inside the church with Eli, as though he has just become her acknowledged spiritual son. It is a reconciliation with the mother, and by extension with female strength and weakness, from which Daniel is wholly excluded. He remains at the outer edges of this intimacy, which flows in the wake of a dreadful recognition and cleansing. Soon Daniel will stand outside the doorway of the church again, losing an argument with Eli about what "should have been done" for Joe Gundha. Daniel loses the argument by losing control of his temper. Eli, meanwhile, quietly consolidates his own just-earned calm as he admonishes Daniel for "avoidable accidents" and "the unblessed well" where Gundha perished. Eli seems to derive extra sustenance from Daniel's flailing; he stands at the threshold of his chapel, maintaining home advantage. Daniel, for his part, gets verbally caught on a single phrase ("blowing gold all over the place") that he obsessively repeats. He takes the exorcism he has just observed and converts it into an oil image. The well must be allowed to produce, to disgorge wealth. The repetition of the phrase builds in pressure and becomes a gusher itself. This verbal eruption covers over, perhaps, for a time, further concern with Joe Gundha, Ailman, and mother losses that may have led Daniel, almost against his will, to seek out Eli at the church service.

* * *

The third and final death segment I examine is Daniel's murder of his "brother," Henry Plainview (Kevin J. O'Connor), or rather the nameless man—the "no one"—who took over the real Henry's story after this brother died of tuberculosis. "Henry" learned enough family history from the dead man's diary and prior talk about himself to do a persuasive impersonation of Daniel's closest kin. He has appeared in Daniel's life at roughly the point when Daniel has given up hope that H.W. will recover his hearing. Unmindful as always of the depth of his need for contact with another, Daniel is groping for some sort of replacement for the damaged, unreachable child who is proving ever more of a challenge for Daniel to face up to directly and care for.

Henry, the new arrival, is playing at least two roles then, and possibly a third, for the period that Daniel believes in his kinship. He takes over many of the tasks and "services" H.W. used to perform for Daniel, providing companionship, physical nearness, automatic agreement, and loyal, quiet following of the sort that H.W. had been trained for. He also supplies Daniel with a vital link to his childhood in the form of a scarcely remembered younger brother, who can restore a dim dream of home and the possibility of regaining in a better form what has been left behind. As the brother from another mother, Henry is also arguably fused with that replacement mother figure. He possesses her desired attributes of selfless nurturing and unconditional love. This mother-brother would fit right into the lavish Hollister house that Daniel fiercely coveted as a boy. He reveals to Henry, after they have bathed in the Pacific Ocean, how the house offered a complete fantasy of belonging and security. He wanted "to live in it, and eat in it, clean it, and even as a boy I wanted to have children . . . to run around in it" (shooting script, 91). When Henry

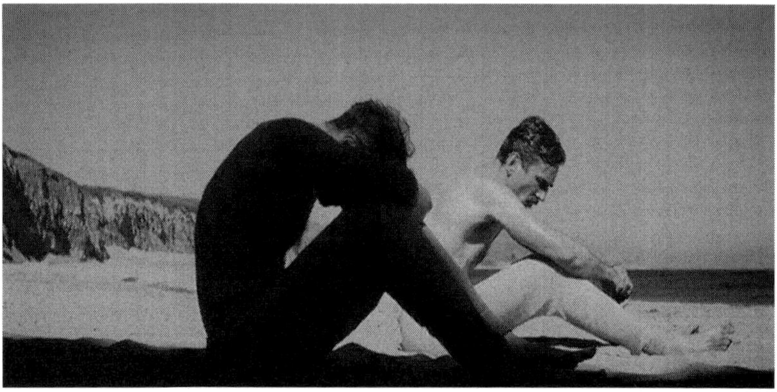

"Henry" (Kevin J. O'Connor) and Daniel as long-lost brothers. Daniel suspects treachery in *There Will Be Blood*

asks if the house he will build for himself now that he is rich will look like that one, Daniel promptly repudiates his boyhood fantasy as being utterly insufficient to contain the person he has now become. The Hollister house "would make me sick now if I saw it" (shooting script, 91).

Anderson's shooting script includes episodes involving women in the Henry section that do not appear in the final film, including scenes with Mrs. Sunday, Mary, and a "vixen" whom Daniel pays to submit to a desolate session of cunnilingus. Daniel also confides to Henry, in the shooting script, that H.W. is not his biological son. He comes close to breaking down as he pathetically divulges: "my cock doesn't even work, how'm I gonna make a kid?" (79). It is typical of Anderson's procedure throughout the final editing process that he pares away nearly all the scenes that present female characters and Daniel's hobbled interactions with them directly. Anderson elects instead to endow gentle, reserved, passive, and accommodating Henry with as many conciliatory maternal attributes and functions as possible. During his first meeting with Henry, Daniel is moved, among other things, by the fact that Henry has made the long journey to seek him out because he needed to reclaim the lost tie with his brother. Daniel is further struck by Henry's avowal that he "likes to be with him." This *liking*, moreover, is proven by the fact that he "needs no favors" and will ask for none.

When Daniel makes his lengthiest confession to Henry, under the influence of alcohol, he juxtaposes a statement about the "hatreds" he has "built up . . . over the years, little by little" (as though they were the holdings he most prided himself on) with the acknowledgment that "having you here gives me a second breath of life." The man who "doesn't like to explain myself" takes advantage of his "second breath" to uncover for Henry's consideration the limited number of things, mostly having to do with antipathy, that he allows himself to dwell on (shooting script, 75). When the two later swim together in the Pacific, the camera is placed in such a way that we see the men's exposed bodies both above and below the water surface simultaneously. The submerged half seems erotic in its relation to the portion of the men disporting above the waves in daylight. This creates a subtle tension with their scrupulous observation of the masculine decorum of taking a dip together. The waterline demarcates what has been gradually coaxed to stir and assert itself during the pastoral interlude of imagined kinship, especially on Daniel's part. What lies beneath and spreads joyfully is gradually overcoming the resistance of the taut ego that monitors, tests, and guards. As the two men sit beside one another on shore, after being cleansed in the sea, Daniel's fierce, held-in posture seems almost to have melted away. His breathing relaxes and he is fluidly in touch with positive, affecting memories of his youth. He turns his head, viewed in profile close-up, again and again in Henry's direction in order to confirm, smilingly, the substance of his reminiscence. He contemplates building a house for himself in a spot like this one, by the ocean, with the unspoken implication that the two men would share it.

Once Henry has failed, in the beach scene, to recognize Daniel's "Peachtree dance" allusion, we watch Daniel's face work its way from puzzlement, through nagging doubt, to a shocked piercing of his laid-open feelings. His face is agape with a vulnerability that must be instantly, forcefully overcome and shut down. Daniel retreats to the ocean by himself, as though by swimming a second time he can cleanse himself of his mawkish frailty. He stares back at Henry resting on shore, and as he does so becomes, visually, a hard, disembodied head, floating atop the waves. In the following nocturnal scene, which seems to sprout from the sudden darkness of his mood, he watches Henry get drunk in a brothel and notes with icy rancor that Henry is asking him for a favor (money for whores) and drunkenly laughing (at him!) into the bargain. Not long afterward, Daniel wakens Henry from sleep in some isolated terrain, leaning into him like a lover as he presses a gun to his chin. He is intent on having this reconstituted "stranger" tell him who he is. He asks, twice, "Who are you?" "Henry" claims to be "no one," which would seem to make him a fit companion for someone who has so resolutely extricated himself from the bonds of knowability. "Henry" admits to taking over the story of Daniel's brother, who died of tuberculosis before completing his own journey back to Daniel. He has also pored over his diary, memorizing its contents, which Daniel regards as an act of heinousness equal to hearing the private revelations he has let slip into this stranger's possession. But "Henry's" ultimate blunder in his last exchange with Daniel is declaring that he never meant to hurt him, words that inadvertently disclose the hurt that Daniel cannot bear to allow into the light, and that concede to "Henry" the power to inflict hurt if he chose to do so. When he requests permission simply to survive, that survival wish carries with it the necessity of extending Daniel's shame as well. "Henry" cannot be prevented from remembering the intimacy he extracted by illicit means and the hurt he "dredged up." Nor could he be counted on not to broadcast it for others' amusement. Daniel cannot abide the prospect of his hurt and shame being exposed to another's sight for a moment longer, and seems forced by a summons he can't decipher to fire a bullet into "Henry's" skull to put an end to them. After ascertaining that the man who was his "second breath of life" can no longer breathe, he slides away from him in a tilted shot that keeps his face in view as he tries to regain some distance. His expression conveys a mingling of blank astonishment and mad gloating.

"Henry's" death gasp is followed immediately by a series of actions that repeat those that Daniel performed when we first met him. He is once more wielding a pickax and making a hole in the recalcitrant earth, with Jonny Greenwood's astringent musical accompaniment reproducing the same tension that marked the opening. Anderson depicts the burial process at some length, moving from long shot to medium distance as Daniel shifts from working with a pickax to a shovel. The camera is elevated above the action when Henry is dragged and deposited facedown in his shallow grave. A shimmering liquid is present in the hole, lapping the edges of Henry's corpse in a manner strongly reminiscent of oil and the other forms of muck Daniel has repeatedly planted himself in. The liquid seems to swallow up the body as Daniel hurls spadefuls of earth over it, preparing us for the fit of weeping that Daniel will succumb to once his task is completed.

Anderson cuts directly from Daniel's spade filling the hole to a close-up of Daniel's brother's journal being fingered by Daniel's unclean hands. Here we have yet another of Anderson's telling ellipses—a festering gap and dissonance between an insensible closing up of a hole to conceal a criminal deed (and a disavowed relationship) and a tender, fearful opening up of a volume teeming with revelations and expressions of hope from another lost relationship. The words scrawled on the pages that Daniel's hands diffidently excavate and that his gaze absorbs draw possible lines between the phrase "my brother" and the exiled man who reads, who is striving now to plumb these verbal depths. The written testimony plots a journey from Daniel's dim early memories to an imagined live reunion that has been thwarted. "Henry," the journal's previous reader, had gradually transformed himself into its surrogate author. The *aspiring* brother who gladly traded his own "no man's" identity for the rambling story enclosed in these pages lies buried at Daniel's feet as Daniel surveys the relic text. Daniel permits himself no release of feeling on behalf of the "known" figure who had appeared out of the blue and claimed to be his kin. This treacherous vortex of intimacy, after all, had no legal standing. He was a fictive brother, in the same fashion that Daniel is a fictive father to H.W. Nevertheless, the reading of the journal distresses him mightily. He sighs heavily in acknowledgment of his reinforced aloneness. Then, as he examines a photo of a small child unknown to him, he gives way to a fit of sobbing. Grief has at last taken complete hold of him. "Who are you?" He might well address the anonymous boy in the photo with the same question that he put with such vehement repetitiveness to the false Henry Plainview. The image offers a composite child to his searching glance, a child that is, in the widest possible sense, "missing." The figure is partly his brother, partly H.W., partly the fraternal feeling that betrayed him and that he just destroyed in an act of revenge, and partly himself. The latter is chiefly implied in the photograph's suggestion of somber-faced abandonment.

Daniel's campfire is nearly expired as he returns to drinking, and he has almost arrived at his goal of passing out. The hands that grasped the journal are now otherwise occupied with a flask and a pistol, respectively indicating willed oblivion and the eradication of human bonds. A prolonged blackout ensues, at the end of which another father, William Bandy (Colton Woodward), looms up, confronting Daniel with "too much knowledge" in the morning light. In the background hovers another filial presence, Bandy's son. He waits distractedly by a tree for his father to be done with his present business, so he can resume following him somewhere else. The son is a mirror of H.W. and Henry, and their unprotesting manner of shadowing Daniel as he makes his rounds. Bandy Sr. demands a baptism from Daniel, a cleansing of the blood and a willingness to humble himself before the Lord. He seems entirely mindful of Daniel's recent killing—producing the murder weapon as evidence—but appears oddly willing to barter his silence (silence, of course, being Daniel's specialty) in return for Daniel surrendering his corrupt will to his heavenly Father.

In the last ellipsis we consider here, Daniel is propelled from a state of groggy corneredness beside Henry's grave to his baptism ceremony in the Church of the Third Revelation. Eli will exact his revenge on Daniel for his history of mistreatment, contempt, cheating, and other deceptions. He verbally *drills* him for everything he is least emotionally prepared to say aloud—to morally own up to and lay claim to. This showdown, which I touched upon earlier, is the scene in the film where Daniel's greatest guilt, and the grief encasing it, are brought home to him. Daniel plans to adopt a fraudulent role in the church service, which he is confident he can bring off—a variation on the cagy swindler who tricks others with his smooth rhetoric into believing he is dealing in good faith. He has resorted to this persona on countless occasions. But his role quickly proves unmanageable because he cannot write the script nor recognize how close its requirements come to his buried emotional core. On his knees before a cross of light, he is made to repeat the phrase that Eli hurls at him in front of the assembled congregation. Eli's accusations and demanded admissions hack away at Daniel's inner bulwarks like a pick cracking through rock in a mineshaft. Daniel is called upon to say that he abandoned his child in his sickness. He is obliged to say it repeatedly, in an ever-louder voice, the repetition mimicking his own earlier reiterated query to Henry: "Who are you?" In the course of this humiliating ritual, he gradually seizes the assigned words, usurps them like the plunderer he is, and screams them out to the audience in a combination of wrath and an immense purging release of pent-up, guilt-infused sorrow. He does enter deep into his own unilluminated places here, taking on the weight of hitherto unclaimed sin and loss as his essential property. "*This* is what I own." There is shame, to be sure, in receiving the "blood" in the form of violent slaps from Eli, who is both casting out Daniel's ghosts and demons, and clearing space, despite his private vindictive intentions, for the blood of forgiveness and the radiant fissure of atonement. But a strange jubilation in Daniel counterbalances, for an interval, the meting out of shame. He briefly allows himself to welcome these blows as a fitting punishment, and to gaze unblinkingly at his deepest failure; he experiences, and perhaps comprehends at some level, the paradox of a blood that protects and restores rather than annihilates. His striving will breaks against the image of willing sacrifice.

Daniel is penetrated by this knowledge from an alien sphere despite Eli's blind, crazed malignancy in the performance of his own role. But such light as streams through the tight Daniel Plainview barricades is but another ellipsis—a confounding gap—in a campaign of darkness that will soon resume on its old terms. When Daniel sits down after his ordeal, Mary Sunday (Colleen Foy), who is seated directly behind him, extends her arms to enfold him, but it is already too late for Daniel to turn and acknowledge her, to have the rock rolled away from the mother space within him. The most he can do is almost involuntarily, dazedly pat the reassuring hands with his own hand for a momentary confirmation: "I sense your presence." The good that is unearthed in Daniel here is not remembered at the end of the narrative, certainly not by him. It shines forth in an uncharacteristic rupture of pattern, and is hidden again, by a seeming necessity, in the very act of being brought to light.

Form and Formlessness in *The Master*

> "Unlike Picasso's firm outline, Schiele's chalk lines participate in the unformed realm they depict the traveler embarking toward, even if the

traveler doubts that formlessness is the direction toward which she has embarked, formlessness the shore her vessel is skirting."

—Wayne Koestenbaum, "Odd Secrets of the Line"

"There is no way to where we are."

—Alan Watts, *Nature, Man, and Woman*

The Master (2012) is a film centrally preoccupied with a single relationship, whose terms and logic become less clear the more time we take to examine it. It is a relationship that ends without its issues having been fully understood by either of the participants, or, in any conventional sense, resolved. Freddie Quell (Joaquin Phoenix) and the eponymous master Lancaster Dodd (Philip Seymour Hoffman), never articulate what they need from each other or what causes their peculiarly intense connection to thrive, for a time, and then fail. Moreover, the actual stakes of their messily conjoined spiritual quests are exceedingly difficult to determine. The form of their story, and its internal development, are opposed throughout the film by Paul Thomas Anderson's strong commitment to the possibilities of formlessness.

Anderson began his career as a director with a film that resembles *The Master* in its exploration of an intense, ambiguous relationship between a guardian who seems to know all, appearing out of nowhere, and a younger man without roots or purpose. In *Hard Eight* (1997), a mysterious father figure benefactor, Sydney (Philip Baker Hall), "adopts" a floundering innocent, John (John C. Reilly), then devotes himself to looking out for his interests until John is minimally able to take on the risks of independence. They part ways after some erratic progress has been made, though the protégé is still emotionally lost, and the wise benefactor remains enclosed in a darkness and troubled aloneness that his "son" never suspects. *Hard Eight* eventually discloses a secret that partially accounts for Sydney's long-term bond and sacrificial involvement. The older man has killed John's father and seeks to atone for his deed by taking over the vacated paternal role. *The Master* seems like a reworking of *Hard Eight* on a much larger scale. The later film is nearly epic in its attention to wrenching cultural shifts (the Second World War and the unacknowledged trauma of the turn to peace and prosperity that followed) and in its brooding about fundamental U.S. themes, yet like *Hard Eight* it is obsessively tethered to the confusing relationship between a young man and an older one who wishes to instruct him about life. In both films, the secrets of the master figure, even if partially known by the viewer, are never disclosed to his apprentice.

After *Hard Eight*, Anderson made two "extroverted" films, *Boogie Nights* and *Magnolia*, both teeming with characters, hyperbolic incident, and life energy. Structurally, these films resembled Robert Altman's panoramic, decentered narratives, whose themes, topsy-turvy reworking of Hollywood genres and casually linked characters endow their sprawling, hellzapoppin' looseness with sufficient shape and story progression. At the same time, *Boogie Nights* and *Magnolia* offered journeys to substitute homes, or return journeys to embargoed homes. In *Boogie Nights*, though the subject is film pornography, nearly all of the energy in the film's first half partakes of innocence. A boy finds a more understanding set of parents in the homeland of porn, and these parents encourage and channel his talent. The natural gift of a large penis becomes the equivalent of singing or dancing ability in the similarly utopian world of the musical. Anderson invites us to think of this mom-and-pop sex film business as a kind of Garden of Eden, gradually undone by the terrible imposition of a new set of industry rules, capitulation to more dangerous forms of excess, and the fatigue that sets in when a grand party has gone on too long. But at the end, home is reclaimed and innocence, with only a modest dose of irony, is reborn.

In *Magnolia*, the return of various wayfarers to the not-quite-unsalvageable remnants of home requires the dispensation of a preordained miracle (an innocent biblical downpour of frogs). The teleology of this miracle, redemptive in its effects, presses up against the pervasive forces of contingency and randomness let loose *in Magnolia*'s world. As I argued in the introduction, the powerful fantasy of order and the impulse to integrate warring elements relentlessly confront an equally strong impulse to untie whatever has been tied. *Magnolia* hurtles back and forth between scenes of breakdown and regrouping movements toward an accepting stillness. Order in this film tries to make itself real by continually finding fresh areas of resistance to itself, by looking for trouble, by wending its way, barely defended, through hubbub and mayhem. Its task is repeatedly to thread the needle of chaos. *Magnolia* is, in some respects, a millennial variation on Terrence Malick's *The Thin Red Line* (1998).

It exhibits a similar drive to resolve rifts and splitting, which proliferate at every turn, in a world of senselessly twinned beauty and terror. Like Malick, Anderson makes an Emersonian appeal to collective oneness, as though all the characters (and, by extension, the film's spectators) are fragments of a single, shattered psyche attempting to sing the same song. The narratives make apparent binaries into mirrors, and by that means restore (within their different deadly battlefields) a sense of soul unity. The spectator reclaims, potentially, his or her pre-shattered, Humpty Dumpty position of precarious repose on the wall—teetering, teetering, but not (this time) fallen.

The Master recalls the populous, decentered *Magnolia* in its wandering focus, but in *The Master* the wandering is not from one alienated soul to another in a somehow spiritually unified field. It is about "wandering" *within* a bewildering obsession. We concentrate, for most of the film's length, on a single relationship, but although we are given piece after piece of resonant action and reaction to consider, the pieces never seem like quite the right ones we need to figure the relationship out. As this human connection develops, it refuses every traditional support that orderly, coherent progression customarily provides. Malick's influence again strikes me as decisive, both in the dreamy amorphousness of *The Master*'s story, and in Anderson's gesturing toward a possible transcendental form that renders conventional story mechanics expendable. When Malick shot his second feature film, *Days of Heaven* (1978), he was originally working with a dialogue-heavy screenplay that he had written himself, in which there were many large-scale scenes of character conflict where characters revealed themselves through beautifully shaped lyrical speech. As actors and crewmembers have attested, many of these dramatic scenes were shot pretty much as written. However, when he came to edit the film, Malick made the radical decision to eliminate most of the film's dialogue and its structural reliance on firmly articulated scenes. He converted his narrative into a stream of fragmentary episodes with less discernible linkages and an emotional progression that seems built on evocative glimpses rather than on carefully delineated psychology.

The most pressing feature of *The Master* that must be acknowledged and accounted for is its seeming determination to thwart our desire to get *inside* its narrative. The so-called dramatic action of the film is strangely reluctant to allow us to enter in emotionally and become fully oriented, comprehending participants. When viewers are absorbed by screened events to the extent that they feel inside them, they are necessarily split between the sense of what is present to them—through emotional investment and participation—and what is absent—the fact of literal separation from the image, distance, and perhaps friction with certain elements in the fantasy mix. The screened world coaxes us to supplement our sense of presence and to make the dramatic spectacle more intimately available. We are offered inducements to believe what we are seeing more fully. The frame, both window and mirror, teases us into a state something like a "waking dream." As we become integrated with the spectacle, we become more committed to filling in gaps that will heighten the reality effect with "necessary-for-belief" details that are not actually there. We partly fill in the gaps with inferences about character psychology, story logic, environment. We consider how the parts are arranged, notice repeating patterns, and find the most fitting ways to think about the plot. But mostly it is ourselves (a roiling mass of feelings and contradictions) that we mine to fill in the gaps. It is our imagining self, our living presence, that seals the cracks and most powerfully animates the moving picture. Many films take their time opening up to the spectator and affording intimate access. Few, however, keep renewing the difficulties that stymie our assessment of what is chiefly at stake for the main characters. The distance between watcher and spectacle in *The Master*, while reduced at times, is never entirely overcome.

* * *

Anderson begins *The Master* with a high-angle view of churning ocean waves, with attendant associations of voyaging out. The water is captivating in its swirling, white-capped flow and the pattern the unseen vessel pushing against it produces, but we feel keenly the distance separating us from this turbulent, dancing surface. The second shot grants us the perspective of a man in an army helmet. We see only the upper part of his face. The rest of him is screened by a protective barrier (wooden or metal). I think we are encouraged to assume that this man is one of many on a landing craft, perhaps en route to a combat zone. We are given a great deal of time to contemplate this face, and assign an emotion to it, as the head stays still, then moves back and forth, the eyes shifting their gaze and then drifting toward sleep. As our attempt to decipher his state of mind and location continues, we attempt to place the figure in a putative dramatic context. But the face peering out in our direction repels closeness. We are not able to secure attachment either to the action he is connected with or his emotional response to it. We could project onto this baffling face the conventional attitude of pre-combat fear, but fear doesn't catch the quality of the face's impassive remoteness. The man's gaze does not register clearly whatever might be in front of it. We are not so much beholding a disposition or an intention as a mind adrift—yet the drift does not strike us as linked to imminent peril or even the need to stay watchful. It is half a face cut off from its immediate situation, whose circumstances we aren't privy to. The man cannot approach, in any fashion, the vibrant water surge presented prior to his appearance.

The blocked or diverted act of connection posited between these first images—where a joining feels likely, almost actualized, and then thwarted—offers us in miniature the structure of *The Master*. The film's crucial terrain is the space between someone looking, with insufficient presence and attentiveness (but with an obscure pressure building up) and what this someone is on the verge of discerning and being joined to.

Freddie's (Joaquin Phoenix's) disembodied head is waiting for war in *The Master*

The answers to the questions the master addresses to Freddie—about his world, his memory, his imagination, his emptiness—are perhaps near at hand, and drawing closer as Freddie waits, with a mixture of aversion and slipshod readiness. But they never quite arrive.

Freddie Quell and Lancaster Dodd manifest a perplexingly deep mutual need, but for all their striving and their sometimes overwhelming encounters, they cannot release each other's secrets (in a freeing way), cannot find what they perhaps rightly intuit the other holds for them. They make each other some sort of offer or challenge in their first meeting (which is, typically, only reported to us after the fact). However, though they both seize the other's "opening bid" and are eager to raise it, they subsequently fail to make good on what their partner requires. They nevertheless are bound, for mysterious reasons, to keep playing the game they have started with each other, until they discover the correct moves. Neither is free to opt out.

Freddie and Dodd use all the resources that drama has at its disposal—episodes of testing, confrontation, recrimination, risk-laden confession, boyish play, breakdown, healing, advancing emotional dependence, and abandonment—but the yield of these varied, demanding maneuvers never includes (for the viewer) a sense of having moved inside the relationship. Anderson is grappling in this film with the question of whether failed togetherness can be the basis for a large, consequential story. Suppose that the distance the two men can never successfully overcome is replicated in the film's form. The film will not open up to the spectator and let him or her cross over and experience the relationship from the inside precisely because the barriers to "getting inside" and "allowing another inside" prove too formidable for Freddie and Dodd. Anderson would have us be disconcerted watchers, repeatedly balked and thrown back on our own isolation throughout *The Master*. We are marooned in a space we know from our times of greatest felt separation from others, an interior sense of distance that can't be willed away.

In Malick's *Days of Heaven*, a similarly daunting watching space is created for the spectator, deliberately encouraging the feeling that the characters are too small in relation to the landscape and situated too far away from the camera to grant us the privileges that come from ready emotional access and adequate understanding. In Malick's film, the source of emotion is subtly displaced from immediate character concerns to nature itself. Though the characters' needs and actions are not ignored, it is more often than not the vast fields, immense, overarching sky, the river, the covert movements of wildlife, and the solitary house beckoning in the distance—as they are all caressed and buffeted by light and wind—that suffuse us with longing and with the force of presence. The very thing that holds the characters at a remove from the spectator as well as apart from each other—the inhuman space—finds a way to move inside us and to make us fleetingly at one with nature's rhythms and process. We go in and out of synchronization for the full length of *Days of Heaven*, continually readjusting our perspective (micro to macro, person to surroundings, then reversing) and sense of where we stand in relation to what transpires. Our stake in the narrative proceedings steadily oscillates between effortless abiding (being at home anywhere) and sorrowful exclusion, a state of exile. The fact and pathos of distance, of losing our place in what we see and not belonging to it links up with the bewildered striving of the characters. Most of the scenes in *Days of Heaven*, as I suggested earlier, have an in-between quality, a feeling of transition, as though we have arrived not in the middle of things but in the interval between dramatic happenings, when mindful activity and willed effort are in abeyance. The characters, in these reprieves, slip unawares into unself-consciousness and begin to play as children play, walk with no apparent destination, or simply take note, in a manner that holds them transfixed, of some little occurrence, a piece of what is going on unobtrusively at the edges of normal perception, an uneventful event. So here, in Malick's panorama, our insideness is secured by filling in the space, the ever-shifting distances of nature, with ourselves.

Anderson's emotional placement of the spectator in *The Master* rarely aspires to that kind of unfretful, contemplative fullness. The film instead documents a straining for transcendence that continually collapses under its own weight. The film follows Lancaster Dodd's lead in his "treatment" of Freddie, a prolonged, unsuccessful attempt to do away with brute, frenzied edges that stubbornly persist. Our position as watchers is almost always unsettled, anxious, without reliable external guidance for how to interpret our tumultuous impressions. As in *Punch-Drunk Love* and *There Will Be Blood*, we are deprived of the kind of access to character interiority that we crave (including motives), and because of this deprivation we are left, spiritually and psychologically, out in the cold, with only our own dubious skills for sorting, intuiting, and integration to consult. Anderson's script revisions in all three films reveal a deliberate paring away of reliable clues to character motivation. We absorb, by a kind of contagion, the characters' predicament of being at a loss: we don't know what to do with ourselves as floating, stymied viewers, and we don't know what is expected of us. We may well experience our own identity moorings temporarily loosening as Dodd takes the ornery, recalcitrant, but often guileless Freddie through the processing session. Starting with his name, Freddie is made to repeat basic life data aloud. As a result of relentless repetition and querying, the person (Freddie Quell) seemingly enclosed by that data appears to melt away. As we listen to and observe this "breaking down" of resistance, we may find ourselves becoming strangely less *there* as well—less a part of the dramatic spectacle in front of us, but also less sure of our relation to our own psychic territory . Perhaps we are mistaken in our basic assumption that we know ourselves well enough to be inside our own living. The spectator may very well wish to be *cured* of the assigned duty of watching *The Master* (on edge, from the wrong distance), as his or her own identity position weakens.

Our sense of being "outside" *The Master* as spectators, with a simultaneous yearning to be situated inside Anderson's dream, strongly aligns us with Freddie, the one who cannot break through in order to achieve proper placement. It doesn't matter that we can't identify with him emotionally. It is more an issue of assessing our troubling distance from events, the realm where "real things" happen. The guideposts presented to Freddie and the viewer are nearly sufficient to bring us all the way in as indoctrinated participants. But Anderson repeatedly revokes the promise of enduring, reliable orientation. Tangled in delusion are both Freddie as the incorrigible agent of chaos and Dodd as the half-charlatan visionary offering the cure of a system of integration. We will not find a secure refuge by favoring the mellifluous soul-therapist or the "running-amuck" outcast in their alternating displays of will and devil-may-care demolition. We can't confidently assume either man's position for more than brief interludes, since we are granted no persuasive access to their motives. Nor are we able to make a moral evaluation of how their actions might illuminate the value of their goals. Freddie and Dodd's persistently evasive and opaque maneuvers keep both of them ahead of our knowing. We know that each man is in possession of secret knowledge, but since we don't have a clear insight into either secret, we don't know what sort of mental treasure either is striving to pry loose from his partner-adversary.

I am reminded here of Dodd leading Freddie on an apparent goose chase through the desert to retrieve a treasure box of his buried writings. The box proves to have a literal existence and is successfully dug up, but whether the writings inside are valuable or "fool's gold" is never divulged. Throughout *The Master* we are in the very unusual position of watching a pair continually showing one another things, things that may be linked to consequential "inner unveiling" or coming to terms, but the showing somehow blocks comprehension in the process of laying bare. The atmosphere of scenes is regularly charged with a "Now *they're* getting somewhere / Now *we're* getting somewhere" urgency, but the language and experience of decisive connection are exposed as inadequate. It is not a matter of both men lying or being elaborately deceptive (the latter surely one of the most tired of movie gambits). Freddie and Dodd have an equally genuine, large stake in revelation, but the language and gestures at their disposal will not do for the colossal task at hand.

* * *

Ali Smith's speculations on form in what she describes as a "fictional essay," *Artful*, offer a richly illuminating way of thinking about the relationship between Freddie and Dodd. She begins by reviewing some of the definitions of form, both the familiar and the neglected:

> Form, from the Latin *forma*, meaning shape. Shape, a mold: something that molds or shapes; a species or kind; a pattern or type; a way of being; order, regularity, system. It once meant beauty, but now that particular meaning's obsolete. It means style and arrangement, structural unity in music, literature, painting, etc.; ceremony; behavior; condition of fitness or efficiency. It means the inherent nature of an object, that in which the essence of a thing exists. It means a long seat, or a bench, or a school class, and also the shape a hare makes in the grass with its body for a bed. It's versatile. It holds us, it molds us, it identifies us, it shows us how to be, it gives us a blueprint in life and art, it's about essentiality, and several of us can sit on it at once. It

can mean a criminal record and it can mean correctness of procedure, both at once. Form can be right and it can be wrong. (68)

Smith goes on to talk about form and formlessness having a relationship that is a kind of dialogue (67). Formlessness argues with form ceaselessly and often makes it difficult for form to find connecting bridges, to find the right shape to "quell" the unifying urge. But Smith's preliminary net of definitions acknowledges that the dialogue cannot be understood as merely an exchange between a stable entity (form) and an unstable one. Her inventory recognizes boundaries but also their permeability. One meaning of form reaches out to another or to many others and draws fresh power and capability from the related (but not strictly related) associations.

As we move down Smith's list, form itself becomes ever more unruly and contradictory—not a settled shape or order or idea, but a field of metaphor. It grows increasingly difficult to hold on to the original, more or less clear impression that the word *form* (as molded or crystallized shape) made on us. We can go back and begin again with shape and mold as things, but this point of security has been clouded over with insubordinate shades of meaning. A shape can bend and be misshapen. This possibility is present even if one simply postulates that form signifies both a shape and the force or intent or practice that does the shaping. Form has to clean up its act, however, and appear disciplined and united whenever it is set against formlessness. Formlessness sounds absolute in its refusal to sanction anything but disorder. When form is placed next to this binary opponent, form instantly snaps to attention, remembering how to behave itself and achieve the stillness of repose.

In the realm of aesthetics, form is often posited as a harmonious end result, a completed artifact—following a complex salvage operation from chaos. Form takes what it needs from formlessness, through disciplined but also fortuitous selection, and then overcomes the irresolute, wandering tendencies the secured elements possessed in their original jumbled condition. The mess or turbulent excess of the formless state submits, in cases where artistic rendering prevails, to refinement, clarity, patterned wholeness. The shapeless is redeemed in the act of releasing, after a period of struggle, a shape that coalesces. In so doing, the shape may assert a kinship with beauty or truth. Formlessness, arguably, possesses its own truth claims and hovers near beauty, but we imagine that the character of beauty or truth alters when form has been apprehended and caught.

Form's traditional role in art is that of *master* in relation to formlessness. Formlessness can exert enormous resisting power in its dialogue with form, and often threatens to *be* the master. But art's mastery of its materials calls for a vanquishing of the claims of formlessness *for now*. In a line by Ezra Pound, which Ali Smith cites, it is a matter of "knowing the truth of things unseen before" (81). And there is a stability that form attains from the knowing made possible by an unprecedented feat of vision. That stability or coming to rest, "the momentary stay against confusion" that is form's animating desire, must not be won too cheaply. Art can turn counterfeit, negligible, or vaporous if form closes the dialogue with formlessness prematurely, or if it too readily accepts those elements that the artist has previously "used up" because they are manageable and familiar. The quest for the hidden, exacting form demands no less than a full exposure to the perils, indeed the terror, of formlessness. As many artists have testified, form must not know too well what it needs in advance of the time of making. Like the underworld reclaiming Eurydice, the desired shape rising out of darkness can so easily slip back into the lower depths before it is embodied and granted definition. The compulsion to be certain of what one has, as Orpheus discovered, results in the briefest of backward glances, a transgression that loses all to formlessness.

Early in *The Master*, Lancaster Dodd makes a strange speech to the assembled guests at the shipboard wedding reception for his daughter. He invokes a dragon, a death-force allied with the pervasive human fear of darkness and captivity, that kept marriage, and much else in life, "awful" before "the Cause" was revealed to him. He explains how he conquered this fearsome dragon, with dreadful teeth "dripping with blood" and "red eyes" (plainly a creature created by the projection and delusion of humans in their endless servile state) after a strenuous bout of internal wrestling. Dodd claims to have reached the stage of awareness in this violent contest in which fear of the dragon, in all of its manifestations, has been overcome. The now-docile dragon submits to his commands, and even where death is concerned, is gradually bending to his will. The dragon is being taught the trick of "rolling over and *playing* dead." That's what becomes of death and chaos as a result of the new *form* of things that Dodd has beheld in a vision and proclaimed to his followers.

The Dodd-Quell relationship can obviously be approached in terms of the struggle between form and formlessness that I have outlined. Their recurrent impasse or standoff mirrors the threat to form posed by the wandering narrative structure of the film as a whole. What we cumulatively behold is a defeat of form's concerted long-term effort to control, or at least find an enduring shape for, the dragon of chaos. Dodd, though a figure split up, as he tells Freddie, among many different callings ("I am a writer, a doctor, a nucular [*sic*] physicist, a theoretical philosopher, but above all a man, a hopelessly inquisitive man, just like you"), is integrated by the form and discipline of the Cause, Anderson's quasi-fictionalized version of Scientology, which Dodd has "uncovered" through his relentless inquisitiveness, and now imparts, in moderate doses, to others. What Dodd claims to have achieved, and what no one else could do without the master's sovereign example, is the "quelling" of fear altogether.

Freddie presents Dodd with a human vessel shattered by encounters with his own dragon (war and other darknesses in his past). Enough pieces of Freddie have been haphazardly bundled together to allow him to function at some level and to navigate the periphery of civilized gatherings. Yet something is drastically amiss—indeed, many things are—that anyone who has dealings with him must soon come up against. His crooked smile attests to his accomplishment of brokenness. He is a self-made scrap heap, a ruin dedicated to formlessness. Freddie's body is so oddly mixed up that it resembles an expressionist painting. It seems to operate by arrhythmic, unpredictable jerks, fits, and starts. His face seems to have its wrong side up, with its underneath exposed. Scrutinizing him, I often find myself involuntarily striving to correct mentally the proportions of mouth, gait, arms, misshapen back.

Freddie is intermittently mindful of the "wrongness" in himself, of his desperate lack of coherence and direction. Even more undeveloped inwardly than Barry Egan or Daniel Plainview, his aggressive outbursts and reckless drinking are an attempt to hold his place in the world through aimless, defiant negation. These are the gestures that mark his territory and that make him the master of his own defeat. To move in accordance with someone else's straight line or recommended pattern is to give himself away to alien dictates. His only strength, as he sees it, comes from warding off those who would infringe too closely on his fierce turmoil. A healing would rob him of his vital suspended relationship to the uncompleted, now-impossible tasks he abandoned when going off to war. Paradoxically, resisting others' plans for him is a way of keeping alive all the galling incapacity to connect in his early life, as though refusal had always been the point, the defining need.

Dodd's project with Freddie is to fix all his unfitted craziness, to let nothing within him rest until it is brought back to balance, inside a system that Dodd has invented more than discovered. Dodd's system is nearly as much a patchwork as Freddie himself. Dodd feels driven to imbue the ultimate deformed man not with a form answering to Freddie's needs, but with the master's own form, something tenuous that he insists has perfect solidity. Scientology as a subject attracts Anderson mainly as a primitive, confidently irrational dream of making sense—a new and higher sense. But the Cause is a diversely inflected dream of making higher sense in which outbreaks of nonsense are a recurring feature. It is more the sound of sense that Dodd masters than the fact of it, or whatever might count as fact in the realm of spirit. Yet, as Dodd shares portions of his teaching at various stages of the narrative, it is important that not only his disciples but the film's spectator be caught up in the mellifluous flow of the master's utterances. We are meant to experience the force of his calm, piercing gaze, his stillness, his push to take us through the looking glass of ordinary language to a space "beyond." He is never presented as a mere object of satire. The sound of the master's sense conveys sense on the verge of arriving, almost coming into the clear, but never quite getting there. Sound is a noisy aircraft circling above meaning as if it were in a threatening fog, with Dodd brashly and expertly sitting at the controls, waiting for his opening to bring his "flying sounds" in for a perfect landing. The confident circling stands in for sense.

Writing about the use of sound in Wallace Stevens's poetry, Helen Vendler points out how words and phrases are "almost always deflected" from their common references, but so slyly that a reader can miss the way the poem's act of "telling" something has become unmoored: "The appearance of 'telling' is superficially maintained . . . but one gets nowhere reading Stevens in a spirit of straightforward communication.

The assertions, the language, and the syntax are all too preposterous for that . . . Stevens's art is always about to refresh itself at the well of nonsense. Sound for him is the locus of the primitive" (quoted in Gudas, 147). What Vendler terms the "primitive" force of sound disrupts the flow of language making. Sound seduces with the impression of accessible sense, while also derailing sense: "refreshing itself at the well of nonsense." Yet a concern with higher truth, higher, more capacious *form*, is always in the air of a Stevens's poem. In the same way, we feel the strength of pending revelation when Lancaster Dodd holds forth, and the preposterousness does not crowd out the possibility of consequential epiphany. Dodd's belief in a new container for the human soul, better than our old ones, has surprising power when his words are animated by the force of his knowing, ecstatic, *and* nonsensical presence.

Dodd would persuade Freddie that he is master of the form, which is to say master of the dream of making sense, and that with Freddie's cooperation he can bring him all the way inside it. Freddie's formlessness, as I've noted, is this lost wanderer's stubborn claim to integrity. He knows himself to be "outside" whatever life structures others manage to occupy or settle into. He does not dispute the conviction many people have that they are inside their own existence, on terms that are foreign to him. He intermittently acknowledges that his alarming distance from any sustainable feeling of belonging or connection is a source of distress, and maybe a proof of illness. He dislikes being utterly adrift and beset, alternately, by great pain and equally great numbness. Although he fears the "inside" that Dodd promises as a cure, and he instinctively sabotages the efforts of any figure who would claim authority to help him, Freddie is nevertheless prepared to enter Dodd's dream—to exchange formlessness for the dream of form—if he can be led to believe in it. If Dodd proves strong enough to wrest Freddie's defiance, listlessness, brawling unbridledness, and skepticism away from him, he can almost see himself as a willing captive, a yielding disciple. But there always seems to be a road forking away from Dodd's prescribed path and back into the psychic underbrush for Freddie to seize upon when moments of choosing arrive, even though (or precisely because) this divergent route offers no palliative. Freddie is a man who requires obscurity and is continually seeking a deeper darkness. He has by no means reached the furthest limit of his possible estrangement.

* * *

In "Ordinary Twinship," Kenneth Gross offers a provocative and illuminating examination of sociologist Georg Simmel's concept of the *dyad*—a basic relationship between two "partners" that lies at the foundation of social order.

> Simmel borrows the term, I suspect, from basic mathematics; for Pythagoras the dyad—Greek for the number two—is the first true number, representing as it does the fall of the monad, of original singularity, into time and difference. For Simmel the dyad is a kind of analytic abstraction, a minimal unit of social order. It refers to any partnership formed by the choice of two persons, a partnership that serves both to *protect their freedom and to secure a secret*. The dyad is a fragile association or entity, since it never, like other, larger social units, attains a sense of superpersonal life. It does not by itself produce a structure that grows beyond the two constitutive participants. As a social unit, the dyad is thus peculiarly threatened by death; it is both endangered and irreplaceable. The dyad in Simmel's sense undoubtedly works as a form of refuge; in it a member's singular egotism can be suspended even as it is protected. The relation indeed enhances rather than blocks the individuation of its members. At the same time, the dyad creates peculiar conditions of mutual exposure, since it represents a relation in which one member cannot hide from the other, cannot pass responsibility for some action onto a larger group or impersonal ideal. In a dyad, Simmel writes, "there is no majority which can outvote the individual." (27, emphasis added)

The dyad is a suitable label for the enchained, world-devouring connection into which Dodd and Quell stumble. One of Gross's most interesting glosses on the dyad, Simmel's "speculative entity," has to do with the coupling of mutual exposure with the impossibility of transferring responsibility for individual actions onto a "larger group or impersonal ideal." It might seem that Dodd's entire association with Freddie has to do with the larger framework of the Scientology-like Cause. Dodd's main desire for Freddie is that he be cured, meaning that Freddie must find himself within an age-old captivity and then gain release from fraudulence and fear by accepting Dodd's vision of freedom. However, as the partnership proceeds, it quickly moves beyond the explanatory powers of the Cause or the requirements of therapy. The confusion *The Master* engenders in viewers is in part due to the falling away of our sense of the external world as a given, that is, as a reality that has a freestanding existence beyond the dyad. We can't measure the delusions and deformities the dyad gives rise to by the standards of a normative, outside perspective. Once Freddie and Dodd's paths converge, the features of the world they inhabit, independently of their dealings with one another, become steadily more amorphous: still tangible, but chimerical in their effect on the spectator. Their partnership, with its many unresolved conflicts, overrides every other narrative component as a transmitter of meaning. The dyad, in effect, becomes our main material reference point: it tells us what counts as being present—that is, what stands in some sort of immediate, feeling relationship to the central pair. Everything else is fluttering stage scenery. Objects acquire the status of real presence only insofar as they contribute to the dyad's evolving form, or threaten to undermine it.

In his examination of the dyad, Gross fascinatingly shifts emphasis from the dyad as an abstract idea to the dyad formed between twins, and even more specifically between himself and his own twin brother:

> I can be frightened to see weariness, or fear, or unresponsiveness on my brother's face, to watch it blank out or withdraw. If I am frightened for him, I am also, in a peculiarly immediate way, frightened for myself, since I see my own face so clearly in his, because nothing conceals it from me. I see the traces of thoughts and feelings that expose me nakedly, pitilessly to myself, to what is both present and possible in myself. Sympathy here involves not so much an escape from narcissism as an occasion for a more troubled and self-doubting narcissism. . . . Nothing is hidden. . . . Such changes of attitude or voice or character as inevitably emerge . . . may thus confront a twin sibling with a peculiar kind of shock, even with a sense of being betrayed. (28)

Gross's account of imbibing his twin's facial expressions and anxiously registering every gradation of feeling there is perhaps most remarkable in its conflation of the capacities for sympathy and narcissism. The close encounter with the other, "exposed" member of the dyad seems, in Gross's experience of twinship, to return the condition of twoness to the monad state of singularity. The revelation of the partner's most protected secrets leads not elsewhere, to a larger realm of acknowledgment and sharing, but back to the solitary self, pitilessly reduced to a smaller state. Form and formlessness, though not synonymous in any familiar way, come to seem like twins in *The Master*. That is to say, like Freddie and Dodd shouting at each other through the bars of their adjoining jail cells in one of the film's signature moments, they oddly mirror each other, especially in episodes of contention, and their separate qualities appear to mingle and decompose whenever the issue of their "difference" from each other is most strongly asserted.

Anderson establishes the mirroring-decomposing dynamic immediately prior to the prison scene when police officials abruptly arrest Dodd for "operating under false pretenses" outside the law. As the arrest scene unfolds, Anderson presents us with a prolonged set of contrasting views of Freddie's and Dodd's responses to the demands of interrogation when the police arrive. We note as well their split reaction to the sudden imposition of alien authority and the mechanism of arrest. Dodd sedately enacts a beatific certitude as the agents of the law converge on him. His surest path to inner peace, his manner suggests, comes from facing down skeptics. He is restored to full strength, both in his need to uphold his honor and his license for righteous indignation in the face of public opprobrium. As he is manhandled, put in shackles, and hauled off the porch ignominiously, he protests principally against the officers' ill treatment of Freddie. Freddie, on the other hand, is on a rampage from the moment Dodd raises his voice to challenge his accusers. We watch Freddie's pose of detachment disintegrate into a batty, fist-flailing fury as the police strive to subdue him. It seems as though Dodd absorbs energy to become steadier and more self-controlled from watching Freddie fall to pieces. Dodd takes on all the attributes that Freddie casts off in his spectacular public shedding—no, *shredding*—of dignity.

The pattern of contrasting views continues in the prison scene that follows. The frame is evenly divided between two adjoining jail cells. In the right hand cell stands Dodd, clad in a sport jacket and dress slacks, leaning calmly against his upper bunk watching the tumult unfold through the bars that separate him from his fellow prisoner, Freddie. Freddie has been hauled by policemen down a long corridor, while offering vehement physical resistance, to his own cell in handcuffs. No sooner has the door closed on him than he fiercely head-butts his upper bunk, destroys his toilet, wrestles loose from his shirt, and bangs his head against a rear wall. The contrast between the civilized, rational observer (Dodd) and tormented animal (Freddie), is nowhere in the

Freddie and Dodd (Philip Seymour Hoffman) in one of the mirroring scenes in *The Master*

film more sharply drawn. The division, in its stark simplicity, holds for a considerable length of time. It is Dodd who eventually decides to reduce the distance between realms, urging Freddie to draw *closer* to his master by acknowledging that his "fear of capture and imprisonment is an implant from millions of years ago." Dodd sees Freddie as an embodiment and resurgence of ancient, unreasoning fear. Freddie is nearly reduced to crawling on all fours, a fear vessel blindly stuck at the beginning of the process, controlled by a "push-pull mechanism" that has nothing to do with his spirit and the freedom it craves. Dodd wants Freddie to recognize that his master, despite his seeming confinement in a jail cell identical to Freddie's own, is not, in fact, imprisoned at all. Fear and the "push-pull mechanism" live entirely separate from Dodd, in Freddie's adjoining cage. Dodd insists that the perfectly symmetrical cells in no true sense mirror each other.

Freddie recoils from the barrage of language Dodd presents to him as a gift, especially the diagnosis of his own fear and captivity. He repudiates the freedom that Dodd implies he not only possesses but incarnates, then offers to share. Freddie forgets about the adversary policemen and the brute, material facts of his cell and begins to redirect his battle against Dodd himself, screaming a demand that the master "Shut the fuck up!" When Dodd redoubles his linguistic efforts to "capture" Freddie, Freddie stubbornly negates the substance of the words used against him, repeating the skeptical phrase previously employed by Dodd's son, Val. "You're just making it up as you go along," Freddie yells, grabbing this charge almost randomly, like a small child mimicking grown-up discourse. At this point, the mirroring force of the twin jail cell composition begins to operate more directly. The potent binary (civilized disengagement versus animality) collapses as Dodd helplessly sacrifices his "above-the-fray" advantages. He is no longer able to observe from a distance as Freddie acts out all the outrage that is part of his own exposure and public humiliation. Freddie regards Dodd's verbal dismissal of his "primitive" enslavement to fear as another version of a cop laying hands on him, or another jail cell to kick apart. It is never hard for Freddie to *disown* his connection to language, to reassert that he has come to no agreement with it. As Dodd surrenders to the impulse to abuse Freddie in language that coarsely matches his own, the bastion the master has built around himself crumbles.

Freddie is the obvious underdog in any contest of words. He often conveys the impression of scarcely knowing what talking is for. Whenever he is obliged to resort to speech to make some intention known, he appears to be faking it. The words that issue from him seldom evince a convincing relation to the person he is. And, of course, it is an ongoing enigma whether Freddie should be labeled a "person" at all, at least in the familiar senses of the term. Words mainly serve to camouflage the fact of his apprehensive disconnection from them. He is mouthing sounds handed to him by various authority figures, sounds whose power of reference and meaning have not quite been internalized. Language is exclusively foreign language, just as Freddie's bodily gestures seem weirdly askew as natural expression. Words even more than gestures belong only to others, never truly to him.

No sooner has Dodd finished insisting that Freddie can be free if he accepts Dodd's narrative about what freedom actually consists of and where it comes from, than he is seized by a compulsion to throw a tantrum. His semblance of freedom evaporates as he explosively taunts and shames Freddie, imitating the terms set by the one he has identified as "captive." Dodd commences his litany of abuse by assigning Freddie weaknesses that he clearly shares with him ("a lazy-ass piece of shit"; "a drunk"). He retorts to Freddie's wounding claim that he is hated by his own son with a mirroring and escalating claim: "I am the only one who likes you." Dodd finally gains his adversary's attention with this repeated pronouncement. Once Freddie is rendered vulnerable to the threatened removal of the last straw of human kinship, he gives physical expression of his need for one human tie by shrinking back from further conflict. Dodd calmly declares that he is "done" with Freddie as soon as there is clear evidence that Freddie is not free to be done with him.

* * *

Is there an "order" to be found in the "great disorder" of Freddie's fractured activity? Is a return to someone's idea of order worth the sacrifice of whatever mystery percolates in his incapacity to adjust, adopt beliefs, or be at home anywhere? These concerns no doubt preoccupy Dodd during his systematic breaking down of Freddie's disordered nature and planned reconstruction of him in terms of a different, less chaos-driven freedom. Freddie might be regarded, in Wallace Stevens's resonant phrase, as a "connoisseur of chaos," someone whose continuity is to be looked for in the varieties of confusion he engenders, and at times revels in. He is linked to Anderson in this role as well, since the director willfully sabotages one fantasy of order after another as each temporarily gains ground in his narrative. He wants to snap the linkages that might bind things together, as though binding were tantamount to a betrayal of imagination's ongoing need to leave the main highway.

Well before his first meeting with Dodd aboard the yacht *Aletheia*, Freddie plays the role of director in his one "respectable" job: studio photographer in a department store. My focus in this segment of the narrative is on how Anderson—using Freddie as his surrogate director—also breaks down the somewhat reliable protections of visual convention and cultural form for the first time in the film (the earlier war scenes gave no preliminary signals of safety zones). Freddie will prove in short order to be a director who relinquishes control of his "sphere of competence" in a manner that bewilderingly mingles willfulness and crazed compulsion.

When we're introduced to Freddie in the department store, he misleadingly strikes us as having successfully weathered the transition from wartime psychic injuries to some degree of social readjustment. Clad in a nondescript suit, he is also sporting, in a not-too-ungainly fashion, an extrovert's flamboyant striped tie. With composure and confidence, Freddie guides those posing for photos through a prepared script. He instructs his customers to *look at him* before he makes an exposure. We see at close range samples of his portrait work, which glow with their achieved blend of security and placid integration. Every figure in the series has found a comfortable fit within the preordained scheme of domestic felicity. The colorful, vibrant backgrounds supplied for each framed subject make safe haven into a realm of magic. Freddie, in his limited domain, appears to be a kind of master, as well as a stand-in for Anderson himself. He has somehow learned the tricks of the trade and projects a security himself while steering others to their proper placement, pose, and expression. Freddie's provisional hold on the world depends here on honoring the frame that has been set up for him, and the mode of vision it requires. He is the servant of the soothing, artifice-insulated image effect that he produces and reproduces. His air of mastery, therefore, is somewhat vitiated by the necessity for assembly line consistency in the pictorial results. It is of little consequence whether or not Freddie keeps faith with what he is doing, as long as he performs the specified task efficiently.

Anderson's camera veers away from Freddie after exhibiting his skill and apparent adaptation to the demands of a structured job. We are gracefully swept into the looming department store work world. Before leaving Freddie, we may have time to register the oddity of his having been given nothing resembling a studio. He is situated in the open in a busy area of the store, and there are no visible boundaries to his assigned space. Anderson's camera detaches itself from the "static frame" of the portrait taking and proceeds to wander in the company of a salesgirl named Martha (Amy Ferguson), who is walking around the store modeling a coat for prospective customers. Her work, to a certain extent, parallels and overlaps with Freddie's. She is expected to strike conventional poses and briefly hold still as potential buyers judge the effect of the coat being opened up. Her display is intended to reveal not only the coat's appeal, of course, but its fantasy linkage with the dress and body it enfolds. Martha's job conveys a spirit of ease and modest freedom in her wandering that Freddie's fixed position lacks. Anderson's

Freddie is in control when lining up a shot in *The Master*

mobile camera entices us with the spectacle of the model working her way dreamily through the large, richly illuminated department store space of glamour consumption. Martha's quasi-autonomous wandering through the aisles in Freddie's vicinity (in marked contrast to Freddie's fixed position) establishes the prospect of both a meeting between them and a pursuit. Freddie may be tempted to "break the pattern" of his static placement to enter this wider female domain. But there is a gentle dream continuity between the space of Freddie's idealized family portraits and the glide of the enchanting model to outlying, exotic precincts of the store. The two employees seem to be ministering to kindred fantasies.

Once Martha halts at Freddie's station and intimates (surprisingly) that some sort of romantic connection already exists between them, we commence the disruption of initially planted, misleading clues for understanding Freddie's situation. We are given just enough time to become convinced of Freddie's wartime isolation naturally persisting, perhaps augmenting in his new job, as he creates images of domestic tranquility for others to inhabit, when Martha joins him at his lonely post, overturning the impression of his aloneness. Clearly, he has adjusted more quickly to his new circumstances than we would have thought possible, and Martha's attraction to him promptly removes, or drastically reduces, the prior stigma of the freakish misfit. Their comfortable meeting and Martha's flirtatious, eager agreement to meet him during her break create a positive second frame of reference for "reading" him, suggesting that Freddie is taking form as a character with intelligible goals and reasonable hopes of attaining them. Before returning to work, Martha poses for Freddie in front of a blank screen, which strongly resembles a movie screen. Removed momentarily from her defining context in the department store, she seems to become Freddie's own projection, awaiting his decision as to which lush background will best suit her image, and then encouraging him to fill it in.

We cut abruptly to a more obscure private space—Freddie's darkroom in the store—where he appears to be carrying on with his wartime experiments of inventing perilous alcoholic beverages. Indeed, he is shown pouring photo developing fluid into the beaker that holds the liquor reserved for his forthcoming rendezvous. When Martha arrives in his cramped sanctuary, there is a temporary return to normative assignation protocol. She good-humoredly accepts a drink from the flask he offers her and initiates an act of undressing that both extends the display work of her previous modeling and also harks back to Freddie prostrating himself before the large-breasted sand woman along the seashore. He laughs, half-drunkenly, as he examines her legs, touches her genitals, and then teasingly pokes her exposed breasts. He seems to teeter here between genuine arousal and a confused, mocking sadism. We can't know precisely what he wants from Martha, though her lack of alarm somewhat neutralizes his hints of strange aggression. They make arrangements to resume their dalliance later at her apartment. The question of what will transpire between them is quickly resolved with a brief shot of Freddie, fully dressed, collapsed in sleep behind Martha, as she stares with deflated hopes at an untouched glass of wine and two plates of food on her small dining table. This shot serves to break another pattern: that of smoothly developing desire or connection between Freddie and a girl who was first presented as a vision beyond his reach and then as someone miraculously available.

We are then brought back to Freddie's photographer's station, where the complete disintegration of the clearly defined cultural setting, as well as Freddie's glimmerings of a potentially coherent psychology, are about to take place. All the stabilizing features of narrative forward motion (one thing leading, through cause and effect, to another) and a recognizable world fall to pieces decisively, with a few impenetrable strokes. Freddie is back at his task of photographing, but his attitude is now impatient, brusque, as though carrying a residual strain from the abortive dinner date with Martha. As Freddie confronts his new customer at the photography site (who is for a time kept invisible to us), he looks perturbed by the fact that this stranger, oblivious to Freddie's struggle simply to exist, assumes that he—the would-be portrait subject—lives comfortably *inside* something. "Are you married?" Freddie asks him, abrasively. "Is this for your wife?" The customer answers "yes" to both questions, as though he is both confident that he *is* married and confident of his power to make his wife happy with a dressed-up image of himself. Freddie turns away from him and gazes into the suddenly out-of-focus store background, a bright, shimmery maze of lights, mannequins, and human movement. When Freddie goes back to his camera, he handles it as though it has all at once become a foreign object, alien to his touch and eye. He grips the camera handle and pans the mechanism on its tripod to the right, breaking out of what would seem to be his customary framing position. He then stiffly approaches the customer, appraises the lighting setup, and proceeds to box him in with hot photo floods. "Don't move," he advises. "Just stay still." It is not until Freddie moves forward that we are granted our first glimpse of the customer. He looks prosperous, beefy, middle-aged, and wears a pricey suit—but most importantly, he bears a striking resemblance to Lancaster Dodd, whom neither we nor Freddie have been introduced to yet.

One should not press too hard to impose clarity on Freddie's motivation for the incident that ensues. One might reasonably claim, however, that he seems to be goading, with perverse deliberateness, the customer to challenge his authority—by enclosing him with hot lights, he pins him into a deeply uncomfortable place with no room to maneuver. This stranger, for reasons unknown, suddenly looms as a threat to Freddie. Perhaps it is his projected sense of entitlement to a social framing that is stable and unambiguous. Freddie's brief, perplexed survey of his department store surroundings perhaps leads him to the feeling that he is not *inside* anything himself. What he attacks, then, is not so much the customer per se, but the fact of his taken-for-granted *insideness*—making the frame he occupies suffocatingly unpleasant, and forcing him to erupt, to break out. The fisticuffs and glassware hurling that Freddie instigates serves to expose the *inside* position as untenable, and likely unreal. How quickly everything can be forced outside of the protective, governing context. A man (who bears the label "employee") pointlessly disrupts the frame that you, as customer, occupy, and the chaotic gesture immediately infects the entire surrounding milieu. One pattern breaks down, and there is a ripple effect to outlying patterns.

Anderson, I would argue, wants the "form collapse" in this scene to extend to our sense of the overall film narrative. We cannot recover the previous imagined order of the department store sequence in a way that makes Freddie's part within it an intelligible progression. Neither does the uproar and wild brawl in the department store cause or logically lead to the next location or time frame in *The Master*. Freddie, having abandoned his fight with the customer without anything having been resolved or made plain, storms off in his hobbling animal fashion past a group of stunned onlookers. He retrieves a dazed Martha in transit, and makes her a seeming partner to his outburst by taking her hand and leading her away. This reincorporation of Martha in the action is itself a non sequitur, because she makes no further appearance in the film. A jarring cut takes us to a field where lettuce (in a parody image of enlarged female genitalia) is being chopped by Freddie in the company of what we identify as a group of migrant workers. Martha, in effect, is done away with by the aggression visited by the machete blade on the passive crop. All that we can readily determine in this transition passage is that Freddie has moved swiftly to a position further down the social scale. He has also moved to a position much further outside the *form* of life that his furious misconduct has shattered.

Later in the film, we have another equally jolting instance of form breaking. After Dodd (but not Freddie) is released from prison, we are promptly taken to an elegant, darkly lit dining room where Dodd has resumed his patriarchal position at the center of a perfectly symmetrical family mealtime gathering. Dodd's previously stated intention to call it quits with Freddie is supported and reinforced by each member of his family, who tactfully raise a host of sensible objections in subdued, deferential voices to Freddie's continued presence in the Cause. Dodd has reverted to his customary role of Freddie advocate, contending that if the Cause proves incapable of helping Freddie, then those belonging to it have failed him. What is most noteworthy about the dinner table scene is its reassuring formality and implicit *visual* argument for the values of balance, calm, and order. Anderson seemingly recognizes our possible need for some sort of "excess" corrective after the chaos of the jail scene, and grants it.

The scene that follows is Freddie's return to the fold—which proves to be a demented variation on the parable of the prodigal son's return. It commences with the Norman Rockwell elements of the dinner episode carried over into a porch setting. Dodd rests in a rocking chair on the open, turn-of-the-century verandah we have already seen. The lighting and long-shot framing of the porch (suggesting a temporal, nostalgia-softened distance from social upheaval) have enhanced the picturesque appeal of this larger-than-life home. The dignified autocrat presiding over his meal now appears to us as a fond elder watching a small child play on her tricycle beside the porch steps. To increase the balance of the composition, Freddie enters from the right, providing a symmetrical counterweight to the girl at play on the left side of the frame. Although Freddie is clearly a man who has been through struggles, carrying their marks, his juxtaposition with the little girl accentuates our sense of his childlike qualities and emotional vulnerability.

Since there is considerable unresolved tension concerning Dodd's current state of mind with respect to Freddie, and his decision of how best to handle him, we await his formal response to his arrival. It is equally possible that he will solemnly forgive or reluctantly repudiate him, in the latter case extending his punishment with a period of exile. What one does not foresee is the instant breakdown of the carefully established visual and ceremonial form of the occasion. It is a John Ford moment of father-son confrontation after a quarrel, but this meeting slides into anarchy before even the preliminary emotional ground is covered. As soon as Dodd descends from the porch and gives Freddie, without hesitation, a reconciling embrace, the two men both fall in the grass and roll around together like dogs at play.

Their form-shattering frolic has a quality of hysteria. It feels like Dodd wildly surrenders the advantages of decorum—for maintaining authority—in favor of excessively high spirits. Neither man seems remotely mindful of the effect that this spectacle might produce on the

Cause members observing them from the porch. Dodd, who obviously has far more to lose than Freddie by this fit of self-indulgence, looks as though he is "finding himself"—in some mad shape—as he tussles ecstatically with Freddie on the lawn, meeting the animal force of his friend on precisely that level. The original Rockwell composition of the porch and sidewalk persists throughout this hubbub, with no cutaway shots. Its powers of containment are bolstered by our memory of the majestically composed dining room scene. These images resonate with long-term cultural associations: a host of cohesive meanings residing in the iconography of American family tradition and stability. The wrestling, laughing, gasping men are disquieting rather than comic, I think, because this scene sabotages the ritual that has been invoked, for no clear purpose. The men's behavior firmly resists a satiric or parodic reading. Nor do we gain easy emotional access to their animal release—this upsurge of giddily homoerotic fellow feeling that paradoxically affords no clues about how the two men understand what is taking place. The compositional form breaks against the incoherent action, and our *sense* of the form's meaning drains away, as though the form had a hidden crack. Dodd's wife, Peggy (Amy Adams), rushes out onto the porch as if to save the situation, but all that she and the other witnesses can do is to play their conventional roles in a reconciliation scene. To carry on, they must turn the action away from its threatening formlessness, whiting out Dodd's fit of abandon in order to convince themselves that what they witnessed did not really exceed the bounds of reconciliation propriety.

* * *

For much of his career, Anderson seems to be exploring the idea that the image itself might not be the site of revelation on film, or rather, that what can be readily seen is not the thing we need to be looking for. He pursues various methods of framing and tracking and cutting that cloud the issue of perspective (or vantage point), often creating spaces and bits of temporality that seem shadow sites, neither subjectively nor objectively authorized, and not quite *there* when we try to pin them down. Malcolm Turvey has written provocatively about a "revelationist tradition" in film, whose artists and theorists are imbued with the belief that "cinema's most significant feature is its capacity to reveal truths about reality invisible to the naked eye." When Anderson (in his introduction to *The Earrings of Madame de . . .*) discusses director Max Ophüls's radical break with moving-camera conventions in that film, he points out how Ophüls conjures up, in his lengthy opening tracking shot, an almost indeterminate space *between* the subjective point of view of Mme. de . . . and the material possessions she is concerned with. We are invited to see both *with* the character and *from behind* her at once, creating a blend of subjective and objective perception, but adding to them a ghostly middle ground, a place where the nature of perceiving becomes mystically scrambled. We have a vantage point, to be sure, but our ability to grasp it—to accurately designate what aspects of seeing belong to Mme. de . . . and what eludes her visual comprehension—is tenuous. It is the point of invisible but still palpable tension between the outside perspective and the character point of view in Ophüls's tracking technique that fascinates Anderson—how Ophüls maintains the precarious balance between a rigorously determinist composition (every moment of which is calculated, and attests to foreknowledge) while the character convincingly holds on to her distracted, thoughtless, carefree freedom.

The Master is manifestly, almost operatically, about the collision of two large-scale subjectivities. We often have the sense that the space that stands between them is unsettled, deceptive in its apparent solidity, in need of revision, reclaiming and higher validation. Dodd frequently implies that the space he occupies is a domain more spiritual than material, and that one must learn to behold it as he does. Recall his instructions over and over to Freddie about crossing a room from wall to window, until Dodd is satisfied that he has done it correctly. The external milieu is treated by both men as a kind of fantasy, or mirage, which must be approached with the right sort of memory and imagination to become authentic. Ordinary perception, Dodd assures us, is blindness. Nothing we engage with our untutored senses is simply there, to be taken for granted. Dodd wants the material dimensions of things to be less dominant; a strong-enough eye can decompose them. Dodd strains to make Freddie agree that the environments Freddie dallies in as a visitor "belong" to Dodd's vision, that he owns their mutual frame of reference. (We would do well here to remind ourselves of Dodd's own visitor and parasite status, though he is at pains to deny it.) Dodd's implicit challenge to Freddie becomes a challenge to the film's viewers. It might be put in these terms: "Do you know where you are and what stake you have in being there? You do not see what you think you do, and until your way of seeing is cleansed of hindrance and obstruction, your life will not belong to you."

Anderson tries to give a quality of indefiniteness not only to scenes but to the spaces they transpire in, verging (despite all the accurate period detail) on phantasmagoria. Screened space as well as the subjective actors vying to disrupt appearances and disclose what is really "present" seem to be in a permanent state of transition and dissolve. I'm reminded of the drawings of landscapes of different countries that scroll past the windows of the lovers' train compartment, creating the illusion of vista and movement, in Ophüls's *Letter from an Unknown Woman*. Who is to say that Ophüls's lovers are not transported to different climes if their imaginations kindle to the game? But *The Master*'s viewer, adrift as Freddie is in the experience of dissolve, can't get outside the compartment of illusion. We lack both a sense of placement in relation to the various modes of reality and unreality, and an awareness of destination. "Transitional scenes" in film customarily provide passage between sites of focused dramatic action and meaning. *The Master*'s transitions take up most of the narrative space. The scenes have a floating, diaphanous feel, displaying a reluctance—despite all the character energy on display—to declare their weight and take solid hold. The transitions supply a kind of movement that substitutes for conventional narrative progress. Since the subjectivities in transition do not reveal progress toward an endpoint we can envision, they gradually acquire a quality of immobility.[5]

It is troubling to be denied our customary access in film to the meaning of subjective states, in spite of an atmosphere thick with psychological clues. Ordinarily, it is the nature of character subjectivity on screen to blossom like a flower under our ministering, attentive, albeit covetous gaze. But, in this medium that is so often transparent, perhaps it is salutary to be reminded that another's subjectivity is, in truth, far more inclined to thwart us than to divulge its secrets. Perhaps we know next to nothing about this business of entering someone else's soul-terrain, and have regularly, lazily depended on fake tools. And perhaps the *ease* of penetrating characters' guises puts us, more worrisomely, at ease with the fantasy of self-mastery. Without thinking about it much, we can suppose that, in our own case, genuine self-knowledge, which *we* can properly manage, is something readily attainable, or already attained. Watching Quell's and Dodd's long-term endeavors to "find a fit" for their respective, hard-to-specify needs is vexatious if our participation isn't rewarded by the sense that our manner of understanding them is somehow helping things along. The third party to the dyad (the spectator) wants to believe that he is *necessary* in the building of rapport and insight. As we find the pattern or possible pattern that organizes the relationship and gets to the heart of its central conflict, we are making a vital contribution to the characters' growth. We may, in fact, recognize the solution to their problems well before they do, and wait for them to catch up with our acute judgment. In this familiar viewing position, we are given a double position—outside the form (as we gradually discern the shape of the drama) and inside the form, almost as a cocreator, making what happens happen, "making it up," as it were, with our lively speculation.

It is rare to encounter so starkly as in *The Master* our own impoverishment of means, our imaginative destitution when we are placed beside characters we might, under different circumstances, "grasp" and inwardly assist. Lancaster Dodd's proclamation to those seekers who *need* the Cause is that their whole approach to seeing, remembering, and imagining is woefully defective. Perhaps ours is, too. A radical transformation must take place inside us before the scales are removed, and we know how to make connection, finally, with the things around us, behind us, ahead of us. Instead of presenting Dodd's wild and woozy Emersonian injunctions as a bamboozlement (plain and simple), Anderson creates a situation of spectator incompetence, akin to blindness, to which Dodd's directives sharply and undismissably point. What sort of dream is this life we are lost in, both inside and outside the narrative, and how should we go about taking stock of our current deprivation and learn to rouse ourselves? *Our* "processing" (to use the Cause term) might commence, as Freddie's does, with the droning repetition of our name. Who belongs to such a name, and in what sense does the named one own it and conceal himself behind it? How much repetition in rapid sequence, and the resultant questioning pressure, can our name (anyone's name) withstand before giving way? Or, jumping to one of Dodd's later sessions, do we know what it means to walk across a sizable room, from a wall to a facing window? What if we were required to declare, again and again, what the open and closed aspects of wall and window consisted of? What does it take for a wall to acquire the properties of a window, and a window to become as obdurately impenetrable as a wall? What is the nature of the sensory obstruction or resistance presented to our imagination by both entities, and what might enable our "seeing" spirit to remake them and pass through them without their literal attributes defeating us?

How, in other words, must we loosen and concentrate our attention for efficacious, imaginative vision to transpire? Gaston Bachelard, in his phenomenological study, *The Flame of a Candle*, describes "maximum existence" as "existence in tension. . . . through this tension . . . the mind is constructed and reconstructed. Every evolution of thought, every prospect for thought, occurs in a reconstruction of the mind" (77–78). Throughout *The Master*, Anderson strives to sustain a high degree of contemplative tension across a long series of phantasmagoric transitional scenes. The tension is focused on the ghostly space between the two men, the space where things have lost their reliable character. It is a space where they dream of bringing back together some portion of what has (for good or ill) been cast into doubt or come apart. The powerful desire for a mind to be reconstructed so that it can be more humanly responsive, more responsive in general, depends for its fulfillment on another person meeting that mind where it is. The "invisible space" where reality dwells and might be revealed under "maximum tension" is most intensely present, in Blakey Vermeule's phrase, where one person stands "at the brink of another person's soul" (*Why Do We*, 110). One hopes to find an entry point there, and equally fears to. Dodd and Freddie, mutually encased in delusion, are nonetheless driven to expose themselves to one another. Heart knowledge of a painful radiance is intermittently attained through their customary two-step of approach and retreat. Sustained exposure arouses anxiety in both of them about subjection and annihilation. As Anderson cedes more and more reality to the dyad in *The Master*, as though that were the one authentic space to be concerned with, he creates an ever-stronger impression that Freddie and Dodd are not just projecting, but dreaming one another. And the viewer, in turn, is not observing them with superior understanding and detachment but rather dreaming both of them, and catching glimpses of the "invisible image sought" in the little, ghostly spaces between them.

The drama is located on the verge, the brink, the edge of their desired exposure, where the bonds of separation might ultimately give way.

* * *

The stage is now set for approaching the segment in *The Master* that poses the most startling and bewildering challenge to the dominance of the Freddie-Dodd dyad: the "A-Roving" musical interlude, featuring a sudden unveiling of a host of naked women followers of the Cause, who sing and dance under Dodd's capricious orders. This episode poses knottier point of view puzzles and raises more questions about how to distinguish between the literal and visionary status of an event than any other portion of the narrative. An extended analysis of this segment is necessary because it powerfully connects the impasse of the Freddie-Dodd relationship with a deceptively submissive-to-the-master crowd of vulnerable women. They are only "*deceptively* submissive" because in the course of their naked revelry they appear to reach a space of freedom beyond the control of either Dodd or Freddie, despite the fact that the spectacle seems to pass back and forth between the two men, as something that both of them perceptually, imaginatively, willfully vie to own. Against expectation, the women who perform as commanded by Dodd and who are simultaneously spied on by an inebriated, prurient Freddie, arrive at a space of freedom from which the men are excluded, a space where ease, openness, and fellowship prevail without striving. I would suggest that women are the unmastered form that Dodd and Freddie need to bring into the dyad so that its demands can be fulfilled, but for either to do so flies against the logic of control and distance the two men are driven to protect.

Once more we reach the near-mystical interval in an Anderson film where a surreal happening seems to "break the vessels" and reverse the flow in a manner similar to that which Aimee Mann's "Wise Up" number displays in *Magnolia*. Before we venture further into the labyrinth of Dodd's song-and-dance ceremony, it is useful to pause and consider how the array of female personages—actual, dreamlike, fabricated, or purely auditory—stake out a territory within the world of *The Master* that is both inseparable from the memories and projections of Dodd and Freddie, and yet, somehow, freestanding, apart from them. These female presences continually generate images of a destination where the two men might dock—the realm, perhaps, of achieved form. Whether as idea or tangible fact, the women flickeringly evoke better stations and better ways of being and experiencing with which they seem to be in touch. These fugitive possibilities elude or defeat the male questers, in part because they are terrified by the prospect of a female taking their power (however illusory) away from them. This takeover is, in fact, what the superficially rollicking "A-Roving" lyric is about.

The female images in *The Master* initially look like objects for use, submitting to coercive manipulation or patriarchal assertion. But the apparent fantasy uses to which they are put conceal a countercurrent—a force of resistance. The "yielding" images demonstrate a quiet refusal to remain in their assigned spot or role, to be persuasively possessed, or in any true sense mastered. The film's first female image, to which we will return at film's end, is the goddess-like sand woman, apparently built by sailors at the sea's edge, during a short reprieve from the obligations of war. It reposes imperturbably on the beach, surrounded by a group of sailors whom we have, only moments before, viewed in another sort of circle, cheering on their comrades who are stripped to the waist as they wrestle with each other. Freddie's discovery of the sand woman occurs after he has been visually established, in isolation from the other men, high in a palm tree chopping down fruit with a machete. We next see him alone on the ground, hollowing out the fruit, and making the first in a long series of experimental potions. Freddie's opening speech in the film, fittingly delivered to an off-screen listener who never materializes, includes references to testicles, pubic hair fire, and the emergency decision to take an ice pick to one's recalcitrant member. As though seeking a cure for genital impairment, Freddie sets out to conquer the sand woman sexually as soon as he catches his first glimpse of it. He proves unsuccessful in his effort to complete the sexual act, however, despite the men's approval. Shortly after, Freddie is viewed from behind, standing in the ocean as he finishes masturbating. Relieved of this burden, Freddie returns to the sand woman, pacified and perhaps repentant, and rests beside its foregrounded breasts, like a child seeking comfort. Anderson returns to this image at the film's conclusion, affording us our last impression of Freddie's placement in the world.

Freddie in repose with the sand woman in *The Master*

For Freddie, the most important female figure from the few scraps of his past he can retrieve from oblivion is his young wartime girlfriend, Doris (Madisen Beaty) whom he left behind. She lives in his memory as a figure both docile and gigantic. Physically she dwarfs him when he recalls them sitting together on a bench, having the conversation that he has long dwelt on and never erased. Here she embodies containment and constancy, in contrast to his own scatteredness and need to escape. Freddie fled from her to the war (the war seems almost like a convenient pretext). He has never answered the letters she sent to him during his time overseas, though he has, with utter sincerity, enjoined her to wait for him and remain in touch. He has also made no effort to contact her since his return to the United States, after the war ended. In spite of all this neglect and apparent forsaking, his memory of Doris singing a song to him, "Don't Sit Under the Apple Tree," is the one incontestably vivid and enduring image from his past that he holds on to. It seems to stand for whatever positive potential his blurred history has planted within him, and he still feels there may be time to show that he has remained faithful to it, and honor his pledge. Although I say more about Doris's

Doris (Madisen Beaty) about to sing "Don't Sit Under the Apple Tree" to Freddie in *The Master*

song later, for now, let us note that Doris's performance is linked with a sequence of songs by female vocalists of the 1940s and 1950s that are prominent on the soundtrack for *The Master*, in the spirit of Aimee Mann's presiding presence in *Magnolia*. There is also a parallel and contrast between these songs and the song that Dodd performs with such imperial manic gusto in the "A-Roving" sequence that we examine later.

In addition to "Apple Tree," three romantic ballads sung by war-era artists are heard almost in their entirety in the course of the film: "Get Thee Behind Me, Satan," sung by Ella Fitzgerald; "No Other Love," sung by Jo Stafford; and, at the end of the film, "Changing Partners," sung by Helen Forrest. Vocally, these performances all express the sweet containment of forceful feeling. Whether the lyric addresses sexual temptation, unshakable fidelity in love, or waiting for an absent dance partner's return until change proves necessary, there is no hint of turbulence in the singers' professions of intent. The singers demonstrate in their beautifully calm, even styles, how to hold their position, against any sort of challenge, without strain. Their voices supply proof that a realm exists somewhere in which deep feelings can attain stability and effortless cohesion. A romantic purpose can be delicately sustained and bring everything associated with it into a unified state. The vocalists silence doubt and apprehensiveness with an all-encompassing smoothness of occupancy of the lyric's terrain. Jo Stafford singing "No Other Love" with the majestic fervor that might accompany a church hymn engenders a sound image of inviolable truth in *The Master*, a narrative otherwise rife with dislocation, unsteadiness, and flimsiness. Throughout the Second World War, Stafford's singing voice powerfully combined yearning and a consoling strength of constancy, striving to be an answer to the great confusion of the war's endless losses. The four songs that women sing in the film, taken together, crystallize perhaps the one sure thing that Freddie can lay hold of from the miasma of his past: a girl's voice pledging her abiding love as she stays fixed in a precise, imaginary location—under the apple tree. The network of soothing female singers reinforces the single moment that holds together for Freddie. A point of repose dwells within him as well as outside him, in a blossoming backyard of time. It is a point that he can mentally return to, continue to imagine and build upon. The Doris moment gives his life a potential *form*, which he will eventually seek to actualize.

The figure of Martha, the department store model who briefly pursues and attaches herself to Freddie in the photography sequence discussed earlier, is associated, like Doris, with a song: "Get Thee Behind Me, Satan." It accompanies her as she makes her rounds of the store, seeking out possible buyers, in front of whom she pauses, opens the coat she is displaying, and seductively intones "$49.99." Ella Fitzgerald's smooth-as-silk rendition of the song includes repeated purrings of Satan's name, mischievously connecting Martha's tour of the department store aisles with a perhaps daredevil loosening of restrictions. Martha is an avatar of Doris, to whom we have not yet been introduced. Like her less worldly prototype, Martha seeks out Freddie and seems enchanted by him. Since Freddie lacks the will to initiate his own voyage back to Doris, this postwar surrogate seems to be voyaging to him, tainted perhaps with a knowledge of worldly temptation and compromise that Doris, at least in Freddie's mind, is protected from. Freddie's apparent comfort with Martha is deceptive. He cannot be reached by her, emotionally, no matter how much she seeks him out, or beckons him to come nearer; he cannot reciprocate her willingness to open herself to him. He instantly forgets about her once he leaves the structure of the department store job, though she seems a benign alternative to the chaos he leaves in his wake. She does not recoil from him after his frenzy of destruction, though she has every right to.

For Dodd, the most significant female presence is his wife, Peggy. He downplays both his attachment to her and his dependence on her whenever he performs the role of the self-sufficient visionary leader to his disciples in the Cause. But Peggy is the unwavering strength of law, hidden behind Dodd's audacious rhetoric, his confident vaporings. Although seeming to comply with his lordly whims and impetuous reversals, she is the one who supplies form and consistency to their life together. What clarity of direction Dodd manages to find emanates from her.

The female characters in *The Master*—whether projection, living entities, or a combination of the two—give the ideas, values, and attitudes that Dodd and Freddie are struggling to make sense of a temporary radiant focus. Doris is imbued with grace, innocence, and empathy; Peggy embodies loyalty. She can also live sedately amid contradictions, and she wields decisive authority from the shadowy sidelines without fanfare. Mrs. Solstad (Lena Endre), Doris's mother, whom Freddie encounters in his long-delayed attempt to find her daughter, seems in touch with the beauty and reality of home, emerging from her lodging at the top of a magical, yet sturdy flight of stairs in a place teeming with fresh floral bloom. Helen Sullivan (Laura Dern) is a generous provider of funding and accommodations to Dodd's Cause, and, in her relation to the master's teachings, is ablaze with curiosity and a hunger for genuine transformation. Freddie and Dodd, meanwhile, in their increasingly stifling dyad, deal with their attending female allies and witnesses mostly through distracted, capricious exploitation. Always distrusting solid ground and proudly at odds with ordinary life, they remain caught in the vortex of "unfettered" inward and outward expression. Dodd wants to solve the metaphysical engineering problem of Freddie's chaos. Chaos, of course, is notably resistant to engineering.

The Master's women, linked to order rather than chaos, are obliged to operate on the periphery of the narrative, where they provide intermittent, vivid flashes of emotional centeredness, attained definition. Dodd and Freddie try to press into service what the women "emanate." Both men are chiefly enamored by the images the females in their orbit release in them, and of the effects of these images as thought emancipators, or in Freddie's case, impulse emancipators. The spaces where the women exist in their own right, as freestanding agents, are closed to them, though they both associate women with the breaking of onerous bonds and with the tantalizing freedom of beauty, expansion, rebirth, acceptance. Again, the songs on the soundtrack, under the sway of the female voice, give the images that accompany them temporary, sustained contact with an almost-celestial balance.

I'm reminded again of Terrence Malick's *Days of Heaven*, and how the story, such as it is, is held together by the voice-over of a secondary character named Linda (Linda Manz), who possesses only limited access to the central love triangle on which the plots turns. However much this triangle's dynamic troubles or brings harm to her, her voice-over continues to sound entirely separate from it. Her scanty "inside" knowledge of what the other characters are going through does not make her anxious to know more. Instead, she seems enviably detached from their turmoil. Her voice is free to wander off at any point from their concerns and to register, with beautiful unconstraint, whatever impressions of the larger world may strike her. The voice-over passages create an alternative realm of fanciful musing. Linda's voice, rather than aligning logically with the film's extraordinary images of nature, or echoing their mood, lightly brushes against them, seldom commenting directly on what the spectator sees. She is surprised by a sudden association, which she arbitrarily pursues, taking something to heart or wondering at its import before inconclusively breaking off. Most intriguingly, Linda evinces little interest in making sense of her own part in the overall story. She is like a vocal shadow, or a soft breeze, rippling across the fields, seeking above all not to impose.

The female forces, skirting the edges of *The Master* narrative, and providing the incontestable auditory proof of self-possession in the voice-over songs on the soundtrack, hint at various points in the film that a solution might be found to the Freddie-Dodd deadlock. In the "A-Roving" dance sequence, the two men attempt to harness a communal female

Seeking control in the "A-Roving" scene in *The Master*

force in different ways, literally removing the "veil" of material covering (the women's garments) and coercing from their respective positions—Dodd out in the open, Freddie a concealed Peeping Tom—the dancers to do their bidding. It is perhaps at this juncture in the narrative that Dodd first conceives of making the imagination rather than memory the basis of freedom in his new, second Bible for the Cause. In any event, Dodd and Freddie seem engaged here in an effort to will themselves back to the *beginning* of seeing, becoming, roving. They devise a catalytic hide-and-seek game with a lost female center that they hope to recover and gain control over. The logic of this game is to meld the lost female center, once it has been conjured up as a compliant throng of bodies, with the male's own sovereign will. In the narrative of every childhood, there is the moment when the infant first grasps the "mother" as someone with the power to leave the child's room, her power to abandon and perhaps not return. "A-Roving" is the fantasy of calling the deceptive mother back from her journey of absence, and making her dance to the imperial son's tune. She must emerge, in this game, as a figure with nothing to hide, no concealed weapons (of mind or matter). Suppose the son were to reverse the order of things, and make his own escape before the mother has "seized the power" to leave him.

Zbigniew Herbert describes the son's escape fantasy, and its complications, in his great poem, "Mother":

> He fell from her knees like a ball of yarn.
> He unwound in a hurry and ran blindly away.
> She held the beginning of life. She would wind it
> On her finger like a ring, she wanted to preserve him.
> He was rolling down steep slopes, sometimes
> He was climbing up. He would come back tangled, and be silent.
> Never will he return to the sweet throne of her knees.
> The stretched-out hands are alight in the darkness
> Like an old town.
> (quoted in Hofmann, 155)

The "A-Roving" song sequence in *The Master* is preceded by a characteristically lengthy medium close-up shot of Freddie as a silent audience member of one of Dodd's impromptu talks on love in Helen Sullivan's Philadelphia mansion. Dodd is quite possibly delivering his speech while under the influence of one of Freddie's dangerous drinks (a daunting mixture of alcohol and more worrisome secret ingredients). Dodd begins his observations about love in an antic mood, suggesting that we have all experienced love and then referring, almost tauntingly, to his love for his wife, Peggy, as though this bond were an inferior version of the fabulous entity he aims to illuminate. We confirm the hurt and possible mortification that Peggy experiences from his glancing ridicule during a close-up of her reaction, in which she visibly tightens up, like a parson's wife under the congregation's scrutiny.

We hear next to nothing of Dodd's address on love, apart from his preliminary assurance that "when we're in love we experience pleasure and extreme pain." As he offers this statement, we in the audience are permitted to study Freddie's face, which appears alert, receptive, but also slyly knowing, in the manner of a fellow conspirator, and as he continues to listen, noncommittal. Perhaps he feels that Dodd is speaking directly to him (though he is not looking in his direction) and divulging a secret. We might also deem it likely that Freddie is still responding to the sudden, discreet sexual overture made to him by Dodd's daughter, Elizabeth (Ambyr Childers) just moments ago. While the camera holds on Freddie, the soundtrack separates from Dodd's speech and leaps ahead to an indeterminate later point as Dodd is getting ready to perform a song. The effect of this sound disjunction is to amplify our sense of disconnect in Freddie's "present" act of witnessing Dodd. The speech being delivered in front of him proves unable to keep him absorbed. A distracting noise is rising up from elsewhere, perhaps within him. The requirements for making sense of things have swiftly shifted ground, dividing us between two locations (one visual, one auditory) while Freddie straddles both realms. As this split is accentuated, the image of Freddie is subtly distanced from the action that the sound anticipates; he seems to be left behind in the room.

The singing scene that is ready to begin as we join it reveals Dodd surrounded by another audience, predominantly composed of women, in a double space consisting of a music room and a sitting room. Dodd, now more obviously inebriated, begins singing a seventeenth-century sea shanty, "The Maid of Amsterdam (A-Roving)." It is an amusing, bawdy round about a sailor beguiled and comically done in by someone he mistook for a careless, carnal but naive "fair maid." The song has obvious associations with Freddie's time as a seafarer and his own "lost love," Doris. More importantly, it hinges on a split point of view. The speaker tells a tale of confident male seduction in which the intended female victim is, in fact, many steps ahead of him from the outset, leading him into the darkness as he playfully woos her. The maid is finally an unknowable figure who winks at us from behind her mask before vanishing from the sailor's life, triumphant.

As the "A-Roving" performance begins, Anderson leads us to suppose that the camera narration is offering an objective or neutral perspective, as though an actual event were being documented, without fantasy distortion. At first, the gathering reveals no peculiar features. The women in attendance are dressed formally, as are the men. The crowd is no longer seated, as it was during his discourse on love. Only pregnant Peggy remains in her chair, in the second room, which is farther away from us. Her placement renders her inconspicuous. There is no hint of impending Bacchanalian revelry or a summons to flout rules of decorum.

Freddie, the hidden observer, is seated in a small curtained alcove whose precise relation to the large performance is indefinite. He now appears to be more withdrawn, physically and emotionally, than in the previous lecture scene. He looks sullen and sleepy, quite possibly the result of his own furtive drinking. He wears the same vivid blue shirt that he had on during Dodd's remarks on love. (Freddie's blue apparel always harks back to his naval uniform from the World War II prologue, as well as to the aimless turbulence of the blue ocean in the film's opening shot. The seaman's uniform was Freddie's nearest approach to a clear public identity, and has obvious parallels to Barry Egan's blue suit in *Punch-Drunk Love*.) Recall that immediately prior to Dodd's impulse to sing, we watched him getting ready to explore, in his lecture, the contrast between love's lighthearted pleasures and its "extreme pain." Judging from Dodd's gleeful disposition, he is now situating himself on the pleasure ground of love and has chosen to banish from sight, like a benevolent magician, the "pain" he has previously dealt with. But as we light upon Freddie, we are put in touch with something painful. His expression is combative and unresolved. He is trying to process Dodd's activity from his cubbyhole, but he also seems to be drifting toward slumber, or falling under the hypnotic spell that envelops Dodd's audience.

We are meant to be jolted by the next, unmarked transition from Freddie's sleepy spying to an interval somewhat later in the sea shanty where the women's attire has been entirely whisked away. The main questions for the viewer as Dodd performs the song is where the control of the spectacle actually lies, and what sort of *reality* is being established in the images. We are also meant to be engaged, throughout this strangely "held-in" licentious display, in a tug-of-war between three divergent authority perspectives. We are likely to be most conscious, initially, of Dodd, who cuts a commanding figure as the master of the revels. It could be argued that it is the influence of Freddie's "hooch" that gives Dodd the mad whim to stage his sea shanty and then, exerting his full authority over his followers, push the women to "expose" themselves, like exultant daughters of the song's "fair maid," to the new truth about love he has disclosed in his lecture. Dodd's power is further enhanced if we assume that he knows precisely where Freddie is located, and that the song is secretly aimed at him rather than at the bewitched participants in the dance. Although he does not grant Freddie so much as a single glance, Dodd is, after all, calling forth the silver memory of a love who has taken advantage of the sailor's romantic trust and vanished after cleaning him out. The array of sportive, compliant maidens can be regarded as a supplication to Freddie from the master to come forth from his lover's place of concealment and be similarly "stripped bare," unafraid. But we attend as well to the authority of the hidden observer, Freddie, whose seeming puzzlement matches our own. This spy and conceivable fantasist has the power to divert Dodd's alluring music hall turn to his own voyeuristic purposes, and he may be hatching a private daydream scandal that suits his needs and crude appetite. To complicate matters still further, a third point of view—belonging to Peggy—insinuates itself in the viewer's struggle to determine whose perspective on this scene should take precedence. As the performance of "A-Roving" continues its dizzying, rapturous build, Peggy sits unobtrusively in the background, pregnant and naked. Her eyes firmly locate Freddie—which is to say, where the camera is, with its privileged vantage point, and where the film's viewer is. Peggy's gaze seems knowing and stern, making Freddie's manner of looking, and also perhaps his contribution to Dodd's feverish state as performer, cause for reproach.

Three points of view now vie for control of the viewer's understanding of what is taking place. Is the activity on display fact, fantasy, or some ineffable blending of the two? Female nakedness is a strong, if intermittent, preoccupation of Freddie's, given that *The Master* begins with his effort to establish a viable connection with a naked maternal sand sculpture. The sand woman's ephemeral nature—she will vanish in the next incoming tide—resembles the solid but vaguely apparitional mass of women, covering a substantial age range, who present themselves briefly in carefree fellowship in the "A-Roving" scene. Most startling is the fact that they maintain their previous roles as musicians and engaged, clapping listeners in a casual, unselfconscious spirit. They pose no obstacle to his joining in, though there is an air of self-sufficiency to their revelry. They have no *need* of his involvement and, apart from Peggy, take no notice of him. They echo the sand woman's impassive apartness from him. He must ultimately *submit* to the sculpture's detached presence, as he does to the vision of bare women. Yet the mother in the midst of this group, heavy with child, seems able to read his mind from a distance and to brand him as some sort of failure: a failure in his watching, in his passivity, in his drunkenness, and his attempt to hide. Possibly it is something more than these shortcomings that makes Freddie culpable in Peggy's eyes. In any event, she appears to wrest control of the fantasy, if we can confidently call it that, away from Freddie. By asserting her vigilance and judgment so forcefully, she makes her state of awareness a firmer ground of reality for a viewer's reading of the scene, despite the fact that she too is naked. Her perspective seems, for the moment, to discredit the possibility that the entertainment is a mere hallucination. Dodd's Svengali feat of getting the women to disrobe is no sooner dismissed as Freddie's hallucination than Peggy's point of view restores its plausibility, and the spectacle attains an eerie foothold in the realm of the Cause's "under wraps" practices.

We have a pressing need to settle the question of what we have just witnessed, because of its surpassing strangeness and extremity. Yet the more we attempt to stabilize the episode, the more it oscillates. On reflection, we may conclude that Freddie is a somewhat unlikely author of a fantasy of this kind: a collective mental undressing of all the women present, with no discrimination on the basis of age or attractiveness. He does not exploit his prerogative, as fantasy orchestrator, to make himself part of the salacious game or to exert his power over anyone his glance happens to favor. It is a peculiarly self-effacing vision, one that acknowledges and extends Dodd's authority at the expense of his own. His willingness to leave odd adornments and personal items (such as a necklace) in place on some of the female "objects of scrutiny" suggests a delicacy of touch in his observation, and an attunement to small, individualizing distinctions. This imaginative refinement seems an almost inconceivable attribute of Freddie's way of looking, drunk or sober. On the other hand, Anderson's elaborate highlighting of Freddie as a half-drunk, half-asleep discoverer of the saturnalia should not be discounted.

Anderson introduces a flutter effect in Freddie's perception of the altered circumstances of the musical performance, which is crucial to our growing sense that his consciousness not only dominates but directs the spectacle. The transition from sleep to entranced wakefulness suggests a man on the edge of dreaming, visited by a possibly alcohol-induced optical hoax. This eruption of images (like the "Pink Elephants on Parade" sequence in Walt Disney's *Dumbo*) would square with our earlier findings about the fearsome liquids mixed together in Freddie's demon concoctions. Freddie being startled, as we are, by what he unaccountably witnesses, is a smooth cinematic entry point to the women's metamorphosis. Then it seems logical that we "flutter" during his prolonged spy attentiveness to the alternative possibility of Freddie secretly running the lurid show and keeping it going by force of will. Peggy's incriminating look to Freddie (and to us) completes the idea that Freddie has been caught in the act of Peeping Tom wrongdoing. Like a mother with magical clairvoyance, Peggy catches her "child" doing something stealthy and shameful, and she makes him mindful of her authority. But Peggy is also staring directly at *us*. Does her look not root us out of our own place of hiding and make us, briefly, partake of Freddie's sense of discomfort in exposure? Something inadmissible in our own "playing around" with interpretation as the naked women dance and clap, vulnerable to our predatory interest, leads us to sever ties with Freddie's position and to make him the source of all dubious gazing and troubling manipulation.

I described Freddie's discovery of the Bacchanal as a "flutter" effect. For the viewer there is a similarly delayed capacity to see what is actually happening in front of us. Narrative context and expectation often operate with such force in film that we continue to see elements that have already been established as behaving in a manner consistent with our previous sighting and visual expectations. The clothing, or anticipated continuation of "women clothed," remains present in our imaginative memory and we lurch at the sudden need to revise our impression of what is confronting us. It is almost as though the dresses are dissolving as we watch, and are not simply gone. Freddie's unmistakable signs of drowsiness as he reclines in the alcove when the entertainment is still proceeding in a normal fashion allow us to interpret the point-of-view ellipsis and the brief halting of sound that accompanies it as the "lost time" of sleep. In this version of what took place, the inebriated Freddie's consciousness has slipped away in a doze of indeterminate length. When he snaps back to waking attention, it may seem to him that only a few moments have elapsed. The viewer is similarly confounded by how much missing time and activity must be accounted for, since Dodd is still involved in performing the same song.

Perspective authority is returned to Dodd, and we see what might come from a scenario in which he oversees the crucial puzzling variables. One might infer that while Freddie was asleep, Dodd proposed an experiment to the women in attendance—both the musicians playing for him and the female members of his audience. Possibly, in his discussion of love's higher freedom and courage, he offers the simple truth of exposure as one antidote to the "extreme pains" of love that he has delineated. When his followers have complied with his request, Dodd takes up the song again with a different purpose, meaning, and set of stakes. He has granted the women access to the "fair maid's" superior wisdom and power. Dodd has persuaded them to exchange self-consciousness for a relaxed acceptance of the shedding of all false coverings. They can joyously embrace nakedness as a state of ordinary being, thus facilitating their own rebirth. I have, of course, invented a spiel for Dodd, which might or might not enable a crowd of formally dressed women to find ease and euphoria, rather than humiliation, in the casting aside of their garments. Questions of power and trust are inescapable here. What are the consequences of eliminating the awkward, tentative, potentially humiliating preliminaries to the naked frolic and moving directly, through Freddie's mediating perspective, to an assured, crowning display of unconstraint? We naturally take our cues from Dodd, who is unquestionably the exuberant ringmaster of the remarkably playful carousal. There is a calm evenhandedness in the revealing of the female dancers and musicians. They are physically distinctive but emotionally unified in their powerfully unintimidated enjoyment of Dodd's cavorting and song.

Significantly, it is Dodd who somewhat lags behind the serenity that surrounds him. He appears winded from exertion, sweating and alcoholically boisterous. He is striving for an effect of ease, rather than experiencing it. The man who has devised the *form* of this rite is laboring mightily to be in the midst of his creation, but he is not in full sync with it, perhaps as much an outsider, with respect to mental placement, as Freddie is. As we scan the women's activities in the dance and their responses to Dodd's ribald clowning, they appear to be equally shielded somehow from both the prurient intent of Freddie's spying and from Dodd's manipulation as group leader. They have "come into the light" that Dodd often alludes to, and their performance of exposure attests to at least a temporary transcendence of social regulations and to a cleansing of social form.

Many perceptual paradoxes, gaps, and perplexities are released in this scene with quiet, stunning speed. Behold the joy that casting off masks, inhibitions, and other sorts of bondage can usher in "in the blink of an eye." But, as I have argued, Freddie is excluded from having a seeing conversion of his own because of Peggy's censuring look back at him. He does not get the benefit of loosening his own shackles by contemplating the innocent display of beauty opening before him, a revelation aligned with the mystery of the sand woman on the beach. The space that the women's exhilarating, nonchalant delight therefore creates is a fourth perspective within the scene. They present a standpoint that is within our imaginative reach but elusive.

This alternative space and mode of being excludes Freddie and Dodd in roughly equal measure. Something is taking form in a positive spirit that exceeds the capacities of both men to absorb. This form (prodigiously female) stands at a utopian remove from the blocked seeing, immoderate appetites, machinations, concealment, and desperation that Dodd and Freddie separately resort to. Dodd poses and preens as an unfettered master while the women gathered around him achieve grace and naturalness by other means, which they have made their own. Dodd depends on the "fair maids" being caught up in an illusion he has conjured up, but his own authority is unable to get him beyond sleight of hand, as his female believers manage to. His authority protects him from entering into the sacred space, but protection of that sort is fear-based and drastically limits him. Freddie's alcoholic potions are Dodd's substitute for an expansive release of spirit. Dodd is instead drawn downward to the tempting chaos Freddie presents to him. He urges Freddie to admire the order he contrives in his strenuous cavorting with his subjects, even though the order is a sham for him; he cannot lay hold of it or make it real. On the form-formlessness divide, the desired entity appears to be taking shape right before their eyes, but neither man can find a way to connect with it.

The atmosphere as the scene draws to a close is thick with culpability and impending collapse. Peggy's probing gaze into the camera, from her chair in the far distance, impales Freddie, and the viewer, with a reprimand whose burden of meaning resists easy explanation. Anderson creates a perceptual impasse for the viewer at the heart of literal exposure. Nakedness becomes a floating unresolved question, at once the product of manipulation (either Dodd's or Freddie's, or both in succession), and mysteriously free of that manipulation. For either man exerting control by looking, there is no getting at the place where authentic unveiling, untrammeled beauty, and naturalness live.

* * *

Anderson's favorite pattern of scene juxtaposition, as I argue earlier, involves a movement from a scene of eruption—where unforeseen images and possibilities explode into view with a density and speed that outpace our capacity to process what is shown—to a scene of containment, where calm is restored by an appeal to a different kind of pressure. In the bathroom "containment" scene that follows the disruption of the "party," Eros assumes a new "domestic" guise and presses back the spectacle of wildness into a narrow, more familiar channel: a limiting order. The scene consists of a lengthy static shot in a bathroom. Dodd is shown bending over a sink, with his back to us, apparently grappling with the effects of a painful hangover. Above him is a prominent mirror. As the scene commences, the "A-Roving" music continues in the background, a kind of memory echo that links the bathroom to the concluded festivities. The composition of this shot provides an alternative answer to the question posed in the closing shot of the dance sequence: "What does Peggy see?" We have just experienced Peggy looking directly at us and Freddie. She appears to be gazing beyond the confines of the frame from a privileged sitting position; she neither participates in the dance nor watches it. By following Peggy's point-of-view perspective with a shot of Dodd turned away from the camera (half-hidden, in effect, as Freddie is), we are momentarily led to suppose that she has actually made visual contact with her husband. That deception of the eye is noteworthy, although we swiftly exchange our mistaken impression for the realization that Dodd occupies a different setting at a later time. The look that Peggy sends out from the dance scene is eerily replaced in the new setting by an image of Peggy's face materializing in the mirror positioned above Dodd's head, as he leans over the sink, gazing down. We first catch sight of her approaching Dodd—a bit disorientingly—as a mirror reflection. Within the mirror we watch her crossing toward Dodd in profile, then her head enlarges as her physical form arrives behind him. No longer naked, she is now clad in a nightgown. Her body materializes on screen *after* the arrival of her face in Dodd's mirror. Peggy's reflected face establishes continuity with Peggy's look from the dance, as though she is still bearing the look's message for its intended recipient.

As the "A-Roving" music fades away, Peggy stands beside Dodd, a comforting, maternal presence. She places her arm around his shoulder as she leans over him to kiss his shirt. Complicating the mirror image further is a striking reflection of a framed print of swans gliding on water, and another hanging wall mirror reflected below it. Both frames, we gradually figure out, would be situated on the wall behind Dodd and Peggy. I allude to the destabilizing features of the image because they work to compromise the reality effect of the bathroom itself. Without the estranging peculiarities, the bathroom setting would convey the idea that things have returned to normal, that the saturnalia hallucination—if that indeed is what it was—has ended. Peggy in her nightgown, initially expressing gentle spousal concern, is clearly a more intelligible, down-to-earth presence than the disporting maidens we have just left behind, but her arrival through the mediating mirror reflection turns her greater solidity into doubt.

Everything in Peggy's subsequent interaction with Dodd is bewilderingly double-sided, a vortex of mirror reversals. The least contestable point in her exchange with him is the one with which we might at first be most disposed to argue. In her opening comments to him she seems to be mildly reproaching him for his excesses as a philanderer, a criticism that lends credence to the view that the implausible, dreamlike vision we have witnessed was not a chimera or an exaggeration of actual events, but literal truth. While Peggy's voice is a calm, softly reassuring whisper and her visible arm tenderly clasps his shoulder, her unseen hand begins almost immediately to grip his penis and force him toward climax. As in the case of two other oblique elements (her mirrored entrance and the emphasis on Dodd's mostly hidden face), Peggy's sexual offensive is rendered deliberately obscure in its early stages, and we become aware of it—with a sudden shock—after it has been in progress for some time. Peggy's talk accompanying the hand job emphasizes Dodd's *freedom*, but she maintains utter control of him throughout. His ashamed, turned-away placement in the shot, his hungover rumpledness, and his confused acquiescence to Peggy's quiet demands accentuate our sense of his diminished authority since his impresario stance at the party.

Peggy's other major theme in this one-sided conversation is knowledge. Dodd's freedom to do "whatever he wants" is dependent, according to the rules Peggy lays out, on her being kept in the dark about it.

He is at liberty, she informs him, to go beyond the bounds of what she knows about his dalliances, or of what she might hear about his escapades from others. Yet one is struck by the sheer unlikelihood of his doing anything that would escape her vigilance or her ability to gain whatever knowledge she seeks. Thus, Dodd's permission to "go a-roving" is no sooner granted than it feels severely curtailed. She sanctions his need to indulge himself as he sees fit, all the while retaining control of his penis. The vision of female bounty that has so recently been set before us is reduced in the bathroom to a shabby, brutish outcome. Her manner of handling him physically is aggressive and punitive, though her tone of voice throughout remains affectionately accommodating. Eros becomes a tiny, groggy spasm, overseen by spite.

Anderson appeals to our desire for a return from the perceptual disruptions and enigmas of the party to something we can more readily comprehend. In effect, we want Peggy to lay down the law as a remedy for our feeling too adrift, too much at a loss. Sex needs to be put back in a place where it obeys certain rules and thus behaves sensibly—so we can decipher it by reference to conventional signs. The shamefulness and grubbiness of Dodd's mere urge to be relieved, and the mechanical servicing of that urge, are a kind of necessary reprisal for his prior confounding audacity—venturing without compass or map into questions about love where everything turned mysterious. Shorn of all the trappings of power and confidence, Dodd is a creature exposed, naked in his stupefaction and physical weakness. As Peggy goes through the motions of consulting with him, she effectually strips him of his defenses, while reading his mind and making it over into her own likeness.

Peggy advances still further into the realm of maternal power when (later the same night) she pays a visit to Freddie, who is sprawled on a couch, asleep, and wakens him. This experience of being brought back to consciousness parallels Freddie's sleep and confused waking progression in the "A-Roving" scene. Peggy functions as a third element in a number of scenes in succession, intervening to stabilize the volatile, uncertain field between Dodd and Freddie by proposing a clarity that is seldom available when the two men are alone together. She strives to define Freddie's role in Dodd's life as highly conditional. She possesses a narrative of her marriage with Dodd in which everything is subordinate to the Cause. In the logic of her story, Freddie is an interloper without rights, who has no notion of how expendable he is. He is troubling to her because he has no sense of his place, of his real standing. He has no language of respect, and he is not governed by either his attachments or his unearned privileges. Peggy seems to have gone directly to Freddie once she has finished using a towel to wipe Dodd's ejaculate from her hand. Freddie, passed out in one of the mansion's public chambers, is still wearing his blazing blue shirt. His drink-induced stupor as Peggy summons him to wakefulness matches the forlorn, bedraggled condition of Dodd in the bathroom. In a film characterized by odd, slantwise encounters with indefinite aims, Peggy's two missions feel like a dream of lucidity breaking into a larger dream of obscure promptings.

Peggy no sooner gains Freddie's cloudy attention than she voices the viewer's likely shared desire that he discover a clear goal: "I'd like you to place something in the future for yourself that you would like to have. . . . It's there waiting for you. And you can go and get it whenever you're ready." Peggy insisting that he find a compelling image for his future, something he can imagine and keep firmly in his mind until he gets it, is pointedly linked with Freddie's most positive, indissoluble image from the *past*. Young Doris Solstad has, as I noted earlier, sung a song to him on a park bench before he leaves her for overseas naval duty in wartime: "Don't Sit Under the Apple Tree with Anyone Else But Me." This song is the one unambiguous moment of emotional fidelity and tenderness in Freddie's otherwise hopelessly muddled recollection of things past. His face makes powerful contact with a yearning and a claim on him that feel whole rather than a blurred fragment when he recalls, during one of Dodd's processing sessions, her singing to him just once, long ago and far away.

Wayne Koestenbaum writes brilliantly about the voice of a female singer entering, immensely, the "dwarfed" body of a listener in his study of opera and homosexuality, *The Queen's Throat*. Though Doris sings to Freddie only in the space of memory, her voice is fully present to him and brings the rest of her person in its wake until she is toweringly restored—a complete entity—within and beside him. "The listener's body is illuminated, opened up," Koestenbaum writes:

> a singer . . . exposes the listener's interior. . . . Her voice enters me, makes me a "me," an interior, by virtue of the fact that I have been entered. The

> singer, through osmosis, passes through the self's porous membrane, and discredits the fiction that bodies are separate, boundaried packages. The singer destroys the division between her body and our own, for her sound enters our system . . . and I begin to believe—sheer illusion!—that she spins out *my* self, not hers, as Walt Whitman . . . implied when he apostrophized a singer in "Out of the Cradle Endlessly Rocking": "O you singer solitary, singing by yourself, projecting me, / O solitary me listening, never more shall I cease perpetuating you . . ." (43)

To further the notion of the singer, Doris, "spinning out" Freddie's self rather than her own, consider the lyrics of the song she sings. The implied character in the song who issues the plea to "wait" is a soldier worried about his girlfriend's fidelity while he is away. Doris takes on this male persona when she presents the song to him, one who begs his beloved not to replace him with another suitor. Doris's manner of performing it, with a near unearthly, trusting innocence, converts the soldier's entreaty into a young girl's binding promise. The song crystallizes perhaps the one sure thing that Freddie can lay hold of from the miasma of his past: a girl's voice pledging her abiding love as she stays fixed in a precise, imaginary location—under the apple tree. The soothing female singer stretches out the single moment that holds together for Freddie. But perhaps Freddie is also terrified of this memory image of Doris—so perfectly composed in its promise to endure—terrified that it will fail him, like every other shelter and safeguard, if he puts it to the test of real earthly demands. His own sickness, with its many obscure components, may have made it unthinkable for him to seek out Doris anywhere except in a small shrine in his mind. In any event, something in this remembered constancy—this soft, beckoning music of a figure who has not forsaken him, who waits without reproach on the threshold of an unlived, unclaimed life—is hard for him to face.

When Peggy tells Freddie to place something in the future for himself that he would like to have, the memory of Doris is the one bit of salvage that he can imagine lying ahead of him. It is a point he can mentally return to, continue to replenish and believe in. The memory that haunts him so unfathomably and with such binding stasis reverses direction. Doris now looms on the horizon as his future. She waits, an antidote to his shattering, at the end of a road he has still to travel. When they reunite, and the future commences, she will make it possible for him to bear staying together, not only with her but with himself. She will somehow find order among his multitudinous, berserkly warring fragments and start to assemble him, coherently. The Doris moment gives his life a potential *form*.

* * *

Dodd's plan for Freddie is somewhat different from the one Peggy offers. He aspires to fix the "push-pull" mechanism that holds Freddie captive, but to an even greater degree he aspires to preserve Freddie's obscure wildness and unreasoning insubordination. Freddie accuses Dodd in the subsequent prison cell scene of "making it all up as he goes along," though this is hardly a *personal* accusation, since Freddie has randomly borrowed the words from Dodd's disillusioned son, Val (Jesse Plemons). Dodd and Freddie are alike in their drive to "make it up as they go along," though Dodd wants his improvisations to have the force of discoveries that endure, while Freddie hastily loses sight of his actions before he has time to "make" something of them. Freddie lives without the satisfaction of internal continuity. Dodd, in contrast, needs to build a new world from his beliefs in the act of imposing them on others. The imposing is what keeps them substantial and alive in his own mind. Freddie, immersed in chaos and free from any communicable conviction, strikes Dodd as a true improviser. Whatever primitive impulses guide Freddie in his way of imagining things, he appears sovereign in his degree of removal from outside influences.

Thus, whenever Dodd wears Freddie down during a confrontation and successfully coerces him to submit, he feels simultaneously a sense of progress and failure. In the prison scene, for example, Dodd finally gets Freddie to settle down, momentarily scaring him with the thought that, except for Dodd, Freddie is utterly bereft. There is no one else in the world for him to turn to for understanding or alliance but Dodd ("I am the only one who likes you"). Freddie has been kicking a shard of the toilet he broke as he frantically circles his cell. In his separate cage, Dodd makes a lordly show of having a still-intact toilet of his own to meet his "animal" needs. While Dodd urinates, releasing a triumphant, lengthy, and loud stream into the porcelain bowl with his back to him, a chastened Freddie lies down on his lower bunk and agrees through his act of turning quiet and passive to submit to "parental" law. "I will stop misbehaving and lie still," his body language attests, though he tries to mask the extent of his capitulation with mild kicks of residual protest against his bed, like a small child. Dodd has won, but we feel that he may prize the obliterated toilet more than the functioning one. He understands that Freddie can embark on a wholesale destruction of the amenities, with no sense of consequences; he can go too far, unmindful of how to protect himself.

Studying Freddie may well be the decisive reason that Dodd stakes everything on imagination as the new lynchpin of his spiritual system. Freddie remembers almost nothing, yet his strange improvising imagination allows him to proceed, giving the world serendipitous novel shapes with every passing mood. Imagination, as Denis Donoghue argues in his discussion of Wallace Stevens's "chaos," is "the only force that defends us against the terror of reality" (200). Reality burdens our senses with "things as they are that come to us without invitation or apology, often to be thought of as chaos. . . . The past and its traditions are mere souvenirs, the structures of belief have dissolved in mid-air, and there is now (Stevens says) no authority 'except force, operative or imminent'" (190, 191). The imagination becomes the hero in this contest with reality's indifferent sea. It redeems whatever is left and worth clinging to in our tenuous traditions, verifies what is real in relation to our needs, and makes a new world out of its own vital materials. The imagination must have all the strength of "the outside"; it must arise from an unpacified, lawless disposition to accomplish its world-renewing task and lead us through it to

> another life,
> A life beyond this present knowing,
> A life lighter than this present splendor,
> Brighter, perfected and distant away,
> Not to be reached but to be known,
> . . .
>
> (Stevens, "The Sail of Ulysses," V, *Opus Posthumous*,
> quoted in Donoghue, 214)

When Dodd starts over with Freddie after his disciple's return from jail, his aim is to turn the "cage" of his arbitrary defiance, abounding contradictions, and unappeasable nature into a fortress of the imagination. In the lengthy sequence in which Dodd demands that Freddie repeatedly walk back and forth between a wall and a window and relate each time what he sees, the closed and open object are equally frontiers of vision—thresholds, not limits. A wall can become as receptively see-through as a window, and a window is by no means reducible to the components of the vista it happens to frame. Dodd is less interested now in tracking down Freddie's memory demons than in permitting whatever arises in him to unite without fear with imagined possibilities. As a connoisseur of chaos, Freddie will potentially create a fittingly wild no-man's-land of the untutored spirit, unbeholden to outworn forms. Dodd's teaching role has altered. It now has to do with both "unleashing" all of Freddie's form-shattering impulses and at the same time making him aware that he is responsible to this imagination he finds and gradually recognizes as his own.

What rekindles in Freddie as his imagination begins to coalesce and a semblance of selfhood appears feasible to him is a belief in his ability to love someone. He conceives of his life as a vague mythological tale in which his fate, after untold years of being ensnared in a violent perplexity, is to reclaim Doris, the innocent who once sang to him. Like Odysseus's Penelope in the mists of Ithaca, she awaits his return. She stands with increasing vividness as the single immutable figure in the far reaches of his mind. Being responsible to his own imagination comes to signify reclaiming his responsibility to her. Perhaps the image of the sand woman, which, as a wartime fantasy surrogate for his lost love, he grotesquely violated in the presence of witnesses, has somehow blocked access to Doris as a living possibility. One projection has become an obstacle to reaching the other projection (a symbol of purity) behind it. Something within Freddie, of which the fearsome sand woman is the indecipherable sign, demands propitiation and atonement before he can venture in a direction of his choosing.

When Dodd takes Freddie out in the desert for a motorcycle ride to demonstrate the expanded range and sweep of his imaginative vision, Freddie races his vehicle past any marked destination in the visible terrain and disappears from view. He turns up, eventually, at Doris's old house, where he is convinced a place is still being held for him, which a visit will make real. The muddled questions Freddie has been putting to himself about where he is going with his life can be extended outward if he locates Doris. She can direct him to a spot he actually feels he belongs to. And in her company it can enlarge. But Doris, Freddie learns from her gently considerate mother, has met someone else and gone off to be with him. The apple tree where time stands still is no more. One can arrive too late for starting over, too late for love and clemency.

We find evidence that Freddie's imagination has nevertheless continued to make headway in the next crucial episode of *The Master*, one appropriately wrapped in dreams. Freddie is discovered seated alone in a vast movie theater where the off-screen voice of the cartoon ghost child, Casper, is engaged in his customary scenario of making contact with a real child who will, for a short time, befriend him. In every Casper story, the harmless outcast is readmitted temporarily into the realm of children's play that occurs on the imaginative fringe of life. At no point do we catch a glimpse of the screen Freddie faces, nor do we have any sense of what he is absorbing from the cartoon, or whether he is responding to it at all. He has apparently dozed off. The ghostliness of Casper's recurring quest for human connection seeps into the theatre at large. As Freddie gives evidence of coming to, he is, in fact, sinking deeper into a dream, though one that incorporates his actual physical circumstances. The fluctuating impression of where in the waking life-dream continuum Freddie is actually located persists throughout the movie theater scene, just as it did in Dodd's musical performance with the naked women.

The dimly lit theater, with its melancholy Edward Hopper glow and cartoon soundtrack, has a convincing weight and definiteness. It helps ground the surrealistic action, which commences when a uniformed usher hands Freddie a telephone, with a presumably endless cord. Dodd has managed to find him in his cinema hideaway and contact him via transatlantic call. Dodd's voice at first sounds a trifle off as Freddie listens through the receiver, as though it were a half-remembered version of Dodd attempting to gain access to his memory. "He" speaks in a style that amalgamates Dodd's interests with those of some other lost father figure. Dodd bypasses saying hello, immediately offering instead the strong, sentimental declaration, "I miss you." Freddie does not resist the emotional appeal, one that suggests that all transgressions have once again been forgiven. He is moved and vulnerable to an extent that we've rarely witnessed in him before. Freddie inquires quietly, incredulously, how Dodd has been able to find him. Dodd succinctly disposes of that mystery by reminding Freddie that "we're tied together." Time and space, as the founder of the Cause has often asserted, aren't very important, and pose no obstacle in the face of the psychic bond Dodd alludes to.

Whether Freddie is dreaming the conversation or not, he seems powerfully attuned to Dodd's likely concerns, and even intuits the master's whereabouts. Dodd has relocated to England and opened a school there. What is emphasized throughout the unearthly exchange is a growing capacity for reciprocity in Freddie, extending his availability to others' emotional presence and to their speech (as well as their intended meanings) that we have already observed in his porch visit with Doris's mother. One senses that Freddie's amplified and deepened imagination enables him to acknowledge and sustain a living connection with Dodd in his mind and heart. Imagination unites with memory to soften, in the words of George Saunders, "the borders between you and me, between me and me" (quoted in Mason). A change of heart has occurred, or rather a reopening of a heart that has been sealed up for the longest time, "softening what is rigid" in Freddie's mind (ibid., 31). The dream conversation contains more persuasive awareness of Dodd's presence and a greater capacity to respond to his questions and expression of caring than Freddie has summoned in face-to-face encounters.

Dodd promptly invites Freddie to join him in England: he reveals that he has a "matter of such urgency" to deal with and that Freddie's assistance is crucial. It may, he tantalizingly concludes, enable him "to cure insanity once and for all." "Insanity" is a word to linger over here. It has almost never been employed by Dodd—certainly not in his sessions with Freddie. The dream-speak gist of his direct allusion to it is that the insanity in question has chiefly to do with the pair's relationship and that Freddie's visit is required to bring about the desired remedy. He also tempts Freddie with the prospect of an answer to the riddle of where (in the vast time-space continuum) they originally met. All the specific facts that Dodd refers to in the dream phone call (the new school in England; the desire to reconnect with Freddie; the request for a cigarette brand unavailable in England; the solution to the riddle of where, in their "past lives," they first formed an attachment) are borne out in the more reality-based, final meeting between them that ensues. Freddie is fully aware, as he informs Dodd in the course of this meeting, that he *dreamed* the phone call, but that realization poses no obstacle to his taking each of its directives literally and to heart. Nor is he mistaken to do so.

What, then, is the nature of the place that Freddie has arrived at in the movie theater? Freddie has a dream that notably takes place in a movie theater, accompanied by a movie dream, with its assertive off-screen voices and half-presence. He awakens to find the dream's circumstances real, despite manifest impossibilities. Some sort of important integration is transpiring. Freddie is shifting ground—from the chaos of poisonous drink; blind, contradictory impulses forever at war; and the impersonation of speech and bodily expression, since neither agency seems to be *his*—toward the healing inducements of form. Listening to his own imagination, Freddie becomes responsive in a fuller way to the possibility—indeed, the strong likelihood—of another's reality. This path to another's reality is linked to his earlier memory possession of Doris, a "saving remnant" he can attend to and inwardly transform.

As Félix Ravaisson writes in his groundbreaking 1837 defense of habit as a value (*De l'habitude*), "the idea becomes being. . . . Habit becomes more and more a *substantial idea*" (quoted in Fried, 66, emphasis added). Although Doris is confirmed as gone and Freddie is resigned to never finding or having her, his imagination survives the loss. He has acquired the *habit* of imagining, in a manner that steadies him. It is no longer the whirlwind of brutal, maddening fantasy that widens the chasm between himself and a tenable, credible world. The habit of imagining *connectedness* has been acquired: "this immediate intelligence [of habit] where subject and object are confounded, is a *real* intuition, in which the real and the ideal, being and thought are fused together" (quoted in Fried, 66). Freddie Quell imagines his way back (in sleep) to his habitual relationship with Dodd, but although the dream conversation makes reference to the past and the riddle of origins, it is also a summons to advance, to meet Dodd in a new, future place where he is waiting for him, and "missing" him. They both acknowledge the mutual benefit of this strange partnership, and that their roles are structured on meaningful repetition. The dream talk recapitulates Freddie's creative imagining in his earlier therapy sessions as he repetitively moved back and forth between wall and window. In this simple, habitual pattern, the imagination was both grounded and free to open. In the imagined movie theater scene and the previous actual encounter with Doris's mother, Freddie's unreflective instincts are slowly surrendering, inwardly, to the curative force of habit. Freddie has previously depended on blind assertions of defiant refusal and incomprehension, akin to an untamed animal's freedom from social constraints; he fears nothing more than the coercion of fixed response. What seems to shift, markedly, in the movie theater, is his need to rebel against the role he has been assigned. In his completed journey to Doris's old home, he has ceased to rebel against the memory image of Doris, a girl who "laid claims" by counting on him to answer her letters, expecting him to come back and "do his part," and meet her halfway in love. Now, in his phone conversation with Dodd, he seems to recognize that his freedom to flee has perhaps interfered with a better freedom, the freedom to accept and repeat the role he has, for sufficiently good reasons, been directed to play by the master, because he needed its boundaries, its often painful limits. From the depths of his newfound imaginative being, he receives a call from Dodd to come to England, and he heeds that call, repeating a pattern he himself has established.

Anderson visualizes Freddie's trip to England as a repetition of the high-angle view of the sea waves, churning with whiteness, which opened the film. Initially the waves were succeeded by an image of a wary, lost soldier, peering out anxiously, bracing himself for unspecified disaster. The waves returned again during Freddie's first voyage on the *Aletheia*, with Dodd and his wedding party. The chaos of the sea, in our final sighting of it, gives no hint of taming, no lessening of turbulence or indifferent immensity. But as a repeating, reclaimed image, it enters into a dialogue with form. Freddie possibly recognizes, as we do, that his retreats and returns constitute a pattern, that he is not merely a storm-tossed creature, a heap of fragments, sheltered alike from habit and any knowledge that "sticks." He arrives at the grand English building where the school is housed with something of his phantom nature still intact. He seems indefinite in his aims, unsure of himself, but arguably less at war with the fact of his ongoing confusion. It is not clear why Freddie has made an ocean voyage to look up Dodd again, apart from honoring the master's dream invitation to rejoin him. Possibly what has impelled him to embark on this journey is the same drive that led him to seek out Doris: a need to go back and find if something "real" in relation to himself awaits him there. He may be trying to square his present, highly tentative sense of himself—this person that now has an outline he can provisionally imagine—with the puzzling welter of past circumstance. Freddie has developed an "internal spectator," a phrase of David Hume's that Vermeule examines in her discussion of Hume's theory of pride, to evaluate attributes of himself, "creating in essence a formalized, internalized version of the 'personal' relation" (*Party*, 177). This internal spectator, though only partially formed, moves Freddie in the direction of self-awareness.

Dodd once cautioned his fellow shipboard passengers to "watch their step" as they debarked, passing from a steep, slippery gangplank to solid ground. What we have noted Freddie doing is watching certain "steps" he takes as he enters the mammoth school, with Dodd's vaulted, cathedral-like office. Freddie recalls taking the photograph of Dodd that appears on the school brochure, and claims it as his work when speaking to the female staff members at the table in the school entryway. Once he has been admitted to Dodd's imperial command post, he playfully discloses to Dodd his gift of Kool cigarette packages as though it were contraband, thus honoring Dodd's phone call request, and demonstrating that he has held on to the details—even if they are merely dream details. He then steps behind Dodd's desk to initiate a reconciliation embrace, and attentively wipes off the dust and dirt that his hug has left on Dodd's suit coat. He also tests the immaculate cleanliness of Dodd's desktop with his fingers, immediately after the coat brushing, as though performing a witty comparison of the former insubordinate apprentice, soiled by the debris of experience, and the spotless grand desk of Dodd's "settled place."

In his subsequent interview with Peggy and Dodd, Freddie inquires of Peggy about the current welfare of Elizabeth, her daughter, with whom he has had some clandestine romantic involvement. Here again we see Freddie acknowledging human linkage in small but meaningful ways. He displays his newfound habit of imagining himself as someone with a past to call his own, a past that connects with the present moment. Freddie does not accept Peggy's verdict that he is "ill" simply because he doesn't "look well." He tells her that the way she says he looks is not how he is. Such a statement implies that he has acquired at least somewhat more stability in self-assessment and that he has become mindful of the effect he produces on others. When Peggy departs the room after declaring that he still shows no willingness to "get better" and that further dealings with him are "pointless," he placidly quips to Dodd that she "hasn't gotten any softer." This is another demonstration of Freddie making a memory comparison. More importantly, he is able to assess Peggy's determined opposition to him without resorting to resentment or an outbreak of temper.

Alone again with Dodd, Freddie rather quickly comes to the realization that there is no position for him with the master that he could bring himself to accept. Floored by this revelation, Dodd begins to deride Freddie's sailor's notion that he is free to go wherever he pleases, and his delusion that he can proceed to live his life in some "landless latitude" without a master, a feat that so far, in Dodd's estimation, no one in human history has ever accomplished. Freddie, unrelenting, replies by requesting that Dodd settle the question of where they first met, which Dodd had promised in Freddie's movie theater dream. (Freddie refers to the dream as "dream" but still assumes it was a shared experience. Topping the peculiarity of Freddie's sense of what Dodd must remember from the dream phone call is Dodd's instant acquiescence to Freddie's conviction that such a pledge was indeed given.) Dodd's account of the first "long-ago" meeting extends the chimerical logic of the shared phone call. The meeting transpired in a previous life, before any of the horror and damage of *this* existence had broken Freddie to pieces. Dodd recalls their time together in the Franco-Prussian war of 1870–71, when Paris was under siege and they were both message senders, working side by side as "members of the pigeon post." Their task was to send balloons bearing mail and dispatches through the fiercely maintained Prussian "communication blockade." Dodd lays particular emphasis on the fact that only *two* mail balloons of all they sent out failed to reach their destination. These were simply lost, for undetermined reasons. As Freddie and Dodd sit one last time regarding each other on either side of Dodd's judicial desk, stymied by Freddie's decision not to return to Cause service and by Dodd's answering threat to be his merciless sworn foe in any meeting they may have in a "future life," they become the two lost mail balloons of Dodd's reminiscence. Like these message-laden flights that went astray and came to naught, Freddie and Dodd have ultimately proved unable to penetrate the dense "communication blockade" arrayed against them. All of their anomalous, futile efforts to discover what joins them and to make that bond secure have "come to naught."

In this scene, note that Freddie does not strike the viewer as cured either *of* Dodd or *by* him. We are somewhat at a loss to determine what such a persuasive cure might entail or look like. It is arguably the case that Freddie's slow advance toward a form of his own is chiefly notable for not accommodating any form that Dodd might now prescribe for him. Freddie repeats his familiar action of turning away, but not in a manner that rebukes Dodd or renews his largely helpless, ineffectual rebellion. He has come back to Dodd, in effect, "to see what he can see." Freddie's visit to the English "school," as a nongraduate dropout, can perhaps best be accounted for as an attempt to test the validity of his own dream of Dodd. He is "watching his step" as he consults a functioning internal spectator, trusting his still-primitive imagination to verify a "personal" relation to the things he has been through. He wants to look hard enough at Dodd to actually recognize him as someone other—someone outside of himself but also, crucially, someone inside. This is not a simple distinction for Freddie to arrive at. He needs to give this majestic phantom further edges.

When Dodd, after realizing that things are impossible, begins to sing "I'd love to get you on a slow boat to China," we are once again ushered into one of those half-awake, half-dreaming spaces that *The Master* abounds in. It is a deeply intimate communication that feels continuous with the movie theater dream, Dodd's hornpipe with the naked bacchants, and Doris singing her way under the unfading apple tree. Once more, we cannot settle the question of where precisely we are. Dodd's song truthfully conveys his consistent but peculiar yearning for exclusive possession of Freddie and his need "to melt his heart of stone." One believes that the song, as in opera, would make its large, unhidden acknowledgment only at this juncture, because the two men have reached the close of their time together. We can also accept the likelihood of Freddie being vulnerable to the gift that Dodd is offering him. Dodd chooses to sing his devotion rather than to retreat, vindictively, unappeasably, behind his mask of authority. Freddie maintains eye contact throughout Dodd's impassioned lullaby and absorbs certain phrases so piercingly that a solitary tear is released and slides (after how much pent-upness and withholding) down his cheek. And yet the air of enchantment is strong throughout this performance. The nautical theme of the song; Dodd's tender handing over of mastery; his sudden capacity to express everything previously kept secret through a sentimental lyric teetering on the verge of comic collapse—all seem to proclaim some spell at work from the "landless latitudes" of fantasy. But which figure is more the source of the fantasy, if fantasy is what it is? Perhaps, like the movie theater telephone call, they own it jointly. And this dream-waking event manages formally to make a nest for Dodd inside Doris's first mythical (or, to put it more grandly, mythological) act of singing. The lyric of "Slow Boat to China" hauntingly braids together the wistful anticipation of a voyage that would have time enough to remedy all ills, with the resignation that, alas, it will never take place. (The two men's first meeting *in this life* took place on a ship named *Aletheia*, a name that joins "truth" with "unclosedness" in Greek.) Freddie's release from the captivity of the Doris image after he takes the trip that makes her absence real to himself is repeated with Dodd's song, where *everything* is beautifully made to coincide with *nothing*, before vanishing from sight. It is as though Freddie has at last succeeded in taking a memory photograph that serves his needs—a keeper!—of Dodd as himself, rather than as the posing master.

* * *

The Master's ending expends considerable effort keeping the conflict between form and formlessness alive for the spectator and refusing the distinct advantages that endings usually confer. Let us identify the persisting tensions at work in our last sightings of Freddie, starting with the severance of his ties with Dodd. Perhaps he lacks even a dim understanding of why he refuses Dodd's offer to rejoin the Cause. Perhaps he declines on a mad whim, because "no" is the reflex response of his jumbled temperament, his familiar, incoherent fallback position. Freddie's imagination is preparing sturdier ground for him to occupy in the visit to Dodd, as I have already argued, but Peggy's dismissive view of him as a permanent lost soul is not easy to cast aside. We might quarrel with her Cause-based assessment of Freddie and yet have stored up sufficient frustration with him and doubt that we cannot dispel the mostly disconcerting image he projects. It is certainly not difficult to be put off by Freddie's near-silence during his final meeting with the Dodds and his lingering air of indecipherability. Freddie's wandering amble down a country road following the meeting is shadowed by hints that he is once more entirely adrift, that his movements are aimless, and that he has no clear sense of purpose or destination. His ongoing "contrariness" might appear a condition not so much chosen as ineradicably determined, something unexamined still and at odds with his fitful intimations of incipient selfhood. The possibility remains that every thought Freddie takes in will soon fall by the wayside, dissolving as opposed to gaining hold within him. His country ramble, followed by an appearance in a tavern, might well incline us to believe that his burgeoning imagination has already failed him now that he is once again almost helplessly, involuntarily on his own. Stopping at the first convenient place to get drunk is hardly a fresh initiative; he chaotically revives a destructive pattern that he hasn't enough presence of mind to identify, much less repair.

We have here sizable evidence of Freddie's persisting formlessness, demonstrating the unlikelihood that form will secure a victory for him—even one so fleeting as Robert Frost's "momentary stay against confusion." Yet in the fog of Freddie's recurring scatteredness there are meaningful flashes of something akin to grace. Some furthering of the habit of imagining personhood is visible in Freddie's increasing concern with closeness, and the recognition that other lives have a direct and important bearing on his own. Shortly after arriving at the pub, Freddie invites a woman (Jennifer Neala Page) to join him for a drink. His request feels more relaxed than insistent. She smiles back, unintimidated. The way in which she's framed against a dark background in warm light creates the sense that she is some sort of memory image. She reminds Freddie of someone, though we cannot place her ourselves. She might, for all we know (as first-time viewers) be a minor character who figured briefly in a previous episode, but if so, we have forgotten who she is. Freddie, in other words, appears perceptually ahead of us in what he intuits, recognizes, feels.

Abruptly we cut to a shot of the two of them in bed in a room suffused with a blue that conjures the sea, and with a vaulted ceiling that echoes the grand edifice to which Dodd's church and school have relocated. The woman, who is more corpulent and appealingly ordinary in appearance than Freddie's earlier female "prey," is astride him, and they are in the midst of slow, gentle intercourse. This is the first instance in the film when we witness Freddie engaged in sex with a living person. Until now we have been granted glimpses of him ravishing and jerking off on the sand woman, engaged in drunken foreplay with Martha (which apparently comes to nothing), masturbatory fantasy combined with voyeuristic peeping, and a flagrant proposition to another young stranger affiliated with the Cause, whose precise motive and outcome remain ambiguous. He has also been the target of Elizabeth Dodd's secret physical advances, though that encounter seems a potential instance of waking-dream blurring. Freddie also retains a memory of his farewell embrace with Doris. It is fair to say, then, that Freddie has been kept on the outskirts of full physical intimacy until this final scene in *The Master*. Interruption, self-imposed barriers, and fantasy have broken off all previous overtures. This bedroom scene in England therefore represents another emotional advance (at least in the logic of spectator investment). It is a consummation of sorts, somewhat arbitrary no doubt, but still "devoutly to be wished."

While it is undeniable that danger hovers in the room where Freddie and his new acquaintance are having sex, Anderson includes that feeling of danger as a necessary, indeed vital component of any genuine attempt at human connection. Danger certifies the validity of both the emotional objective and the obstacles unavoidably in play. Freddie has done some preliminary drinking, but he has not drunk enough to sweep away the reality, the human *thereness* of his partner. He is recumbent on the bed, facing upward beneath the woman who is astride him, and visibly content with his submissive position. When Freddie begins to introduce bits of Dodd's remembered processing exercise into their talk, in the manner of an instructor, he remains playful and considerate. Urging her not to blink as she speaks her name aloud repeatedly—"Winn Manchester"—he does not seem intent on giving orders, on wearing down her resistance, or causing her to lose the sense of her name (the latter having been Dodd's tactic with him). His aim is not disorientation but drawing her out further, as she looms above him. She is a curious mixture of shyness, assurance, careful self-protection, childlikeness (without too many romantic illusions), and formidable solidity. Freddie continues to gaze up at her as she agrees to repeat her name without blinking. It seems that in doing so, Winn is making her name more rather than less real to herself, and is pleased to claim it as her own.

Once we give up the thought of danger resurfacing, we may begin to marvel at how Freddie uses the master's remembered words from a cheerfully submissive position. He is not gaining the upper hand; he is beckoning Winn to come closer to him, in her own right, and with an increased sense of the freedom that listening and joining bring. Freddie watches her come into focus as a fragile entity shivering in a body that seeks warmth, quickening contact, and repose, as he does. She appears to have entered that realm of comfort and self-possession in nakedness that the women in Dodd's "A-Roving" dance achieved. And though Freddie is still a watcher, he is not this time at a prurient spy's remove from the experience he observes: he partakes of it as one fully engaged.

Freddie inquires if Winn has "lived before," and she is perplexed but not nonplussed. He asks if what is going on is "maybe just a normal life." She expresses the hope that it isn't that, making a joke of it, which leads him to commend her for her bravery. Might he be referring obliquely to her bravery in revealing herself to him with so little apparent strain or misgiving, as well as her bravery in wanting to push beyond normative boundaries? Neither of them feels disposed to stay serious about bravery, and she smiles, leaning forward and pressing against him as they find common ground for laughter. There is a beautifully casual moment, just before the film ends, when Freddie laughs about his penis having "fallen out" while he and Winn have been chatting, then coaxes her to "stick it back in." The hazards of "feeling unmanned," or ceding control to another, are effortlessly bypassed. He exhibits no need to compensate for any of his recent losses by proving something to her. Nor is there any defensive turn toward excess.

For so much of *The Master*'s length, and perhaps even at the end because his elusiveness remains so strongly in play, Freddie Quell strikes us as a confounding distortion of the human image. Anderson strives to revise the customary balance of power in movie narrative by placing a character who embodies formlessness as convincingly as any in film, decisively and relentlessly in the foreground. The agents of form (Dodd, the members of the Cause, the larger culture) are placed somewhat behind Freddie, and even after a long, concerted struggle to come to terms with what he is and give him a shape they regard as communicable, they never successfully reduce his radical unfittedness nor successfully reclaim the foreground for themselves. We become persuaded, perhaps, that "form" possesses the wrong tools for solving the abiding mystery of this distortion. Freddie is "unfitted," and he may well be unfit for fitting by any known means of social, spiritual, or psychological rehabilitation. Though it is difficult to gain enough sense of Freddie's distorting lens to identify with it (or him), I also think it is hard to dismiss Freddie altogether, even for viewers who grow quickly impatient with his unruly, muddled demands. He is tied, not so much to what is openly or secretly rebellious in us in a conscious way, as he is to what is most amorphous in our cobbled-together notion of who we are. He is the abiding, often monstrous sense of lack; the alien transition spaces between our efforts at adjustment; the multitude of unseemly, inadmissible failures in our solitary confinement within our own psyche and skin; the welter of futile doings with no plan or backing; our perverse uprisings against our apparent best interests.

Anderson concludes his movie with an episode of inconclusive togetherness. Freddie is permitted a last dream memory of the monumental sand woman on the beach. His head rests close to a huge sand breast and its eerily tempting nipple. Behind him a blur of figures move rapidly, part of the bustling, ordinary life of the world, but remote from Freddie and out of focus. The sand woman by the seashore in the waning days of official war is a way station in a trip still farther back: a dream of the first encounter with mother, a chance for the crooked child to start over, this time fully beheld and properly nurtured. Winn's body is invitingly maternal, and her presence has perhaps released this last image to Freddie's imagination in a felicitous fashion. Winn has afforded Freddie a brief interlude of solace, musically confirmed by the song that appears with the sand woman and carries us into the credits: "Changing Partners," performed by Helen Forrest. The song assures us that even if the initial waltz is brief, it can be wondrous, and after a change of partners, or many changes, one can work one's way back to the first partner who held you in her arms, the one who *made* the world. All of Paul Thomas Anderson's films seem to arrive, finally, at some version of the sand woman and can proceed no further. Freddie's imagination is a clamorous, still-evolving infant, acquiring habits of being that may throw light into the obscure depths from which he once upon a time emerged—"scarce half-made up." He is a creature whose connections to things became hopelessly frayed early on, and stayed that way for formless reasons. Once again, by some Dodd-like dispensation, the archetypal mother is near and vivid—its breast is within reach. But if one takes hold of it, it will crumble, and soon the sailor's sea tide will rise again and carry all of her away.

Notes

1. By innocence I mean (for both the Claudia and Jim characters) an open-to-wonder, ardent, almost otherworldly connection with the things that happen to them. Their capacity for imaginative vision and wide-ranging sympathy remains intact, no matter what the internal damage. Phil, the only singer to be paired with another person during "Wise Up," and whose words have only to do with Earl's suffering, is also an innocent of the sort I'm describing—a creature of deep, disarming empathy and love. He appears to have no protection against the flood of fellow feeling brought on by the ordeal of Earl's death struggle. He is most childlike in his lack of adequate safeguards for his own fragility. Phil is an unlikely sort of hospice worker in his unfailing selflessness. His saintly, weeping caregiver innocence seems a kind of fantasy island at the heart of *Magnolia*.

2. Jimmy Gator and Jim Kurring make parallel invasions of Claudia's apartment early in the film. The "unforgivable" father's unannounced arrival at her apartment when she is in bed with a strange man and her shrieking expulsion of him when he attempts to placate her is merged with benevolent *Jim* Kurring's exposure of her in the throes of a cocaine high, and her subsequent efforts to get rid of him (and keep what is hers hidden) as his attraction to her becomes evident. Jim's guileless buildup of romantic pressure during his search of her apartment is presented as an indecipherable (to Claudia, and perhaps to the viewer) variation on her father's earlier visit, although the viewer as yet has no knowledge of Jimmy's guile-filled sexual abuse of his daughter. Jim's decency may prove a workable, partial antidote to Jimmy's history of vile exploitation, but Anderson characteristically makes the potential benefactor and the heinous violator confusingly echo each other. It is as though escape for Claudia is only conceivable through a dreamlike reenactment of Jimmy's malignant violation of her space. An aggressive break-in is an inescapable part of the saving turnaround: Jim's desire to be worthy of her romantic interest.

3. So much of surrealism's freedom was in direct response to the cataclysm of the First World War. The primary Breton question was might the dream life grant us an authentic freedom, a freedom as authentic as death?

4. Intriguingly, this flashback appeared in the shooting script, in which Anderson notes that the death will be shown in "very graphic" detail. In the screenplay,

Gundha perishes in a dirt slide rather than being struck by a falling section of the drill. He slips down fifteen feet after the cave-in to "drown in mud," as Daniel's line reads in the screenplay. Changing the manner of his dying strengthens the parallel with Ailman's death.

5. Time, like subjectivity, is nearly immobilized in this narrative. We are initially alerted that the period is a transition between war and peacetime. The aftermath of the Second World War gives few hints of internal readjustment or settling down. The heightened artifice and commodity fetishism of the "peacetime" spaces seem mainly an instrument of repression. Through the romantic sheen of a bustling department store, say, we catch flickers of disquiet and trauma shadows, like those T. S. Eliot assigned J. Alfred Prufrock, "as if a magic lantern threw the nerves in patterns on a screen," for which there is no available public language. The landscape of peace, in other words, is a set of screens of *false* adjustment. Every ordering frame oozes with the tension of what is suppressed or withheld or denied. Time is itself stuck and must make do with a fantasy of forward movement until it is itself "freed up" somehow. The laws of cause and effect have gone missing, or at least appear to be hopelessly scrambled. Actions inevitably take place in a sequence, but there is no available monitor to account for why *this* follows *that*. Neither dramatic nor psychological continuity comes to the rescue. The war and its aftermath are braided together in a dreadful time-knot. Who can untie it?

Composite Interview

The following composite interview is constructed from segments of various interviews Paul Thomas Anderson has given about his feature films and also interviews with actors (e.g., Philip Seymour Hoffman on *The Master*).

Boogie Nights

The basic bones of the plot is an old backstage musical. Mark is like this kid from the suburbs who gets a big break. He utilizes this one talent to become a porn star. It's an ensemble movie, but the wire running through it is Mark.

—*Toronto's Eye*, 1997

Q: What things determined the style of the film for you?

A: In terms of structure and emotion, it was clear: first half/second half, '70s/'80s. And this is probably more an afterthought, but I felt it should maybe resemble my personal experience of watching a porno film: incredibly funny one second, turns me on the next, then incredibly depressing and so on, up and down.

Q: One of the things that's interesting about *Boogie Nights* is its tone shifts, for instance between dramatic and comic/parodic.

A: Two of my favorite movies are F. W. Murnau's *Sunrise* [1927] and Jonathan Demme's *Something Wild* [1986], what I call gearshift movies, that can change tones [*snaps fingers*] like that. I like to see that in movies because that's what real life is like, and it's also good storytelling.

—*Sight and Sound*, 1998

A: There are younger girls I've talked to in the [porn] industry and you can't get a handle on them. You spend an hour grilling them—nothing. You won't get anywhere. "What's going on with you?" "You know." "Well, how do you feel?" "Oh, you know . . ." It's my theory they will one day burst the way Rollergirl bursts.

Q: That's interesting, because what's striking about *Boogie Nights* is that none of the characters seems to know themselves or have real emotional honesty.

A: I think they have an emotional honesty but there's something stripped and raw and childlike about a lot of them. And that's what I saw in that world, so it's truthful. But for instance Jack introduces himself as "Jack Horner"—I think he's a character who probably forgets his real name. And in the course of five minutes the Mark Wahlberg character goes from being Eddie Adams to Dirk Diggler to being "John." There's no going back for this kid, no way back to Eddie Adams. And then there's a third identity, Brock Landers. In the documentary, he's telling Amber, "I am Dirk Diggler, Brock Landers is a character that I play"—but he's looking in the mirror at the end of the movie and says "That's right. I'm Brock Landers."

Q: This is the core of the film, everyone struggling to become some kind of alter ego and deny the reality of who they are.

A: Well, who wants to be the kid in Torrance being beaten up by his mother?

—*Sight and Sound*, 1998

Q: One scene in *Boogie Nights* that was very effective was when Dirk's mother screams at him and kicks him out of the house. A lot of people who come from dysfunctional families told me that scene was like something out of their lives. Were you surprised a lot of people could not only relate to the scene but also thought it was one of the strongest in the film?

A: Yeah, but I was also surprised by how many people thought it was one of the weakest scenes in the movie. When his mother comes at him like that, she's really crazy and out of control. She's kind of without motivation to a certain extent. I think one of the greatest mistakes that I've made in the past and that a writer can make is, "What's the character's motivation?" Well, a lot of times it's so fucking confused and so polluted that you really have no idea. That woman is pretty nuts, and I think it's sometimes hard for an audience to grab a hold of a character whose intentions aren't clear. You don't really know what the fuck she's yelling about. You know she has an odd jealousy towards him or towards the neighborhood girl that he's banging, so she's upset about that, but her actions are so manic, you can't get a hold of them. I was just really glad that the actress in the scene didn't require a lot of clarity on her behavior, because I couldn't have given it. I really wrote what made sense, and what made sense was sometimes so illogical. There are some people that saw it and said, "That scene doesn't make sense! Why is she going crazy?" And I would just say, "You know what? I've never been able to figure it out." But it sure makes sense, and I've sure been there.

—*Creative Screenwriting*, 2000

Q: Isn't the coda a fantasy redemptive happy ending?

A: No, I tried to come up with the saddest happy ending I could come up with. It would be way too easy to punish all those characters, to have them die or whatever. That's not how I felt about them, and that's not usually the case in real life. The bottom line is that Dirk Diggler and everyone else are preparing to go and make another porn movie. But after this whole journey, what have they learned? If that's happy and redemptive, OK.

—*Sight and Sound*, 1998

Magnolia

When you're writing, you're writing who you are, and your flaws—but you're also making sure to write what you wish you could say. The person you wish you could be.

—*San Francisco Chronicle*, 2000

I hope that . . . [the film is] not entirely specific to the [San Fernando] Valley. The characters are easily found here, but hopefully the themes don't parallel anything that is happening in the Valley. But who knows? There's certainly an interesting sort of grid effect to the Valley that, maybe, structurally, means something to the movie.

—*LA Daily News*, 1999

This movie is trying harder to face up to family a little bit more. It's trying to be a little bit harder on it, in a good way . . . *Boogie Nights* is saying, "Just hang out with your friends, it's a lot easier to hang out there than it is to go back home." This movie is saying, "Smarten up and go home. Or at least try."

—Associated Press, 2000

Writing that scene, when Phil has just dropped the morphine into Earl's mouth, I was crying myself as I was writing it; it was all coming from a true emotional place, and I suddenly realized, I've always wanted to do a musical number, how about right here? . . . And in production, everybody was really curious about, well, is it going to work? Can he pull this off? But every time we'd get to the point of shooting a character's "Wise Up" scene, it was kind of like, okay, ante up. Will it work as well with this person as it did with the other one before . . . and it did, every time.

—*Magnolia* Script Book interview, 2000

I get up early to write and always get coffee at Winchell's [Donut House]. There was this woman who had her car door open and was clearly dressed up from the night before—this was six in the morning—and she was crying her eyes out, playing "I Will Always Love You" at full blast, singing along with it in the middle of the parking lot. It f—ing broke my heart, and it made sense to me that you would sing along and wallow in it at that slit-your-wrist moment.

—*Entertainment Weekly*, 2000

Q: Like the other characters in the film, the character played by Tom Cruise says "I love you" in his own way, that is by saying "I hate you"?

A: Yes, that's exactly what I wanted to hear you say. Frank Mackey [Cruise] feels anger toward his dying father[,] but even when he's saying he's glad he's dying, these are words filled with love that he's pronouncing; he doesn't want him to die, no way. What's even more disturbing about Frank is that he's full of contradictions. Here's a kid whose mother dies and whose father abandons [them]. And he'll be mad at his mom until she dies and mad at women in general since he gives seminars on how to seduce and destroy women. There, you feel like saying "Hey wait a second! Why aren't you mad at your dad? Why is your mother the mean one? It doesn't make any sense!" That's the kind of mistake we all do in our lives. It's universal. That's what makes the strength of the character played by Tom.

—*Cinelive*, 2000

Q: What, in one sentence, would you say *Magnolia* is about? Would you say that it's about life, love and dying? You have Jason Robards [the Earl Partridge character] dying of cancer.

A: Yes, it's about life, love and dying, but it sounds presumptuous if I say that, and people would probably stay away from the movie. Yes, Robards was dying of [lung] cancer, and here I am smoking a cigarette in front of you. But the film hasn't made me stop smoking. I don't really think that movies influence people in that way. I doubt that a movie makes a big change in a person's life—only in, maybe, a very subtle way. There are parallel stories, but I like for the audience to fill in the gaps.

—*Virginian-Pilot*, 2000

Punch-Drunk Love

I tried to make this simple little movie, but sometimes simplicity can be so complicated.

—*Times UK*, 2003

Q: Do love and aggression go hand in hand for you?

A: That question is too big for me. I don't know if that's true. Maybe it is a feeling of being run over by love and not being able to steer it in one direction—not to know how to get control of it again.

Q: In . . . *Punch-Drunk Love* there is a type of catastrophic whirlpool, in which your lead actor Adam Sandler is the catalyst. Where do these ideas come from?

A: From this secret place, where all ideas come from. But the situation, where one is pulled into such a whirlpool, is very old: that is Buster Keaton: the little man in the middle, who has shit always flying around him. One of the proven methods to bring verve into a story is to have a little fun.

—*Der Spiegel*, 2003

Q: All comedians are said to be tragic at heart.

A: I think it's true. It's probably something to do with feeling like an impostor. You beat yourself up and you make yourself feel like you're kinda worthless. It can turn into a rage.

—Ebert, 2002

Acceptance always feels good. But I've always got to ruin it in some way, though, so I don't feel comfortable. I mean, I always feel like an imposter anyway[,] so when (acceptance) fades, I'm always consumed by "what am I doing?" and "what do I want?"

—*Seattle P-I*, 2002

Q: Why Utah?

A: That's where Dean [Trumbull] is from. I'd been to a town called Provo, Utah, which is a really bizarre place. You've never seen anything like Provo, Utah. It's gay and it's Mormon and there are Mexicans and they're all racist a little bit. It's weird. And that's just . . . Provo is a good spot for a phone-sex place. My casting director came to me one day and she said, "Well I found this one guy," then she showed me his picture and she said he's got three crazy brothers that look bizarre and just like him. I thought it'd be so great to have the guy with seven sisters being chased by four blonde brothers. I thought it was a great concept. Almost like a fairy tale. Something really old-fashioned. It got to be like a myth story at that point.

—BAM Q&A, 2003

I wanted just to write a real guy [Barry Egan] not to be afraid of getting caught in the trap of character. Writers are always worried about moments that are "out of character," but everyone does things they don't want to do, where you wonder "where did that come from?" We're all a bit of a mess.

—*LA Times*, 2002

There is an old rule that says you can annoy your audience for two minutes, but don't let them know ten seconds in advance what's going to happen. I try to surprise the audience—they resist that. [Anderson is referring here to his frequent swerves away from conventional narrative sense in *Punch-Drunk Love*.]

—*Der Spiegel*, 2003

There Will Be Blood

All of life's questions and answers are in *The Treasure of the Sierra Madre* It's about greed and ambition and paranoia and looking at the worst parts of yourself. When I was writing *There Will Be Blood*, I would put *The Treasure of the Sierra Madre* on before I went to bed at night, just to fall asleep to it.

—*New York Times*, 2007

To see that [full-fledged greed and paranoia on display] in a film, or see that from these filmmakers, is encouraging. You say, "Shit. You know; okay. That's good." But more or less, too, is that when I look at it, it's an adventure film or it's an action film—but it's really just a play. It's really just these three guys at each other. It's just dialogue and the three of them desperate, and ambitious, and jealous, and greedy, and all those things. It's a play between the three of them, but because of the setting and everything else, it's really an adventure film, an action film. I thought, "Fuck, alright, that's good, you know?" And really, more than anything else, it was a way to figure out how to economically tell a story, because

I knew that to try to tell the story, we weren't going to have that much money to do it. So it was, "How to do kind of an epic story, but in a small way, with a few settings?"

—Museum of the Moving Image, 2007

Q: [Is there] anything you could say about the pacing of the film, a film that moves around through so many different periods in time?

A: Well, a lot of it has to do with Dylan Tichenor, who's the editor of the film. We cut the movie in New York, ironically enough . . . and I think it really helped us, actually. It was great to go from West Texas and the middle of nowhere, and edit the movie in New York City. It was so strange. You know, all these quiet scenes and everything, and all you could hear was horns outside honking, and fucking steel, and metal, and everything else. I don't know, but I think it was good. It actually helped us pace the movie faster. (*Laughs*) Every Wednesday night, we would have steak and vodka night—where it was just steak and vodka; we'd have no sides—and we said, "This is what the movie should be, steak and vodka." (*Laughter*)

—Museum of the Moving Image, 2007

ANDERSON: I saw *Bodysong* at a film festival in Rotterdam on a rainy afternoon . . . and I just fell in love with what he [music director Jonny Greenwood] did for that film. . . . Then when I heard "Popcorn," I just loved the sounds of it, and I just couldn't put my finger on what I liked about it. Because I would always hear it when it wasn't on, like a phantom limb, just the strange sounds of it. I had been listening to it over and over again, and then when not listening to it, would feel like I had left the stereo on in the other room or something.

[JONNY] GREENWOOD: That's mad, because that's exactly why I wrote that! That's really weird, that you saw that in it. The whole idea was about when you think there's some music playing, and there isn't. You know, like when you're doing a Hoover or a vacuum cleaner and you think there's a radio playing as well, and you turn it off, but there isn't any music on. That was the starting-off point for that piece, anyway.

—*Entertainment Weekly*, 2007

Q: The film is dedicated to Robert Altman. Was your experience working with him on *Prairie Home Companion* [2006] what you hoped it would be?

A: I got to watch Bob navigate that film, and I watched how good he was at evading questions, in the best way. He was really good at not committing himself too early to something. He didn't impose his will early. He loved to work with people. He loved to see what they came up with. He would give things time to settle, to rise or to fall, and watching him do that was a great lesson in patience. Because at the end of the day, he invited everybody in to work on this film, but he ended up getting exactly what he wanted, and everyone else felt that they had been part of it, because they had. They really made the film with Bob. How he did that was a lesson to me.

—Onion AV Club, 2008

Q: You've been known to befriend and work with people much older than you, [i.e.] Philip Baker Hall, Robert Altman, Jason Robards. Why is that?

A: A lot of those guys were the same age my father was. I've always loved that group—Bob Ridgely, too, Philip was younger than Bob and Jason. But Jason and my dad were all pretty much the same age. That's what it is, really; an affection for that kind of man. There's a sense of humour about those guys that . . . I was really sad when Bob died, for a number of reasons, but above all because he was the last person like that I knew who went. I felt like, "That's it. I don't have any of them left. I don't have anybody left that was in World War II or had that kind of sense."

—*Mean Magazine*, 2008

The Master

PHILIP SEYMOUR HOFFMAN: What do they [Freddie/Joaquin Phoenix and Dodd/Philip Seymour Hoffman] see in each other? I guess I still don't understand. I don't think they see something in each other, they feel something in each other. It's a sense of each other and I think they identify with each other. They're coming from different places but they're more the same, they're both wild beasts I think. One of them has just tamed it somehow and he's trying to teach other people how to do that. But ultimately that's where the doubt comes in, where the whole reluctant prophet thing comes in. Ultimately, he wants to be wild like Freddie is, so there's this real attraction there over those two very things: wanting to be tame it and wanting to be wild. I think that's basically what life is. I think that's what we'd wake up every morning going, "Fuck, why can't I just run naked through the streets of Venice and just eat and shit. Why can't I just do that and have it be okay? Is it possible that I can just have sex with everyone I see today? No I can't. But I wish that was possible. So I think I'm just going to go find my Master, he'll teach me how not to do that . . ." It's the age-old story of a man who needs guidance, finds a mentor, they become co-dependent, the man leaves, and the one who is actually hurt is the mentor.

—Venice Q&A, 2012

Q: We can quite easily understand Freddie's attraction to the Master—but how do you explain the Master's attraction to Freddie?

A: It's funny—I feel the same way in reverse. It was always easier for me to understand what the Master saw in Freddie—that was always very clear to me . . . I always had to ask myself: Why does Freddie stay around? 'Cause he has such an impulse to go away. And one thing that Joaquin came up with and found was—for a lot of these sailors that had been in the war—when they came back from the war they felt very aimless. Because they didn't have any commander anymore—they enjoyed the part of the military that was very structured, that gave them a commander.

—Paris Press Conference, 2013

Investigating another time when you might have lived is just inherently so hopeful and so optimistic and so sweet to me. You see it in all the things coming out of that time, whether it was music and the songs of that period—everything was about "seeing you again" or "I'll find you someday." . . . You're talking about finding ways to go back in time and to pick up some lost piece—and that stuff is just food and drink to me.

—*Washington Post*, 2012

You know *Casper the Friendly Ghost* we have playing in the movie theater in the film and that's a kind of creation of the '50s. That's like early 1950s—who says ghosts have to be spooky and scary? Why can't they be nice, why can't they try—they're just trying to be our friends. You get into this stuff when you talk about time travel and all that kind of stuff that *The Master* is talking about—*The Master* is going on about linking yourself to the past, and it all feels really good until that kind of moment when you really want to say "Okay, I want to travel back in time. I want to go get that lost love. I want to go hold her hand." And that's when you hit a wall when you can't. It makes it something wonderful that you can do in your mind when you close your eyes, but when you really want to go back and grab that thing, it's not there. You can't do it.

—*Sunday Night Safran*, 2012

Q: I understand that you showed Phoenix the 1955 Lionel Rogosin documentary *On the Bowery* for reference in developing the Freddie character?

A: Yes, it's a great film. We've seen drunks on screen before, but this is something else: the shifts between sadness and hopefulness in the blink of an eye. And also physical stuff: there's not a lot of body fat on those guys—they're men probably 30 years old that look 50 or 60 It was also an influence in the way you're rooting for somebody who behaves destructively. It's like in a horror movie when you know someone is going to go through the door they shouldn't. You know in your bones that these guys are going to keep drinking, but it's still suspenseful in case one of them gets clean—but of course they keep reaching for the bottle. Heartbreaking.

—*Sight and Sound*, 2012

I think that *The Battle of San Pietro* [John Huston, 1945]—to me the best part of that film—yes you have this harrowing war stuff but getting to the end and to see these faces and there's just this kind of relief—not relief, but it's faces. It's not landscapes and explosions—as haunting as that is—the second you see the faces everything comes rapidly into focus. And *Let There Be Light* [John Huston, 1946] is exclusively faces, there's no war footage at all.

—LACMA, 2012

Maybe part of the story [in *The Master*] we were telling is somebody selling transformation and the possibility of transformation. And maybe how either possible that is or how impossible that is so, there's a rub there[,] ya know? . . . If you have a character who, maybe fundamentally is not going to change, then you've got a real screenwriting problem on your hands. And I guess the only thing to do is to invest in *that* in of itself, you know. Invest in a character that cannot change, that maybe the most he can change is to put a suit on him and have him handing flyers on the street and not wallop somebody in the back of the head for not taking the flyer. That's enough of a change. And I suppose it's sort of taking stock and realizing that maybe you're going to tell a story that requires an investment from the audience solely on the characters and at the expense of any possible plot that they might be expecting. And if they do invest with them, then hopefully, ideally, every nuance of their struggle is what makes it dramatic. That every nook and cranny of how that goes can be worth two hours. For some people it probably isn't, you know, it's not enough.

—WGA, 2012

Filmography

This filmography includes short films, feature films, and one documentary film (*Junun*) written and directed by Paul Thomas Anderson.

"The Dirk Diggler Story" (1988)
United States
Producer: Shane Conrad
Director: Paul Thomas Anderson
Screenplay: Paul Thomas Anderson
Cinematography: Paul Thomas Anderson
Makeup: Johann Benét
Principal cast: Michael Stein (Dirk Diggler), Robert Ridgely (Jack Horner), Eddie Delcore (Reed Rothchild), Rusty Schwimmer (Candy Kane), Ernie Anderson (Narrator)
Format: Color
32 min.

"Cigarettes & Coffee" (1993)
United States
Producers: Kirk Baltz, Patrick Hoelck, Wendy Weidman, Shane Conrad
Director: Paul Thomas Anderson
Screenplay: Paul Thomas Anderson
Cinematography: Vincento Baldino, David Phillips
Production design: Kevin Shanks
Principal cast: Kirk Baltz (Douglas Walker), Philip Baker Hall (Sydney), Scott Coffey, Kim Gillingham, Miguel Ferrer (Bill), Michael Harris (Steve), Jennifer Kaplan, Bonnie Fidelman
Format: 16mm, color
24 min.

Hard Eight (1996)
United States

Production: Green Parrot, Rysher Entertainment, Trinity
Executive producers: Hans Brockman, François Duplat, Keith Samples
Producers: Robert Jones, John S. Lyons
Distribution: Metro-Goldwyn-Mayer (MGM)
Director: Paul Thomas Anderson
Assistant directors: Wayne Gee, Rip Murray, Toni Whiteman
Screenplay: Paul Thomas Anderson
Music: Jon Brion, Michael Penn
Cinematography: Robert Elswit
Editing: Barbara Tulliver
Casting: Christine Sheaks
Production design: Nancy Deren
Art direction: Michael Krantz
Set decoration: David A. Koneff
Costume design: Mark Bridges
Makeup: Lydia Milars, Alyson Murphy
Production manager: Craig Markey
Special effects: FTS EFX Inc.
Principal cast: Philip Baker Hall (Sydney), John C. Reilly (John), Gwyneth Paltrow (Clementine), Samuel L. Jackson (Jimmy), Melora Waters (Jimmy's Girl), F. William Parker (Hostage), Philip Seymour Hoffman (Young Craps Player), Richard Gross (Floorman)
Format: 35mm, color
102 min.

Boogie Nights (1997)
United States
Production: New Line Cinema, Lawrence Gordon Productions, Ghoulardi Film Company
Executive producers: Lawrence Gordon
Producers: Paul Thomas Anderson, Lloyd Levin, John S. Lyons, JoAnne Sellar
Distribution: New Line Cinema
Director: Paul Thomas Anderson
Screenplay: Paul Thomas Anderson
Music: Michael Penn
Cinematography: Robert Elswit
Editing: Dylan Tichenor
Casting: Christine Sheaks
Production design: Bob Ziembicki
Art direction: Ted Berner
Set decoration: Sandy Struth
Costume design: Mark Bridges
Principal Cast: Mark Wahlberg (Eddie Adams/Dirk Diggler), Burt Reynolds

(Jack Horner), Julianne Moore (Amber Waves), Luiz Guzmán (Maurice TT Rodriguez), Rico Bueno (Hot Traxx Waiter), John C. Reilly (Reed Rothchild), Nicole Ari Parker (Becky Barnett), Don Cheadle (Buck Swope), Heather Graham (Rollergirl), William H. Macy (Little Bill), Samson Barkhordarian (Hot Traxx Chef), Nina Hartley (Little Bill's Wife), Brad Braeden (Big Stud), Joanna Gleason (Dirk's Mother), Lawrence Hudd (Dirk's Father)
Format: 35mm, color
155 min.

"Flagpole Special" (1998)
United States
Director: Paul Thomas Anderson
Screenplay: Paul Thomas Anderson
Principal cast: Chris Penn, John C. Reilly
17 min.

Magnolia (1999)
United States
Production: Ghoulardi Film Company, New Line Cinema, the Magnolia Project
Executive producers: Michael De Luca, Lynn Harris
Producers: Paul Thomas Anderson, JoAnne Sellar
Distribution: New Line Cinema
Director: Paul Thomas Anderson
Assistant directors: Adam Druxman, Jorge L. Baron, Christina Stauffer
Screenplay: Paul Thomas Anderson
Cinematography: Robert Elswit
Music: Jon Brion
Editing: Dylan Tichenor
Production design: Mark Bridges, William Arnold
Set decoration: Chris Spellman
Costume design: Mark Bridges
Animator: Gray Miller
Special effects: F/X Concepts, Industrial Light & Magic (ILM), Steve Johnson's XFX
Principal cast: Tom Cruise (Frank T.J. Mackey), Jason Robards (Earl Partridge), Julianne Moore (Linda Partridge), Pat Healy (Sir Edmund William Godfrey/Young Pharmacy Kid), Genevieve Zweig (Mrs. Godfrey), Mark Flannagan (Joseph Green), Neil Flynn (Stanley Berry), Rod McLachlan (Daniel Hill), Allan Graf (Firefighter), Patton Oswalt (Delmer Darion), Brad Hunt (Craig Hansen), Chris O'Hara (Sydney Barringer), Clement Blake (Arthur Barringer)
Format: 35mm, color
188 min.

Punch-Drunk Love (2002)
United States
Production: Ghoulardi Film Company, New Line Cinema, Revolution Studios
Producers: Paul Thomas Anderson, Daniel Lupi, JoAnne Sellar
Distribution: Sony Picture Entertainment (SPE)
Director: Paul Thomas Anderson
Screenplay: Paul Thomas Anderson
Music: Jon Brion
Cinematography: Robert Elswit
Editing: Leslie Jones
Casting: Cassandra Kulukundis
Production design: William Arnold
Art direction: Sue Chan
Set decoration: Jay Hart, Lori A. Noyes
Costume design: Mark Bridges
Special effects: F/X Concept, Industrial Light & Magic (ILM)
Principal cast: Adam Sandler (Barry Egan), Emily Watson (Lena Leonard), Philip Seymour Hoffman (Dean Trumbell), Jason Andrews (Operator Carter), Don McManus (Plastic), Luis Guzmán (Lance), Rico Bueno (Rico), Hazel Mailloux (Rhonda), Karen Kilgariff (Anna), Julie Hermelin (Kathleen), Salvador Curiel (Sal), Jorge Barahona (Jorge), Ernesto Quintero (Ernesto)
Format: 35mm, color
95 min.

"Couch" (2003)
United States
Director: Paul Thomas Anderson
Principal cast: Adam Sandler (Couch Testing Man)
Format: Black and white
2 min.

"Blossoms & Blood" (2003)
United States
Production: Columbia TriStar Home Entertainment
Distribution: Columbia TriStar Home Entertainment
Co-Producers: Laura D. Smith, Aaron Ali Tichenor
Director: Paul Thomas Anderson
Screenplay: Paul Thomas Anderson
Music: Jon Brion
Editing: Leslie Jones
Music editor: Jonathan Karp
Dance: Sissy Lake

Principal cast: Adam Sandler (Barry Egan), Emily Watson (Lena Leonard), Salvador Curiel (Sal), Sissy Lake (Hula Dancer), Rogerlyn Kanealii Wakinekona (Lena's Apartment Receptionist), Iris S. Weinkoff (Lena's Neighbor)
Format: 35mm, color
12 min.

There Will Be Blood (2007)
United States
Production: Paramount Vintage, Miramax, Ghoulardi Film Company
Executive producers: Scott Rudin, Eric Schlosser, David Williams
Producers: Paul Thomas Anderson, Daniel Lupi, JoAnne Sellar
Distribution: Miramax, Paramount Vintage
Director: Paul Thomas Anderson
Screenplay: Paul Thomas Anderson, based on the novel *Oil!*, by Upton Sinclair
Music: Johnny Greenwood
Cinematography: Robert Elswit
Editing: Dylan Tichenor
Casting: Cassandra Kulukundis
Production design: Jack Fisk
Art direction: David Crank
Set decoration: Jim Erickson
Costume design: Mark Bridges
Production manager: Daniel Lupi
Principal cast: Daniel Day-Lewis (Daniel Plainview), Paul Dano (Paul Sunday/ Eli Sunday), Dillon Freasier (H.W.), Barry Del Sherman (H. B. Ailman), Harrison Taylor (Baby H.W.), Stockton Taylor (Baby H.W.), Paul F. Tompkins (Prescott), Randall Carver (Mr. Bankside), Coco Leigh (Mrs. Bankside), Ciarán Hinds (Fletcher), Sydney McCallister (Mary Sunday), David Willis (Abel Sunday), Christine Olejniczak (Mother Sunday), Kellie Hill (Ruth Sunday)
Format: 35mm, color
158 min.

The Master (2012)
United States
Production: the Weinstein Company, Ghoulardi Film Company, Annapurna Pictures
Executive producers: Ted Schipper, Adam Somner
Producers: Paul Thomas Anderson, Megan Ellison, Daniel Lupi, JoAnne Sellar
Distribution: the Weinstein Company
Director: Paul Thomas Anderson
Screenplay: Paul Thomas Anderson
Music: Johnny Greenwood

Cinematography: Mihai Malaimare Jr.
Editing: Leslie Jones, Peter McNulty
Casting: Cassandra Kulukundis
Production design: David Crank, Jack Fisk
Set decoration: Amy Wells
Costume design: Mark Bridges
Special effects: Method Studios
Principal cast: Joaquin Phoenix (Freddie Quell), Philip Seymour Hoffman (Lancaster Dodd), Amy Adams (Peggy Dodd), Jesse Plemons (Val Dodd), Ambyr Childers (Elizabeth Dodd), Rami Malek (Clark), Lorelai Hoey (Baby), Martin Dew (Norman Conrad), Joshua Close (Wayne Gregory), Jillian Bell (Susan Gregory), Kevin J. Walsh (Cliff Boyd), Lena Endre (Mrs. Solstad), Madisen Beaty (Doris Solstad), Kevin J. O'Connor (Bill William), Patty McCormack (Mildred Drummond)
Format: 35mm and 70mm, color
144 min.

"Back Beyond" (2013)
United States
Director: Paul Thomas Anderson
Screenplay: Paul Thomas Anderson
Music: Johnny Greenwood
Cinematography: Mihai Malaimare Jr.
Principal cast: Amy Adams (Peggy Dodd), Laura Dern (Helen Sullivan), Philip Seymour Hoffman (Lancaster Dodd), Rami Malek (Clark), Joaquin Phoenix (Freddie Quell), Christopher Evan Welch (John More)
Format: Color
20 min.

Inherent Vice (2014)
United States
Production: Ghoulardi Film Company, IAC Films, Warner Brothers
Executive producer: Adam Sonner
Producers: Paul Thomas Anderson, Daniel Lupi, JoAnne Sellar
Distribution: Warner Brothers
Director: Paul Thomas Anderson
Screenplay: Paul Thomas Anderson, based on the novel by Thomas Pynchon
Music: Johnny Greenwood
Cinematography: Robert Elswit
Editing: Leslie Jones
Casting: Cassandra Kulukundis
Production design: David Crank
Art direction: Ruth De Jong

Set decoration: Amy Wells
Costume design: Mark Bridges
Special effects: Crazy Horse Effects
Principal cast: Joaquin Phoenix (Larry "Doc" Sportello), Joanna Newsom (Sortilège), Katherine Waterston (Shasta Fay Hepworth), Jordan Christian Hearn (Denis), Taylor Bonin (Ensenada Slim), Jeannie Berlin (Aunt Reet), Josh Brolin (Lt. Det. Christian F. "Bigfoot" Bjornsen), Eric Roberts (Michael Z. Wolfmann), Serena Scott Thomas (Sloane Wolfmann), Maya Rudolph (Petunia Leeway), Martin Dew (Dr. Buddy Tubeside), Michael Kenneth Williams (Tariq Khalil), Hong Chau (Jade), Shannon Collis (Bambi), Christopher Allen Nelson (Glenn Charlock)
Format: 35mm and 70mm, color
148 min.

Junun (2015)
United States
Production: Ghoulardi Film Company
Director: Paul Thomas Anderson
Editing: Andy Jurgensen
Production manager: Pippa Robinson
Principal cast: Johnny Greenwood, Ehtisham Khan Ajmeri, Gufran Ali, Shazib Ali, Sabir Bamami, Shye Ben-Tzur, Aamir Bhiyani, Soheb Bhiyani, Ajaj Damami, Nigel Godrich, Hazmat, Afshana Khan, Asin Khan, Bhanwaru Khan, Chugge Khan, Dara Khan
Format: Color
54 min.

Bibliography

Anderson, Paul Thomas. Introduction to *The Earrings of Madame de . . .*, directed by Max Ophüls (1953). Criterion Collection DVD, 2008.

———. *Magnolia: The Shooting Script.* New York: Newmarket Press, 2000.

———. *Punch-Drunk Love: The Shooting Script.* New York: Newmarket Press, 2002.

———. *There Will Be Blood.* Final shooting script, 2006. Accessed at www.pages.drexel.edu/-ina22.

Bachelard, Gaston. *The Flame of a Candle.* Translated by Joan Caldwell. Dallas, Tex.: Dallas Institute Publications, 1988.

———. *Intuition of the Instant.* Translated by Eileen Rizo-Patron. Evanston, Ill.: Northwestern University Press, 2013.

Bergman, Ingmar. *Bergman on Bergman: Interviews with Ingmar Bergman.* Edited by Stig Bjorkman, Torsten Manns, and Jonas Sima. Translated by Paul Britten Austin. New York: Da Capo Press, 1993.

Butler, Judith. *Giving an Account of Oneself.* New York: Fordham University Press, 2005.

Carson, Anne. "We Point the Bone: An Essay on Threat." *Tin House* 13.4 (2012).

———, trans. *Grief Lessons: Four Plays.* By Euripides. New York: NYRB Press, 2006.

Cavell, Stanley. *Pursuits of Happiness.* Cambridge, Mass.: Harvard University Press, 1981.

Cusk, Rachel. *Outline.* New York: Vintage, 2015.

Donoghue, Denis. "Wallace Stevens." In *Connoisseurs of Chaos: Ideas of Order in Modern American Poetry*, 190–215. New York: Columbia University Press, 1984.

Duncan, Robert. *The H.D. Book.* Eds. Michael Boughn and Victor Coleman. Berkeley: University of California Press, 2011.

Fletcher, Angus. *Allegory: The Theory of a Symbolic Mode.* Ithaca, N.Y.: Cornell University Press, 1964.

Fried, Michael. *Flaubert's "Gueuloir": On "Madame Bovary" and Salammbo.* New Haven, Conn.: Yale University Press, 2012.

Gross, Kenneth. "Ordinary Twinship." *Raritan* 22.4 (spring 2003): 20–39.
Gudas, Eric. "Sound-Play in Stevens." *Raritan* 32.4 (spring 2013): 145–59.
Hofmann, Michael. *Where Have You Been? Selected Essays.* New York: Farrar, Straus & Giroux, 2014.
Koestenbaum, Wayne. "Odd Secrets of the Line." *Tin House* 15.4 (summer 2014): 122–134.
———. The Queen's Throat: Opera, Homosexuality, and the Mystery of Desire. New York: Penguin, 1993.
Konow, David. "PTA Meeting: An Interview with Paul Thomas Anderson." *Creative Screenwriting*, January 2000. Accessed at *Cigarettes & Red Vines: The Definitive Paul Thomas Anderson Resource*, http://cigsandredvines.blogspot.com.
Lane, Christine. *Magnolia.* West Sussex, U.K.: Wiley-Blackwell, 2011.
Mason, Wyatt. "Make This Not True." Review of *Tenth of December* by George Saunders. *New York Review of Books*, Feb. 6, 2014.
Nelson, Maggie. *The Art of Cruelty: A Reckoning.* New York: Norton, 2011.
O'Brien, Geoffrey. "A Drifter and His Master." In *Stolen Glimpses, Captive Shadows: Writing on Film, 2002–2013*, 291–300. Berkeley, Calif.: Counterpoint, 2013.
Onstad, Katrina. "Doing It to Music." Interview with Paul Thomas Anderson. *National Post*, Jan. 15, 2000. Accessed at *Cigarettes & Red Vines: The Definitive Paul Thomas Anderson Resource*, http://cigsandredvines.blogspot.com.
Pasternak, Boris. *Safe Conduct: An Autobiography and Other Writings.* Translated by Beatrice Scott. New York: New Directions, 1958.
Phillips, Adam. "The Art of Nonfiction No. 7, Interview." *Paris Review* 208 (spring 2014): 29–54.
———. "Misgivings." Review of True Friendship: Geoffrey Hill, Anthony Hecht, and Robert Lowell under the Sign of Eliot and Pound by Christopher Ricks. London Review of Books 32.14 (22 July 2010).
———. *On Balance.* New York: Picador, 2011.
———. *Promises, Promises: Essays on Psychoanalysis and Literature.* New York: Basic Books, 2001.
Rensin, David. "Twenty Questions." Interview with Paul Thomas Anderson. *Playboy*, February 1998. Accessed at *Cigarettes & Red Vines: The Definitive Paul Thomas Anderson Resource*, http://cigsandredvines.blogspot.com.
Richardson, Joan. "Emerson's Sound Effects." *Raritan* 16.3 (winter 1997).
Ruefle, Mary. *Madness, Rack, and Honey: Collected Lectures.* Seattle: Wave Books, 2012.
Rosenbladt, Bettina. "Doubles and Doubts in Hitchcock: The German Connection." In *Hitchcock: Past and Future*, edited by Richard Allen and Sam Ishi-Gonzales. New York: Routledge, 2004.
Ross, Alex. "Blessed Are the Sad: Late Brahms." In *Listen to This*, 293–314. New York: Farrar, Straus and Giroux, 2010.

Schiller, Friedrich. "The Sublime." In *Essays Aesthetical and Philosophical*, 128–41. London: George Bell, 1875.

Sedgwick, Eve Kosofsky. *The Weather in Proust.* Edited by Jonathan Goldberg. Durham, N.C.: Duke University Press, 2011.

Smith, Ali. *Artful.* Toronto: Hamish Hamilton [Penguin Canada], 2013.

Turvey, Malcolm. *Doubting Vision: Film and the Revelationist Tradition.* New York: Oxford University Press, 2008.

Udovich, Mim. "Lights . . . Camera . . . Hold It, Hold It; Would Someone Please Reattach Mark's Member, Please . . . and Action!" *Esquire*, Oct. 1, 1997.

Vermeule, Blakey. *The Party of Humanity: Writing Moral Psychology in Eighteenth-Century Britain*. Baltimore, Md.: Johns Hopkins University Press, 2000.

———. *Why Do We Care about Literary Characters?* Baltimore, Md.: Johns Hopkins University Press, 2010.

Warshow, Robert "Movie Chronicle: The Westerner." In *The Immediate Experience: Movies, Comics, Theatre, and Other Aspects of Popular Culture*, 105–24. Enlarged ed. Cambridge, Mass.: Harvard University Press, 2002.

Watts, Alan. *Nature, Man, and Woman.* New York: Vintage Books, 1991.

Waxman, Sharon. *Rebels on the Backlot: Six Maverick Directors and How They Conquered the Hollywood Studio System.* New York: Harper Perennial, 2006.

Paul Thomas Anderson Interviews

Unless otherwise noted, interviews were accessed at *Cigarettes & Red Vines: The Definitive Paul Thomas Anderson Resource*, http://cigsandredvines.blogspot.ca.

Associated Press, 2000: Kennedy, Mark. "Whiz Filmmaker Plows Familiar Ground." Associated Press, Jan. 12, 2000.

BAM Q&A, 2003: Lim, Dennis. Interview with Paul Thomas Anderson and Philip Seymour Hoffman. Brooklyn Academy of Music, June 2003.

Cinelive, 2000: Benedetti, Sandra. Interview with Paul Thomas Anderson. *Cinelive Magazine*, March 2000.

Creative Screenwriting, 2000: Konow, David. "PTA Meeting: An Interview with Paul Thomas Anderson." *Creative Screenwriting*, January 2000.

Der Spiegel, 2003: Rehfeld, Nina. "I Wanted to Make Myself Scared." *Der Spiegel*, April 13, 2003.

Ebert, 2002: Ebert, Roger. "Love at First Sight." *Chicago Sun Times*, Oct. 13, 2002.

Entertainment Weekly, 2000: Willman, Chris. "Mann Crazy." *Entertainment Weekly*, Jan. 7, 2000. Accessed at www.ew.com/article/2000/01/07/mann-crazy.

Entertainment Weekly, 2007: Willman, Chris. "There Will Be Music." *Entertainment Weekly*, Nov. 8, 2007.

LACMA, 2012: Mitchell, Elvis. Interview with Paul Thomas Anderson. Transcript by Megan Leddy. Los Angeles County Museum of Art, November 2012.

LA Daily News, 1999: "Anderson Soft on Valley." *Los Angeles Daily News*, Dec. 12, 1999.

LA Times, 2002: Turan, Kenneth. "Crazy for Love." *Los Angeles Times*, May 20, 2002.

Magnolia Script Book interview, 2000: Anderson, Paul Thomas. "Introduction." In *Magnolia: The Shooting Script*. New York: Dey Street Books. Jan. 9, 2000.

Mean Magazine, 2008: Hoelck, Patrick. "Blood from Oil." *Mean Magazine*, January 2008.

Museum of the Moving Image, 2007: Schwartz, David. Interview with Paul Thomas Anderson and Daniel Day Lewis. Museum of the Moving Image, Dec. 11, 2007.

New York Times, 2007: Hirschberg, Lynn. "The New Frontier's Man." *New York Times*, November 2007.

Onion AV Club, 2008: Modell, Josh. Interview with Paul Thomas Anderson. *Onion AV Club*, Jan. 2, 2008.

Paris Press Conference, 2013: Waschberger, Beatrice. Interview with Paul Thomas Anderson. Transcript by Megan Leddy. Paris Press Conference, January 2013.

San Francisco Chronicle, 2000: Guthman, Edward. "The Actor's Director." *San Francisco Chronicle*, Jan. 2, 2000.

Seattle P-I, 2002: Nechak, Paula. "Director Punch-Drunk with Joy." *Seattle P-I*, Oct. 19, 2002.

Sight and Sound, 1998: Smith, Gavin. Interview with Paul Thomas Anderson. *Sight and Sound Magazine*, January 1998.

Sight and Sound, 2012: Bell, James. "The Anderson Tapes." *Sight and Sound*, December 2012.

Sunday Night Safran, 2012: Safran, John. Interview with Paul Thomas Anderson. Transcription by Megan Leddy. *Sunday Night Safran*, November 2012.

Times UK, 2003: Gilbey, Ryan. Interview with Paul Thomas Anderson. *Times UK*, Feb. 2, 2003.

Toronto's Eye, 1997: Patterson, Alex. "Boogie Night." *Toronto's Eye Magazine*, September 1997.

Venice Q&A, 2012: Interview with Paul Thomas Anderson and Philip Seymour Hoffman. Venice Film Festival Press Conference Transcript, September 2012.

Virginian-Pilot, 2000: Vincent, Mal. "Magnolia Blossom." *Virginian-Pilot*, Jan. 7, 2000.

Washington Post, 2012: Hornaday, Ann. "Paul Thomas Anderson on *The Master* and Going Big for All the Wrong Reasons." *Washington Post*, Sept. 12, 2012.

WGA, 2012: Clements, Jim. Interview with Paul Thomas Anderson. Transcription by Nikhil Venkatesa and Isaiah Lester. WGA, November 2012.

Index

George Toles is Distinguished Professor of English at the University of Manitoba. He is the author of *A House Made of Light: Essays on the Art of Film*.

Books in the series Contemporary Film Directors

Nelson Pereira dos Santos
Darlene J. Sadlier

Abbas Kiarostami
Mehrnaz Saeed-Vafa and Jonathan Rosenbaum

Joel and Ethan Coen
R. Barton Palmer

Claire Denis
Judith Mayne

Wong Kar-wai
Peter Brunette

Edward Yang
John Anderson

Pedro Almodóvar
Marvin D'Lugo

Chris Marker
Nora Alter

Abel Ferrara
Nicole Brenez, translated by Adrian Martin

Jane Campion
Kathleen McHugh

Jim Jarmusch
Juan Suárez

Roman Polanski
James Morrison

Manoel de Oliveira
John Randal Johnson

Neil Jordan
Maria Pramaggiore

Paul Schrader
George Kouvaros

Jean-Pierre Jeunet
Elizabeth Ezra

Terrence Malick
Lloyd Michaels

Sally Potter
Catherine Fowler

Atom Egoyan
Emma Wilson

Albert Maysles
Joe McElhaney

Jerry Lewis
Chris Fujiwara

Jean-Pierre and Luc Dardenne
Joseph Mai
Michael Haneke
Peter Brunette

Alejandro González Iñárritu
Celestino Deleyto and Maria del Mar Azcona

Lars von Trier
Linda Badley

Hal Hartley
Mark L. Berrettini

François Ozon
Thibaut Schilt

Steven Soderbergh
Aaron Baker

Mike Leigh
Sean O'Sullivan

D.A. Pennebaker
Keith Beattie

Jacques Rivette
Mary M. Wiles

Kim Ki-duk
Hye Seung Chung

Philip Kaufman
Annette Insdorf

Richard Linklater
David T. Johnson

David Lynch
Justus Nieland

John Sayles
David R. Shumway

Dario Argento
L. Andrew Cooper

Todd Haynes
Rob White

Christian Petzold
Jaimey Fisher

Spike Lee
Todd McGowan

Terence Davies
Michael Koresky

Francis Ford Coppola
Jeff Menne

Emir Kusturica
Giorgio Bertellini

Agnès Varda
Kelley Conway

John Lasseter
Richard Neupert

Paul Thomas Anderson
George Toles

The University of Illinois Press
is a founding member of the
Association of American University Presses.

University of Illinois Press
1325 South Oak Street
Champaign, IL 61820-6903
www.press.uillinois.edu